D0305560

BAINTE DEN STOC

WITHDRAWN FROM
DÚN LAOGHAIRE-RATHDOWN COUNTY
LIBRARY STOCK

RENAISSANCE
NATION

David McWilliams

Gill Books

Gill Books

Hume Avenue

Park West

Dublin 12

www.gillbooks.ie

Gill Books is an imprint of M.H. Gill & Co.

© David McWilliams 2018

978 07171 8075 2

Print origination by O'K Graphic Design, Dublin

Copy-edited by Brian Langan

Proofread by Matthew Parkinson-Bennett

Printed by CPI Group (UK) Ltd, Croydon CRO 4YY

This book is typeset in Adobe Caslon with chapter headings in Prohibition.
The paper used in this book comes from the wood pulp of managed forests. For every tree
felled, at least one tree is planted, thereby renewing natural resources.

All rights reserved.

No part of this publication may be copied, reproduced or transmitted in any form or by
any means without written permission of the publishers.

A CIP catalogue record for this book is available from the British Library.

5 4 3 2

For Sian, Lucy and Cal

ACKNOWLEDGEMENTS

I would like to thank my exceptional researcher Finn McLaughlin. This young man is a one-off and without his extraordinary work this book would simply not have happened. Hats off, Finn!

Thank you to Conor, Sheila and Catherine at Gill Books.

Shout out to my old mate David 'Rupert' Kelly for getting me up on a bike with the Mamils and Swallows. Sinead Caffrey and Clare Ridge for the finer details on Sliotar Mom. Rachel Ray for essentials on The Fringe and The Sleeve. Thanks to the wonderful Deirdre McCloskey for her ideas, corrections and allowing me to see the world a bit differently. Declan Kiberd for his Joycean tips, and Kevin Cunningham for the survey data. Pinchas Landau, Martin Lousteau, Clayton Love, Jono Hill, Carlo Pizzati, Dan Ariely and Vikas Nath for the chats. Eilish Bul Godley for on-the-money urban descriptions. To old friends Charlie and Shenda Anyaegbunam for a great night in the Olympia, at EP and more.

To Sian for her painstaking dedication to detail and for her hours and hours of hard work on the text.

CONTENTS

PART 1
CULTURE WARS

CHAPTER 1

FROM MOVING STATUES TO BOUNCY CASTLES

9 A.M. DOMINICAN CONVENT, DÚN LAOGHAIRE

A patient column of people runs all the way down the street as far as the New Paddy phone repair shop. The only other shop doing business so early on a Friday morning is May's Occasions, which is busy selling communion dresses, tiaras and parasols to cater for the last-minute panic ahead of the big celebratory weekend. Irish citizens might have been about to repeal the constitutional amendment on abortion, but no one would lay a finger on our divine right to host a full-on, over-the-top communion, replete with bouncy castles, gazebos and Instagram poses.

Down here on the coast south of Dublin you can taste the salt in the air. The impressive harbour is the last man-made sight that thousands of pregnant Irish women would have seen from the ferry to England. The polling station at the convent is jammed; the returning officer has never seen anything like it in her 20 years of supervising. By four in the afternoon, turnout has already hit a massive 43.7%. In other votes, it would typically have been half that. Something is afoot.

This is Dún Laoghaire: traditionally, Ireland's most liberal constituency and, for years, the antithesis of 'Middle Ireland'. Here the locals have been baptising and confirming their children for years, without believing a word of it. Being a pro-communion Repealer sits easy here. It's an ambivalent place. But so too is Ireland.

Since the last abortion referendum in 1983, Ireland has moved seamlessly from austere Moving Statue Catholicism to squidgy Bouncy Castle Catholicism and no one really batted an eye. We might change our constitution but we're holding onto our rituals. Welcome to the home of à-la-carte Catholicism for the Tinder age. Why pray when you can swipe?

After a winter of heavy snowfall, the town feels almost tropical in the early summer sunshine. But sunny weekends bring their own maritime challenges. The hotter the day, the busier the cops. Down at the Forty Foot, the toxic combination of Magaluf temperatures, fellas necking cans of discount Dutch Gold at noon and the arrival by jet ski of Conor McGregor isn't going to end well. Such alien incursions upset the local Forty Footers. Like all orthodoxies, the daily swimmers follow a creed, bonded together by feats of demented endurance in icy waters. Hypothermia is their communion. Outsiders are not welcome and fair-weather, heatwave dippers are heretics. Sandycove is their tabernacle and Sandycove has strict rules; Crumlin on jet skis breaks all of them.

This morning sees even these seal-people of the Forty Foot migrate from their rocky habitat to cast their vote.

Campaigners in Repeal sweatshirts are nervous. Some long-war warriors have been at it since 1983; others are first-timers, galvanised by indignation, social media and the desire to do right not just by themselves, their friends and their daughters, but by their grannies and mothers too. They've had enough.

Ahead of the referendum, both sides thought the result would be tight. Liberal Ireland and Traditional Ireland were thought to be neck-and-neck.

The received wisdom was that we were still a deeply divided nation and that in the 'long grass' of Middle Ireland lurked a Silent No. In the final days, the strict guidelines for media 'balance', particularly on radio and TV, bolstered the impression of a country split down the middle.

In the end, we weren't split at all. The long grass was not just liberal, but unflinchingly so. The overwhelming majority, albeit a private and non-vocal majority, were liberal, not conservative. In one generation, to use V.S. Naipaul's phrase about India, 'millions of little mutinies' had kicked off inside Irish heads. The result? The values that Dún Laoghaire held at the time of Pope John Paul II's visit had become Ireland's values by the time Pope Francis addressed a much-diminished crowd in a gale at Phoenix Park almost 40 years later.

This dramatic shift in Ireland's value system poses a few critical questions. How did Dún Laoghaire's liberal attitude, once regarded as an outlier, become mainstream? How did we move from Moving Statue Catholicism, cowed by rules, vindictiveness, superstition and fear, to Bouncy Castle Catholicism – still culturally Catholic, loving the big day out, but morally pragmatic, embracing all comers and energised by ambiguity, acceptance, facts and hope? And how did this cultural transformation affect the economy?

DÚN LAOGHAIRE-ISATION

The last time we voted on abortion, in 1983, Dún Laoghaire was a liberal enclave in a deeply conservative country. We were an extreme outlier, with opinions and norms way out of step with the rest of the country. It was more middle class, more cosmopolitan and more liberal, with higher levels of education. The fact that it also had a higher concentration of the very small Protestant population contributed to the sense that it was that little bit beyond the reach of the crozier. Today, Dún Laoghaire's values, once seen as radical, are mainstream. We have witnessed the Dún Laoghaire-isation of Ireland.

Back in 1983, as a teenager just too young to vote, I remember feeling proud that almost six out of every 10 people in my neck of the woods had rejected the Church and its doctrine. The Church had never played a huge role in our lives. Ours was a suburban semi-D estate of panel-beaten, faded brown Datsuns where people's primary concern was surviving the various and frequent recessions. Sure, there were Holy Joes who lived in a permanent state of moral alert, but they were not the majority. In contrast to the Church's iron certainty, the economy, and thus people's livelihoods, seemed precarious, fragile and much more important.

My own friends were pretty representative. After getting knocked out of an altar boys' five-a-side soccer competition somewhere in Tallaght – then a massive building site – we never went to Mass again. Mass was an hour for mitching, chatting up girls, smoking Carrolls, hanging out with the few Protestants on the road and finding out what the priest said, just in case your mother bothered to ask you, which was rare enough. Like so many others, she was only going through the motions. My Sunday afternoon anxiety had nothing to do with missing the creed or gospel and everything to do with not having the weekend's 'eccer' done.

As we hung around Dún Laoghaire pier, drinking flagons and looking towards England, spiritual home of The Clash, The Specials and Liverpool FC, we were aware that our reasonably 'live and let live' Dún Laoghaire existence wasn't the Irish norm. Our place felt surrounded by another Dublin, defined by the enormous post-modern Le Corbusier-inspired churches built in the 1970s, designed to house the burgeoning faithful for generations to come. These things were the Calatrava bridges of the 1970s suburbs. We may not have built rail links, schools or hospitals in the new suburbs but, by Jaysus, did we build churches! They were built to show off, lest the last few Proddies be under any illusion who was boss. The Church that built these temples was a confident one, assured that the future was vibrantly Catholic.

Past these suburban triumphal arches, somewhere beyond Terenure, the extreme edge of our known world, another Ireland existed. In that other, much bigger Ireland, people saw moving statues and – even more distressing – bleeding statues. Some of our cousins came from out there; we'd heard the stories and had no reason to disbelieve them.

RTÉ beamed that strange country into our homes. It was a world of swaggering priests in soft Dubarry shoes, mad-looking politicians with combovers and something called *The Sunday Game*. During the frequent elections, there were fellas, always in Farah slacks, up on the bonnets of rusty Fiats, roaring gibberish into megaphones. The country was permanently a few short weeks away from bankruptcy. Dads on the road talked about something called the National Debt, which we understood to be big, bad and about to explode. Up North all hell was breaking loose and UTV implored a strange tribe of people called 'key holders' in places called Lisburn and Newtownards to witness their family businesses going up in smoke. Is it any wonder we couldn't wait to get to the exoticism of Finsbury Park?

For a Dún Laoghaire teenager, Ireland was a perplexing place. That other Ireland threatened us. It was close by, closer than we thought. Three things seemed intertwined in that other Ireland – the Church, the 'Ra and the National Debt.

For our precariously upwardly mobile tribe, just clinging on, even in the anti-English climate of the time, Home Counties-sounding names for roads and estates were de rigeur. The estate beside us was called Richmond Park but my own estate went one better, bringing Irish Anglophilia to new heights by calling itself Windsor Park. What could be more Home Counties?

It was clearly appreciated, but never publicly admitted, that any road in Dublin named after a priest, pope or a patriot risked being mistaken for a council estate. Such a class faux pas would never do for those who'd paid for their houses. We all knew you'd never get into a nightclub with an address that sounded like Blessed Oliver Plunkett anything. Such class sensitivities are always more alive and well when a society claims to be classless. So the St Brendan's Terraces, Rory O'Connor Crescents and St Fintan's Parks were not for us. The penny always looks down on the halfpenny. My dad described our street as a place where Protestants on the way down met Catholics on the way up.

My middle-of-the-road, trying-to-get-on neighbours were never virulently anti-clerical by any means, but they did vote against the notion of inserting the eighth amendment into the Irish constitution, a quiet act of rebellion. We in Dún Laoghaire stood defiant, waving our two liberal fingers up at the bishops. Identity for us was confusing, particularly when we were shipped off to the Gaeltacht, protesting in vain to quizzical people from Connemara that we weren't English, by trying to sound all Dub, like Ronnie Drew after 10 pints in Toners.

In fairness, Dún Laoghaire, then and now, comes in all shapes, sizes and sounds. But in the 1980s that didn't matter, and our total ignorance about hurling only confirmed the Gaeltacht lads' ethnic suspicions. We were Jackeens, little Johns – a reference to John Bull or England immortalised in the work of Dalkey resident George Bernard Shaw. We were also too lukewarm on the North at a time when lukewarm meant Orange. We were oddities.

We even had a dope-smoking candidate running on the 'legalise weed' ticket in the 1981 election, while a typically mouthy Dún Laoghaire burgher, Bob Geldof, railed against the Church on the *Late Late Show*. The election numbers didn't lie; we were out of tune. We had different values. Dún Laoghaire was an outlier, an allegedly foreign-contaminated enclave in an insular country that felt like it was going backwards. All that has changed, but it wasn't a victory for old Dún Laoghaire over rural Ireland. Rather it was a fusion of the two, made possible by an economy surging relentlessly forwards.

CULCHIFICATION

In the early 1980s south county Dublin, future home of Ross O'Carroll-Kelly, was seen as the bastion of West Brits: removed and somewhat diffident, looking down our noses at our country cousins. And Dún Laoghaire was the deep south, the Alabama of the southside.

Both the south Dublin tribe and the country tribe were regularly painted as being polar opposites of Irishness. South Dubliners were thought to be cosmopolitan, open, pompous and were not to be trusted. In contrast, country people were inward-looking protectors of deep Irish culture, a culture southsiders knew nothing about.

If there was an Irish bell curve, south Dublin and the Aran Islands would be the extreme outliers, the tails of the curve. So when J.M. Synge headed out from Dún Laoghaire, then known as Kingstown, home to the ranks of the British forces, to Inis Meáin over one hundred years ago as part of the fledgling Gaelic League, he headed to the place he believed was the extreme opposite of his home town.

In Inis Meáin, Synge got his idea for *The Playboy of the Western World*, the play that rocked the country, leading to riots in 1907 because dewy-eyed and frankly misogynistic nationalists thought his depiction of women was scandalous. If Ireland needed more evidence of how out of step the likes of Dún Laoghaire was, it was there in the history of the State's cradle of culture, the Abbey Theatre.

Even the greats of Irish literature attested to the fact that there was a chasm between south Dublin and the rest of the country. Sure wasn't Joyce's *Ulysses* scorned for undermining Irish values and morals? Where did it start but in an English-built Martello Tower and where else but down the road from Dún Laoghaire, in Sandycove.

The Aran Islands, in contrast, were the crib of real Irishness. If there was a stable and a baby Jesus of the true Gael it would be on Inis Meáin, home of the language, sean nós, traditional music and, of course, a GAA stronghold.

Yet in the past few years, a great blurring has taken hold, where these old distinctions have melded into something else. Dalkey, formerly home of retired majors and colonels of the British armed forces, stomping ground of Protestant chroniclers of the relationship between Ireland and England, Shaw and Synge, has become the cradle of Irish hurling. All the while, Inis Meáin, once the holdout of the impoverished Gael, living on potatoes, dependent on turf and emigrant remittances, is today home to one of the most cosmopolitan, high-end fashion products exported from this country, employing Polish immigrants, and has the finest and possibly most upmarket restaurant and boutique hotel in the country booked out a year in advance.

How did that happen?

Let's head to Dalkey to see how hurling, a game relatively unknown in those parts when the Pope came to Ireland in 1979, is flourishing in this former rugby stronghold. Dalkey is now home to the All-Ireland hurling club champions, Cuala, for two years running. On St Patrick's Day 2017 and 2018, legions of locals left deepest south Dublin, decked out in the red and white of Cuala, heading to Croke Park to cheer on a hurling team sponsored by that pillar of south Dublin financial capitalism, Davy Stockbrokers. Yes, you are reading right.

At the beginning of our transformation, in 1979, it was so different. There was always a big local sporting final on St Patrick's Day, but it was the schools rugby final and the sheepskin and hip-flask pilgrimage was to Lansdowne Road, to watch the sons of the local merchant class show their true skill and, more importantly, character on the playing fields. The teams were the local private schools and the prize was Corinthian heritage. This is what this part of the world did.

Had you told us back then that a Dalkey team would be All-Ireland hurling champions, we'd have laughed at you.

For us, hurling was a dangerous game played by fellas from the deep country. It was the foreign game. Soccer was our first love and rugby came second. While some of us may have played GAA in national school, GAA roots were not deep here. The FA Cup final was always a much bigger day than the All-Ireland football final. And whatever about Gaelic football, hurling never even figured. Even most south Dublin national schools, run by GAA-mad teachers, didn't attempt hurling. My own school, Johnstown National School, didn't even have a hurling team. The tiny minority who dared to champion the game were usually the sons of obsessives who brought hurling up to Dublin when they left home to find work in the capital.

In fact, you could say that, back then, sport was genetic. You played what your dad played. The only devotee of GAA on our road was one Des Cahill, who went on to earn fame as a ballroom dancer, amongst other things. The young Des tried repeatedly to convert us from soccer and rugby to GAA with no success. Des's father, a Clare man, was the principal of the local national school.

In the early 1950s, my dad, a Dalkey local, co-founded Dalkey United, so my sport was soccer. In the 1970s and 1980s, Dalkey United shared its ground with a small GAA club called Cuala. Dalkey United was the senior partner in the shared ground. Both cultures lived in harmony side by side, but soccer was king. In fact, the soccer club donated the extra pitch beside it to Cuala out of sympathy for the GAA club, which in the 1960s didn't have a permanent pitch. Further back, Cuala had originally been called the Dalkey Mitchels, named after the nationalist leader John Mitchel.

Fast-forward 40 years and Cuala, the small GAA club of my memory, is ubiquitous in this former rugby and soccer stronghold. There are Cuala red and white flags everywhere from Monkstown to Dalkey. What happened in the past three decades? We have described the Dún Laoghaire-isation of the countryside, but how do we explain the reverse takeover, the culchification of Dún Laoghaire? Neither side won, they blended together.

THE REVERSE TAKEOVER

On a warm Tuesday night, Cuala Academy, with over five hundred kids under the age of nine, is in full swing. This is ground zero for the culchification of Dún Laoghaire. They arrive early in a fleet of Opel Zafiras, each parent with a job to do, each competing in the competence ranking. These mothers could organise the invasion of a world power before breakfast. On the sideline is a legion of dads, waiting to be marshalled into action.

Quite apart from the impressive organisational power on display, the other thing that stands out are the accents. These people were not born around here. Their accents are not clipped Ryan Tubridy or old Dún Laoghaire Ronnie Drew, and not many have the local Bob Geldof spliff-head drawl. These people, or one half of each couple, at least, are from some GAA stronghold down the country. There are some members of local GAA aristocratic families, but in general most of these people have moved here during the great blurring of Ireland.

What we are seeing is the culchification of the professional classes. As only the upper end of the professional class can now afford to live in leafy south Dublin, we are seeing the ruralisation of large swathes of what was once the solitary bastion of liberal Ireland. This is one of the great untold stories of modern Ireland.

The new rural professional caste might be dropping the traditional Catholic moral values of their parents, but they are holding on to something else from deep traditional culture. They are bringing GAA and, more specifically, hurling. South Dublin has become rural and rural Ireland has become all Dún Laoghaire. Ross O'Carroll-Kelly meets the Hardy Bucks and both have a total laugh.

THE CAO WINNERS

Interestingly, the failed bankers of Ireland who were dismissed as 'not very bright rugby players' in the boom were in fact not rugby players on the way down at all. They were all GAA lads on the way up. If you care to look forensically at the backgrounds of the major players in the banking collapse, you will see that almost all the CEOs of the banks that needed to be bailed out by the Irish government went to hurling-playing, free Christian Brothers schools. The fingerprints of Christian Brothers boys were all over the crash, with their corporate boxes in Croke Park, not the much easier-to-lampoon but actually reasonably innocent southside rugby jocks!

So what's going on?

The main economic factor behind the rise of hurling in coastal south Dublin can be traced back to the free education of the 1960s and those who availed of it.

The primary force of the cultural takeover of south Dublin has been the emergence of a rural professional class that has come to dominate Dublin's professions. This is the CAO class, which first emerged in the 1970s when the first generation to benefit from free education came of age. They are members of a ruling caste that I like to call the Testocracy, but more on them later. As Ireland became more meritocratic, exams began to matter more and more and the people who were good at passing exams did best. The sons and daughters of these socially upwardly mobile punters from the country have been the major winners in the Irish professional meritocracies of medicine, the higher levels of the civil service, the law, accountancy and banking.

The class that benefitted most from free education in the 1960s and 1970s was not, as you might imagine and as James Connolly would have expected, the industrial working class, but rather the small farming class. It is their grandsons who now play hurling in south Dublin.

In the 1990s, two economists, Damian Hannan and Patrick Commins, wrote a paper called 'The Significance of Small Scale Landholders in Ireland's Socio-Economic Transformation'. It is our starting point in trying to explain the economics behind the social patchwork that is Ireland today and why south Dublin plays hurling. The writers chart the extraordinary success of the sons and daughters of Ireland's small farmers in the social revolution of the past few decades.

Hannan and Commins found, astonishingly, that the single most important determinant, on a county-by-county basis, of a county's educational achievement in the 1960s and 1970s was the number of small farmers in each county. This is quite extraordinary and unique to this country.

The more small farmers in a county, the better educated the children ended up being. As a tribe, they were very good at exams and did well in their Leaving Cert. The research even found that the single most successful subsection of the Irish population was the children of small farmers in east Galway, the home of hurling in Connacht.

Given that in the 1960s the two most deprived groups of people in Ireland were small farmers and the industrial working class, it's interesting to compare the fortunes of both groups. Compared to their urban, working-class counterparts, 30% more children of small farmers than those of the urban working class did the Leaving Cert and 50% more went on to third-level education. Over time this changed the complexion of the suburbs. Small farmers received the biggest education premium from free education. So we got a huge new class of highly educated country people on the way up.

These upwardly mobile people turned into the teacher aristocracy, bringing with them to Dublin a love of GAA, squeezeboxes and *The Riordans*. Their success in education also catapulted them into the civil and public services in great numbers. They are now retired as the best-paid public servants in Europe. The next generation, their kids, didn't become teachers but went up a notch or three on the social hierarchy to become doctors, lawyers and accountants. They went into the banks and did very well for themselves. Many have adopted rugby, the sport of the old hierarchy, and still support Munster rugby despite never having lived there. However, they have also kept their allegiance to GAA.

This dramatic upward mobility suggests that they are now the only people, the deep professional class, who can afford to live in the coastal parts of south Dublin, where they joined GAA clubs, not rugby or soccer clubs, leading to an explosion of GAA in that part of the world. Many of them also married locals, as there is no better way of establishing class parity – either you marry it, you earn it or both. This is why so few brothers-in-law get on in south Dublin. The gap between the Tim Nice But Dim estate agent, with good pedigree and an acceptable golf handicap, and the upwardly mobile professional or go-getting, business-owning lad from the sticks is just too wide to bridge with drink taken.

As is so often the case in economics, the law of unintended consequences plays out. The unintended consequence of free education and related upward mobility is that, three generations later, Dalkey are All-Ireland club champions. After Cuala won the 2018 hurling final, the town was on fire. There wasn't a cow milked in Dalkey that night!

Incidentally, there was another small game played that weekend. Ireland beat England in rugby at Twickenham. The player who won man of the match was one Tadhg Furlong, not a pupil of one of the private rugby academies of south Dublin, but a native of New Ross in deepest Wexford hurling country. It's a two-way street, this national transformation.

In the traditional Dublin sporting event for Dalkey that day, Blackrock beat Belvedere, so normal service is resumed for the Ross O'Carroll-Kelly brigade. But as befits the social blurring and emergence of a New Ireland, where so much is now possible, guess who is the most famous past pupil of Belvedere of the last 10 years? He is not some latter-day Tony O'Reilly rugby-playing titan of industry. No sir, the man making his name in the world is one Alex Anyaegbunam, a black rapper calling himself Rejjie Snow, whom we will meet later.

CALIFORNIA DREAMING

The year of the first abortion referendum was also the year that a new TV show was launched. Sunday afternoons in the mid-1980s were owned by Vincent Hanley and his unmissable MT-USA. With Fab Vinny in control, MT-USA transmitted images of Van Halen, Madonna and Pat Benatar from sunny, wealthy California into our drab Irish sitting rooms.

California was tolerant, liberal and open to gay men like Vinny Hanley who fled Ireland. Being gay was against the law. Hanley died of Aids-related complications, the first high-profile Irish person to succumb to the disease. As Hanley's health deteriorated in front of our eyes and he grew weaker on screen by the week, some were only too happy to fuel the rumour mill against a dying gay man. There was only one gay bar in Dublin and it only opened on condition that it didn't serve booze. Anything that smacked of sexual self-expression was snuffed out and the 'wages of sin' narrative was never far from the surface as Fab Vinny faded away.

In 1987, the year Hanley passed away, the California that he beamed into our homes wasn't so much a different country; it was like a different planet. California was outrageously wealthy, home to the world's best companies, with an economy that attracted migrants from all over the world. It had a lifestyle that Irish people could only dream of. Its Valley Girls had pearl-white teeth, voluminous blonde hair and accents that inflected upwards at the end of a statement – for no apparent reason, like? It was the home of expensive orthodontics, perma-tanned middle-aged men on the pull and Pamela Anderson lookalikes who had gone up one size too many. Ireland could never become that, could it? Surely not. Back then, movies like *The Breakfast Club* painted a picture of some dream-world far away. Is it any wonder that a queue of hopeful migrants waited every day outside the US embassy in Ballsbridge for that magical US visa, their passport out of this place and into a new life?

But then something happened. Something totally unexpected. Ireland started to liberalise. It was the beginning of our period of glasnost. We started to open. Irish values began to change. We began to afford dignity to people who had once been pariahs. We began to pass laws to allow people to live their lives as they wanted. We started to elect women presidents. The tone of our national conversation changed from exclusion to inclusion, from censorship and punishment to acceptance and encouragement. Values once regarded as outliers slowly became the values of everyone. It was no longer socially acceptable to be homophobic, racist or sexist. Ireland started to stand up for the individual. We started to talk differently. We started to sound like Californians. We began to talk of justice and love and courage and hope.

Some say talk is cheap; it is not. Language tells us what we are thinking and what we are thinking tells us what is going on in the greatest economic dynamo known to man, the human mind. Language is the link between the physical world and the most important source of economic energy and inspiration, our brains. It's the key to how we express ourselves, yes, but also how we make sense of the world around us.

As we began to talk differently, as we began to deploy different words, something else amazing happened: we began to work differently. We began to work smarter. More and more of us went to college, and this education changed the way we thought about the world. The more tolerant, open and liberal we became, the more our once-enfeebled economy started to grow stronger and stronger and stronger. And it didn't stop. In fact, since the late 1980s, the Irish economy hasn't really stopped. We have even recovered from a global crash, which was traumatic and might have stopped an economy in its tracks for decades, as a similar crash did to Japan. But we shrugged it off. It is now history. Even today, the economy is completely different to the once bloated, credit-fuelled binge of the Celtic Tiger years.

During this time between the visit of the two popes – or to put it in a West Coast American context, sometime between the Eagles' 'Hotel California', NWA in Compton and Caitlyn Jenner in *Playboy* – Ireland's income per head grew faster than California's.

I know it sounds mad, but it's true.

The most extraordinary story never told is how Ireland became richer than California. Or to put it differently, how kids born in Irish homes who watched MT-USA in the early 1980s ended up living in a country that has grown more than twice as fast as California, created far more jobs per head and created more wealth and opportunity per head, introduced more liberal legislation and, relative to our population, offered dignity to far more people, than California ever did.

Taking the past 40 years as our timeframe, Ireland has become one of the most liberal societies in the world. And in the same period Ireland's economy has become one of the fastest growing in the developed world.

The open, tolerant society that embraces diversity and difference and affords dignity to all also drives the successful fast-growing economy, because at the heart of economic growth is self-expression and innovation. Innovation stems from the liberated and creative mind which comes from individual liberation, freeing him or her up to venture artistically, commercially and socially.

Free the human mind from strictures and rules, and enormous creative commercial energy is released. Keep the human mind shackled and oppressed, and the opposite occurs: stagnation. Once you allow the innovative mind to imagine a different future, you foster great economic innovation, which drives the economy.

These links from individual freedom to economic expansion explain why today's liberal Ireland is a rich Ireland and yesterday's conservative Ireland was a poor Ireland. Once we opened up, we started to become wealthy.

This is the story of how the Pope's Children – those born in the baby boom of the late seventies and early eighties – became rich. In a world where other countries are divided, their economies stalled, lurching to the extremes, convulsed by existential fights pitting one part of the population against the other, a well-off, relatively chilled Ireland, with a growing economy, surfing a wave of liberal optimism, isn't a bad place to be one hundred years after the state was founded. It's not perfect, but it's pretty damn good and we shouldn't let perfect bully pretty good.

THE LIBERAL DIVIDEND

The repeal result, which represents a huge liberal swing in the country since the year the Pope's Children were born, wasn't a triumph for Dún Laoghaire over the culchies or for cosmopolitan Ireland over traditional

Ireland, but it was a fusion of the best of both, a synthesis of a bit of everything. This new deal allows a person to vote enthusiastically for repeal on Friday, 25 May, and get up the following morning on Saturday, 26 May, the last day of communion season, and sit proudly in Mass overseeing their daughter's entrance into the Catholic communion.

Ireland, so often a place of extremes, has blended into a centre, where old distinctions are blurring. Differences that we thought were set in stone have faded away. The Aran Islands and Monkstown voted almost the same way, in near-similar proportions. West Mayo and Glenageary backed repeal, so too did traditional South Kerry and cosmopolitan Killiney.

In 1983, the year of the first abortion referendum, when Dún Laoghaire was almost alone in celebrating a rare rugby Triple Crown by an Irish team largely made up of local schoolboys, sliotars in Dalkey were about as likely as Roscommon voting for abortion. Yet, 35 years later, both have come to pass. Dalkey's Cuala GAA are All-Ireland club hurling champions and rural Roscommon voted to repeal. In fact, it is provincial, conservative Castlerea in County Roscommon, not urbane, tolerant Dún Laoghaire in south county Dublin, that has the dope-smoking, weed-legalising MEP.

When kids in rugby country excel at hurling, when Inis Meáin and Sandycove vote similarly, and when the once un-Irish ethics and codes of Dún Laoghaire are today the values that Ireland celebrates and that define our new nation, you know you are dealing with something far-reaching.

We are a nation transformed in more ways than you might think. As we became more liberal and more enlightened, we also became much wealthier. Once the society opened, the economy followed. It seems that the white heat of social change energised a remarkable economic transformation because as soon as the shackles came off, the economy started to surge. The link between tolerance and subsequent economic growth – let's call it the liberal dividend – is the story of modern Ireland.

Up to then, dogmatic Ireland suffered from a massive economic systems failure that acted against the interests of the citizens in general. Ireland paid for piety with poverty. However, there was so much pent-up economic energy under the surface that once dogma retreated, the economic potential of the country erupted.

It is often argued that as any economy becomes wealthier, we the citizens benefit from the stronger economic performance and become more tolerant precisely because we are less threatened commercially by people and ideas that are different from our own. This way of thinking is based on the premise that the economy has a mind of its own, as if divorced from the people who create it. A remote, robotic economy, operating of its own accord, somehow delivers the fruit of some miraculous commercial surge, which we then utilise. This view contends that after we become wealthy or more comfortable, then and only then do we become more liberal. Such a conclusion rests on the idea that better working conditions, better health, take-away Indian food, Google, air conditioning, iPads, orthodontist bills and a generally better lifestyle give us the permission to think for ourselves, change our attitudes, drop conservatism and embrace liberalism.

This can only be the case if you believe that the economy and society operate in separate spheres. I'm not so sure this is how it works. It seems to me more plausible that the economy and the society work together and that a philosophical ecosystem that encourages dissent, freedom and questioning is an ecosystem that encourages entrepreneurship and economic dynamism. Culture and philosophy lead economics and commerce. Bouncy Castle Catholicism, the live-and-let-live place we have arrived at, is such a philosophical ecosystem.

Ireland's remarkable period of social and economic national transformation was bookended by the visit of an autocratic pope in 1979 and the visit of a democratic one in 2018, and by the first abortion referendum in 1983 and the repeal referendum in 2018. The transformation suggests a compelling case that economic values and social values are intertwined. It seems reasonable to suggest that the culture war and the economic surge are related and, ultimately, we didn't end up with an absolute victory for one side or the other: traditional versus liberal, right versus left, urban versus rural. Instead, we have witnessed a gradual move from the extremes to the tolerant centre.

Social liberalism and economic liberalism go hand in hand. These two transformative forces drive each other and reinforce each other; they came together spectacularly in Ireland in the years between the visit of the Polish Pope and the visit of the Argentinean Pope.

CHAPTER 2

THE RADICAL CENTRE

VICTORY FOR THE COMMON PEOPLE

Once we are prepared to accept the link between culture and economics, lots of developments we see in society become clearer and we can see larger patterns. For example, economic prosperity is associated all over the world with increases in individual moral, sexual and personal liberty. Economic promiscuity, a little bit of that and a little bit of this, an experience here and an experience there, is the path to commercial virtue. This is the story of the modern world: social liberalism is twinned with economic dynamism. You could say that this is the essence of liberalism which unshackles ordinary people.

Such a contention is not a new idea. After all, wasn't it individual revolution that drove the Dutch to make 17th-century Amsterdam the richest, most creative city in the world, with great commerce, art, architecture and liberalism? From there these Enlightenment values spread. Wherever they spread, the economy tended to flourish. Where the Enlightenment was extinguished, the economy rapidly deteriorated in tandem.

Unfortunately, as we will later see, in independent Ireland through much of the twentieth century, this fruitful font of individual creativity became clogged up with religious dogma, post-colonial ideology and hard-line nationalism, elevating to sinner status the creative entrepreneurial hero, destroying the source of commercial and economic innovation. When looking back at the lifetime of the Pope's Children, it is hard to grasp now just how out of line Ireland once was and how many mutinies must have occurred within the Irish mind since those days to propel us forward.

THE CLERISTOCRACY AND THE CULTURE WAR

Emboldened by the popular theatrics of the 1979 Pope's visit and the resounding victory in the 1983 referendum, the Cleristocracy – the aristocracy of bishops and their supporters in the deep state – pushed on with the divorce referendum in 1986, delivering another victory for the religious right. Ireland was going backwards.

With the benefit of hindsight, the outbreak of religious radicalism which gripped Ireland in the 1980s might not have been a sign of conservative confidence but a symptom of panic.

Given the higher levels of education that free schooling delivered and the fact that the 1970s were a reasonably progressive decade, at least by Irish post-independence standards, the Cleristocracy understood that the Pope's visit was probably the high point. They saw that the relative liberalism of the mid-1970s was an indicator of impending social change.

This tendency happens in all culture wars. A period of liberalism is followed by a reactionary swing to extreme fundamentalism, before the trend towards liberalism starts again. The upswing in Islamic fundamentalism, which only appeals to a small minority of Muslims in an increasingly secular globe, could be seen in this light. The rise of Trumpism, that 'screw you' nativism allied with the religious right in the USA, is the same thing. When movements feel that the ground is slipping from under them, they tend to lurch towards fundamentalism to prevent the loss of further ground. I suspect the same is happening to Unionism in the North, but more on that later.

My line of thinking here implies that in Ireland, before the battle tipped convincingly towards secularism, the Church lurched to the American fundamentalist position on abortion and divorce, dragging the country with it by deploying the great Catholic twin upper-cut and jab: fear and shame.

For four decades, the culture war raged between the Cleristocracy and the individual citizen. While the huge 'Yes' vote to repeal on 25 May 2018 might have constituted one of the final battles of this great culture war, the opening salvoes were fired the day the first Pope came here on 29 September 1979. The first few years of the war saw advances of the Cleristocracy on many fronts.

The more ground the Cleristocracy gained, the more the economy tanked. As Ireland moved to the fundamentalist right at the ballot box, creative people headed for the door. Emigration surged in the 1980s, driven by the faltering economy, policed by rules and regulations.

Sometimes the culture war was an all-out conflict, sometimes low-level guerrilla warfare. Every now and then there would be an event or skirmish which focused the warring factions, but like all long, drawn-out conflicts, the culture war was a gradual campaign of attrition, with both sides acquiring and relinquishing territory, bolstered by incessant propaganda. The territory up for grabs in our culture war was the most precious zone known to any society: the moral terrain of the mind.

It was Cleristocracy against the citizen, conservatism against liberalism, absolutism versus laissez-faire values, insiders versus outsiders, national against foreign, Hibernianism versus cosmopolitanism. But it also pitted dependency against independence and, maybe most significantly, pitted the national collective myth against the sovereign, individual citizen.

At every stage, in every referendum and every vote, each tribe lined up with its placards, posters, emojis and memes. One tribe trying to change the status quo, the other tribe warning of apocalypse and numerous non-specific floodgates. However, as progress tends to unfold one funeral at a time, gradually but definitively rosary-bead Ireland has been edged out by gluten-free Ireland in the crucible of public and personal morality.

The culture war ended with the victory for the independent citizen.

Watching Pope Francis apologise – again and again – to the Irish people brings to mind a humiliated general of a once-powerful army, who realises that survival means accepting the new reality. With the battle won, one way of looking at the visit of Pope Francis is that he came here in August 2018 to sign an armistice with the Irish people to bring the curtain down on a war that was begun by his predecessor in September 1979.

THE RADICAL CENTRE EXCEPTION

The heroes of the great Irish economic transformation are not the wonderful orators, stand-out leaders or messiahs of any hue, but the everyday people who are slow to judge others, who live by their own set of civilised rules, who return lost wallets or mislaid bikes, who pick up their dog's poo in bags and deposit it in a municipal bin, who do the accounts for the local GAA club, who volunteer at the Mini World Cup and who take it upon themselves to start a small business. These are a nuanced people who, rather than rally around an extreme position, are content to take direction from a Citizens Assembly that tries to find the centre ground, acceptable to most, setting the agenda on a centrist rather than extreme course.

These are the common people who, through their tolerance, respect those around them. They can be found in the background, beavering away, and are driven by the expectation that tomorrow will be a little bit better than today, and therefore worth getting up for. This relentless effort, put in every day in every small town, every suburb and village in the country, without the need for acclamation or bragging, is the dynamo of the economic miracle.

These are not the radical left, who may have thought that victory over the Cleristocracy would usher in an atheist republic so beloved of Connolly, Larkin, Browne and others. They imagined a completely post-religious state, a Finland with Guinness. They got something else. Nor did the culture war lead to a strengthening of the radical right counter-revolution of the 1980s with its fundamentalist leanings, as has occurred with the rise of the religious right in America. We ended up not on the extremes but somewhere around the middle.

This middle ground is the Radical Centre, a place of compromise and synthesis. The Radical Centre begins with the common man or, increasingly and thankfully, the common woman. She is the one, tinkering away or revolving ideas in her liberated brain, who makes the difference.

At its core is the respect for the individual which provides the social ballast that prevents lurches to the extremes. The Radical Centre explains why Ireland has arrived in 2018, on the eve of our hundredth birthday, a century after the War of Independence, without any anti-immigration politicians, let alone an anti-immigration movement, no Brexit-style separatist crusade, no Donald Trump figure intent on a nativist agenda. Look around at the rest of the world. Ireland's combination of an inclusive Radical Centre and a flourishing economy is the precise opposite of what is the norm now in our neighbours, where politics is lurching to the radical right or the radical left, all against the background of faltering economies, local people feeling locked out and threatened by newcomers.

Globally, Ireland appears to be something of an exception.

We don't have an extreme left with any material support, such as England's Corbynistas who seem to suffer from Cuba-envy with their undertaking to nationalise UK industry. Nor do we see support for a Le Pen-style white supremacist party intent on kicking out immigrants and demonising Muslims. We have no significant anti-EU party like Italy's present governing coalition. Nor do we have racist, homophobic leaders like in Poland, Hungary and Slovakia.

We are in the Radical Centre. I say 'radical' because the economy is moving at such a pace, at such tilt, that there is an inbuilt dynamic overturning the old status quo. We are innovating, changing, surprising ourselves, commuting, opening, closing, trading, buying and selling at a pace unrivalled outside Asia. I will explore the economic miracle in the next chapter but suffice it to say that on almost every economic metric, Ireland has outpaced our European neighbours, indeed almost all of the rest of the developed world, by a factor of two in the past 30 years. This has been a quite heroic performance.

The independent citizen, the victor in the great culture war, is the star of the show. Personal motivations of self-improvement drive the economy forward. Most of the time these motivations dwell in our brains, and only come to fruition if they are allowed and encouraged by the rest of us, which is why a society that dignifies commercial efforts tends to grow faster. Once we were liberated and animal spirits were unleashed, our economy took off. Social change came slowly and organically, and because it was slow and democratic, it has generally been accepted. It's almost as if nobody noticed.

This is why the country is now led by a gay, half-Indian polyglot, who went to a Protestant school, is a qualified doctor and a fierce intellectual, who works out every morning, practises yoga and takes world leaders jogging rather than drinking. He is also the first ever graduate of Trinity, the university set up by an English monarch to subjugate the colony, to run the country.

Had you predicted this at the time of the first papal visit, the bookies would have taken your money gladly and offered you wild odds. No one would have believed you. But it has happened.

The beauty is that the international press like the *New York Times*, the *Guardian* and *Die Welt* were stunned at the arrival of this new type of Irish leader. Foreign journalists described his elevation to Taoiseach as being indicative of how old Ireland had suddenly changed, making a big deal of his sexuality and his ethnicity. In contrast, no one here as much as batted an eyelid because the victory of Radical Centre values is now complete.

Guess what year Leo Varadkar was born? Why, 1979. So, we have one of the Pope's Children leading the country, one hundred years after the War of Independence fought to give Ireland back to the Irish. But no one thought the Irish would ever look like this.

Welcome to the Renaissance Nation.

TALK MATTERS

The Renaissance starts with new attitudes because attitudes – and here I mean public attitudes – exert an enormous influence on the economy, setting the tone for the society in which the essential economic innovation either takes place or doesn't.

When I first learned economics, we were told data is crucial. Data is evidence. For economists, data means things that you can measure, like cars on the road, cranes in the sky and so on. However, as I get older, I am more and more convinced that attitudes are also in fact data. What you say and what you think matters enormously. Attitudes set the tone and everything else follows. The change in attitudes is significant, and because attitudes are data, they are evidence. Almost to the day that Mary Robinson was elected, when tolerant, curious Ireland first signalled that it was prepared to change the old male domination of the highest office in the land, the economy started to motor and begin its upward ascent. These are not unrelated events.

Our economy soared past those of other countries between 1990 and 2018. What distinguished us from these countries was that Ireland went through a culture war during the same period whereby attitudes changed profoundly. Indeed, you could add that, as Ireland was becoming more tolerant and richer, many of our neighbours were becoming less tolerant and less rich. The essential chemistry and unique aspect of the Irish experience has been the millions of little mutinies going off inside the minds of millions of Irish people, leading to the triumph of an open civic bourgeoisie. In turn, changing attitudes encouraged the notion that the independent citizen could 'have a go'.

Looking back, there was no one big event that turned the tide, no moment when our Berlin Wall came down; rather it was a gradual opening up to liberalism. Over the years, the national conversation became less accusatory, less vindictive, slightly more refined, more tolerant and less interfering. Privacy has become more valued and public displays of anger and national finger-pointing less common. These are all small things, but they change public opinion and at pivotal moments like political plebiscites, a silent accommodating majority stands up and is counted. Every time the extreme voice sounds more threatening, the reasonable liberal voice becomes more persuasive.

The driver of creativity is what lies between our ears and when that thing between our ears is allowed to dream, allowed to venture forth, left alone to do its thing without the interference of governments or priests or protesters, the power of all these brains firing up at the same time is truly electric. Liberalism was the extra ingredient, the missing X factor that kicked in, driving the economy, once the shackles came off.

When you think about it, it is innovation rather than invention which propels the economy. Innovation is the product of the curious mind, which itself is a function of its environment. And that environment exists when society gives individuals permission to be creative or, better still, actively encourages them. This link is why attitudes matter. Consequently, the independent individual in a civilized society is the crucial alchemical link to a successful economy. And it is that link that explains why Ireland has been much more economically dynamic over the past 30 years than the UK, Germany, France or Italy.

When you look at the economic playing field between western EU countries, you see that it is pretty level. So for one country's performance to surge ahead of the rest unexpectedly, something major must have been going on inside that country that was not happening in the other countries.

So, for example, we are all European countries, we all have access to the same markets, we all have the ability to change our sovereign tax rates and we can all benefit from having hard-working immigrants. Education spending is more or less the same in each western European country. Our universities do not stand out, in the main, from each other. All our neighbours have similar protection of innovation and property rights. We increasingly have the same institutions under the EU umbrella. So when you look at most factors that would normally cause an economy to grow, amongst our neighbours, Ireland is not unique or special in any material way, or at least it doesn't appear so on the surface.

These observations beg two questions. First, why was Ireland's take-off so delayed in the 20th century? And second, once it came, why was it so explosive and long-lasting in the 21st?

The answer lies in the attitudes and the link between culture wars and individual commercial creativity, so it is worth noting that, by the 1980s, other European countries had already experienced their culture wars and the victory of their curious civic bourgeoisie, possibly explaining why they all grew so significantly in the post-war period.

Let's consider a country in the news as I write, as it has a radical, explicitly anti-EU government but, unlike the UK, no apparent intention of leaving the EU. When we think of Italy's great awakening in the 1960s, the Dolce Vita, we think of the creative mind of filmmaker Federico Fellini. Fellini loved the absurd, the ridiculous. His movies, with their outrageous cast of Italian eccentrics, captured the booming, confident Italy of the 1960s, 1970s and 1980s. Fellini was postwar Italy's scriptwriter. Fellini's Italy was the glamorous, liberated Italy of Sophia Loren, Carlo Ponti, Umberto Eco. It was the creative Italy that took the world by storm in design, film and literature. By the late 1960s, as part of the liberal wave that was washing over Catholic Europe, from France and Belgium and down to the Mediterranean, the separation of Church and state in Italy was underway.

It was also a time when the anti-commerce movement was spearheaded by the Italian Communist Party. The battle pitted the free-trading, liberal Christian Democrats against the more austere dogma of the Communists. The Christian Democrats won. As Italy became more open, questioning and centrist, the economy boomed. By the early 1970s, Catholic Italy had introduced divorce and in 1978 abortion was made available to all Italian women.

As an interesting contrast in attitude between poor Ireland and wealthy Italy, in 1981, two years before the Irish abortion referendum in 1983, 68% of Italian voters rejected an attempt to repeal the pro-abortion act. Two years later, the same percentage of Irish voters elected to do the opposite and insert an anti-abortion clause in the constitution.

Italy's boom and surge in creative entrepreneurship coincided with the 'millions of little mutinies' in the Italian mind. We see similar stories all over the continent. Continental countries all shared a similar trajectory of recovery from the war between 1950 and 1960, then a culture war between 1960 and 1980, which coincided with their surge in living standards. Their heyday was a similar 30-year period of rapid growth, with national attitudes moving away from suspicion towards tolerance and acceptance. Ireland, in contrast, was isolated and oppressed and we stalled. But then the same thing happened. Like clockwork: culture war followed by economic resurgence. In 1979, Italy was nearly twice as rich as Ireland; today, Ireland is richer than Italy.

In western European terms, we just came late to the party, but we had years of pent-up commercial enthusiasm waiting to be unleashed. And, as is sometimes the way at parties, the last one in the door makes the biggest impression when you least expect it.

CHAPTER 3

THE GROWTH FREAK

L et's take a bit of altitude and look at the longer term picture because one of the lasting consequences of the housing crash and the credit splurge that preceded it, is that we have developed a tendency to tell the Irish economic story solely through a lens of the recent boom and bust. While understandable, this digestible tale of rise and fall misses the real story. The grand economic narrative of this small island is not centred on 2008, but rather the extraordinary performance of the Irish economy over the past thirty years, indeed, during the lifetimes of the Pope's Children. As the austere Moving Statue Catholicism was gradually replaced by an ambiguous Bouncy Castle Catholicism, the Irish economy soared. Ireland's economic transformation during the same period has been one of the most impressive national turnabouts in contemporary economic history.

Economic growth is the gift that allows societies to improve themselves. Without economic growth we don't get improvements in health, we don't get longevity, we don't eradicate diseases, we don't lift hundreds of thousands out of poverty. In the absence of economic growth, people remain uneducated, their standard of living stagnates, women remain in the home and things we take for granted – central heating, electricity, foreign travel, laptops, mobile phones, large-screen TVs, the eradication of TB, the elimination of measles, the flu vaccine, braces, skinny flat whites, avocado toast, bus lanes, burrito bars and the old age pension – are simply not possible.

Granted, there are difficulties with any measure that adds up all the bits of the economy, or at least tries to do so. One figure, whether it is income per head, gross domestic product (GDP) or gross national product (GNP), is never going to cover everything. In addition, such statistics in a small country can be jolted or zigzagged by big movements of multinational profits and other distortions. But if the trend over time is relentlessly upwards, and truly rocketing upwards at a much faster pace than all your neighbours, the benefits that accrue to the citizens are enormous.

Years ago, I worked in the Central Bank on the economic model that forecasts Irish growth. I used to think I understood what drove economic growth, but now I'm not so sure.

I used to think it was simply a matter of adding material things on top of each other like building blocks. From this vantage, the economy is simply an elaborate game of Jenga. The stacking of the blocks seemed largely at the discretion of policymakers, while the overall stability of the structure appeared reliant upon things like the strength of institutions, investment, property rights, public infrastructure, the tax system and economic variables like the rate of interest, inflation or exchange.

Although these traditional factors are all vitally important, I'm not convinced that they alone suffice to explain what has happened to this country over the past thirty years or so. If they were, surely other countries would have sought to emulate Ireland's success and we would see equally impressive economic stories taking place over similar timeframes around the world. But that is not the case. Ireland is an outlier. Therefore, we need to dig deeper for answers.

The fact is that the economy took off precisely when Irish society opened up to new ideas, became more tolerant and provided dignity to people whose lifestyles were previously shunned. Once we valued self-expression, including commercial self-expression, the economy surged. This is simply too big a coincidence to ignore. Undeniably, more traditional economic factors such as the tax system and accession to the European market played a major role in Ireland's transformation, but shifting social values and the millions of mutinies of the mind that took place around the country were arguably the more important driver. After all, plenty of countries have joined the EU and all have their own sovereign tax systems, but none have performed like Ireland.

In the next chapter I will explore what I believe to be the extra, critical factor that makes the economy dance, but before we unpack that link between tolerance and economic reward, let's look at the evidence.

THE EVIDENCE

Given that we are in a period of commemoration of the War of Independence and the foundation of the state, it is perhaps fitting that we look at Ireland's economic and social transformation over the same period. The charts on the following page tell the story of Ireland over the last century. Before you digest the data, a word of reassurance about economics and graphs. Don't worry, there will be very few charts in this book, but some are simply too good to withhold. Emblazoned in ink, we can see the economic history of the state on a single page.

As noted before, a pinch of salt is required when dealing with such economic measures as GDP given that there are so many moving parts in a highly globalised, open economy. But they are the best we have. The data populating these charts has been drawn from the Maddison Project Database, a well-established source of income levels and economic growth around the world.[1]

Let's look back to the year Ireland gained independence and track the evolution of the Irish economy. Figure 1 traces the growth of real Irish GDP per capita since independence, taking 1990 as a base year for comparison, alongside that of our European neighbours and American cousins.

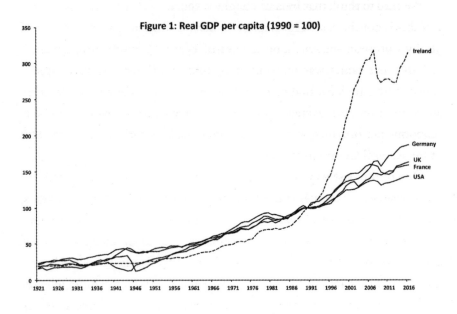

Figure 1: Real GDP per capita (1990 = 100)

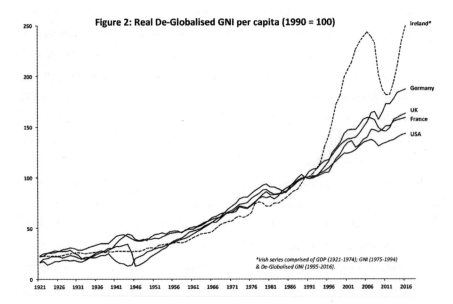

Figure 2: Real De-Globalised GNI per capita (1990 = 100)

*Irish series comprised of GDP (1921-1974); GNI (1975-1994)
& De-Globalised GNI (1995-2016).

We tend to think that Ireland was always poor, at least under British rule. But this is not the case. The fact is that Ireland was actually relatively well-off, by European standards, on the eve of World War I. In 1913, Ireland's real GDP per capita was on a par with that of the sophisticated Swedes and cultured Italians, higher than Norway's or Spain's, and comfortably above the European average.[2] But after independence we blew it, and our economic performance was pretty abysmal thereafter, that is until the rise of the Radical Centre in the late 1980s and early 1990s.

One of the best ways to appreciate how unprecedented the past thirty years have been is to divide the century into two periods: the first seventy years and the past thirty years.

As you can see, from 1920 to about 1990, Irish incomes lagged behind almost everyone else's. This is also when the dogmatic Church and interventionist state ran the show. As I intend to reveal, the more religion meddled and the more the state intervened, the more lamentable our economic performance.

Irish growth rates were just about keeping pace with the UK, by then a country on the decline. And anyway, while we may have been matching British growth rates, we were starting from a much lower base – econ-speak for not having a pot to piss in. Ireland should have been growing faster and catching up with our British neighbours, rather than merely keeping pace. Moreover, growth rates in the UK, and by extension Ireland's economic performance, were poor relative to most other European countries over the first seven decades of the 20th century.[3] So if the UK was the sick man of Europe, what did that make us?

Ireland recorded the slowest per capita income growth of any European economy between 1910 and 1970, with the exception of the UK.[4]

This suffocating trend continued into the 1980s. As you will remember, Ireland took two big conservative leaps backwards with the 1983 insertion of the eighth amendment into the constitution and a bit later with the resounding defeat of a divorce referendum in 1986. If we agree that tolerance is necessary for the economy to grow, it comes as no surprise that in the 1980s, when Ireland was becoming more intolerant, we were also becoming more impoverished.

Ireland was one of the very few countries to experience a recession in the mid-1980s. Within Europe, only ourselves and a few Soviet bloc countries were going backwards.[5] Ireland, wrapped up in its own stultifying conservatism, missed the global economic boom of the 1980s. For a small trading economy, it is quite an achievement to manage to avoid a global economic boom when our two major trading partners, the UK and US, were surging ahead. West Germany also boomed in the 1980s, dragging continental Europe with it. But alone on our little rock in the Atlantic, we continued to export our people and our problems.

Ireland – still in the grip of a Cleristocracy who at that stage (on paper at least) were winning the culture war – was busy stifling individual creativity and self-expression, working very hard at going backwards. In 1979 Irish income per head was around $12,342 compared to $22,053 in Germany, $22,713 in France, $20,500 in the UK and $20,530 in Italy.[6] In crude terms, we had only half of what they had. Compared to the US, which had an income per head of $29,630, we were further behind again. It wasn't good enough to be matching the economic growth of the richer countries – when you are poor you have to grow much faster in order to catch up – but the opposite was happening. By the mid-1980s, as I worked illegally in the kitchens of booming Boston, it seemed that most of the people who had lived on my road in Dún Laoghaire were emigrating after school or college. In the 1980s, for the first time, Ireland experienced mass graduate emigration. We were experiencing a massive brain drain. The influential *Economist* magazine wrote an extremely depressing headline piece about Ireland's lamentable performance, showing a tatty vista under the headline: 'Ireland, the poorest of the rich'.[7] Watching Fab Vinny in America, there was only one route open to us, so the vast majority of my 1988 university class emigrated.

From around 1990 onwards, just when things looked at their most dismal, something dramatic transpired. If you look at Figure 1, you see that, out of nowhere, Ireland explodes from the economic blocks. Globally, only China and a handful of other Asian countries have grown faster since. From then on, an enormous gap opens up between the economic growth rate of Ireland and the countries around us. And with the Irish economic engine motoring, our income levels start to overtake those of our neighbours.

Within the space of three years, from 1997 to 2000, Irish income per head surpassed the French, the Germans and the Brits – the behemoths of Europe – before overtaking the Americans in the early Noughties.

Incidentally, the year 1990 was when Ireland rejected the patriarchy for the first time and voted Mary Robinson – a civil rights lawyer, liberal campaigner and, most crucially, a woman – into the Áras. This was the first concrete sign that something else, something extra, was going on. Typically, if a western country grows much more quickly than its neighbours, it eventually slows down and rejoins the pack. But after the initial 1990 surge, we kept growing, and we haven't really stopped since. Granted there was a significant slump after the crash, but as you can see in the chart, it was short-lived.

Given the startling magnitude of this transformation, you'd be forgiven for questioning the veracity of the Irish GDP figures as a true reflection of life on the ground. As we've seen in recent years, accountants shifting numbers around in the balance sheets of large multinational companies has led to significant distortions in the Irish national accounts, and the term 'leprechaun economics' has caught on accordingly. It is undeniable that these multinationals do form a substantial part of the Irish economy but it is also undeniable that their presence in the statistics is justified. Over 200,000 jobs[8] and the billions in corporation tax paid to the Exchequer each year are real; however, in order to avoid being accused of an over-optimistic interpretation of the growth figures, let's take a figure that seeks to strip out the distortion from the multinationals.

Even when we look at a hybrid index that seeks to strip out the effects of multinationals (see Figure 2, p. 32), the magnitude of Ireland's economic transformation is still staggering.[9]

Before we ask why this happened, and why it happened when it did, it is helpful to put the Irish economic surge (or miracle) into context with a few 'before and after' figures.

While the economy didn't take off until around 1990, just when the Pope's Children were making their confirmations, for my purposes I'm going to start with Ireland in 1979, the year they were born. We saw earlier that we were just half as rich as our neighbours. The case I want to make is that the extra factor, the real driving force of the timing of the Irish economic miracle, was the culture war between the individual citizen and the collective regressive forces of the Church and the state. It wasn't so much an economic policy change, but a value system change encompassing the entire society that drove the economy. Once our values started to move towards liberalism, our economy opened up because we dared to dream of a better future.

Economic dynamism and social liberalism go together.

THE ACHIEVEMENT

The progress the country has made is truly startling. In 1979, when our bankrupt country rolled out the papal red carpet, Ireland was the 42nd richest country in the world. Today we are the eighth richest in the world. Now Ireland is up there with the likes of Denmark and Sweden. Back then at the 42nd richest country in the world we were keeping company with Gabon. Our income per head in 1979 was the same as Botswana's is today.[10] Given what had happened in the previous seventy years since independence, there was no reason for any young Irish person, even if the Pope told us he loved us, to expect the future to be any different. There was no historical basis for optimism. The best most of us could hope for was more of the same.

But that's not what happened.

In 1979, the year the Pope's Children were born, the average Irish person had a budget of €7.29 per day. Today the average Irish person is spending €53.49. This is a huge increase in daily spending power. Of course, things cost a lot more now, but nonetheless the figure is impressive. That's a lot more asparagus tips, Zara strappy dresses, kitchen islands and university MBA places. To put this in context, the rise in the Irish standard of living from spending €7.29 per day to spending €53.49 has been double the rise experienced by our neighbours in Germany (€14.51 to €57.47), France (€12.24 to €51.32), Belgium (€13.14 to €53.77), Denmark (€14.94 to €64.33), Netherlands (€13.30 to €51.49) and Sweden (€14.35 to €57.30) over the same period.[11] All these countries were so much richer in 1979. We came from a much poorer position and have overtaken most of our neighbours.

I remember going to Germany on a schoolboys' football tour with Dalkey United in 1980 and feeling poor. Everything in Germany was so desirable and impressive. The German kids we played against had much more money than we did. Twelve-year-old boys notice things like their cool Puma football kits and top-of-the-range Adidas boots. We usually changed in the Dublin rain on the side of the pitch; their clubhouse looked posher than the Shelbourne. The family homes we stayed in had stuff that we could only dream of. Their cars were new and clean and their roads smoothly asphalted and beautifully marked. Now, when we look at the data, we can see that these boyhood impressions were accurate. They weren't just a bit richer than us; they were twice as rich as us. Irish people had on average €7.29 to spend per day, whereas the average German had €14.94 to spend. Their standard of living was twice as high as ours.[12]

Today our standard of living is about the same level as the Germans, having grown twice as fast on average as Germany over the period. We came from behind and overtook France, Italy, Belgium, the UK and a whole host of other wealthy, colonial countries. For a former colony that isn't too bad.

We are living through truly exceptional times. And because we are living through them, we sometimes don't appreciate how remarkable these times are. The Irish pie has become much bigger and it became much bigger, much faster than anywhere else in the developed world. Only the likes of China, South Korea and India have had more impressive growth stories in the past generation.

GROWTH AS A GIFT

Economic growth in itself is not the objective. In fact, there is a weakness in seeing growth as the be all and end all. Growth is a gift that facilitates progress. Economic growth provides the resources to achieve other goals. Growth rates that are running twice as quickly as your neighbours allow you to catch up on many other levels. On a much broader basis, economic growth has allowed daily life to improve dramatically in Ireland, for the vast majority of the population.

Based on the UN's Human Development Index, Ireland has surged from being the 24th most developed nation in the world in 1990 to the fourth today.[13]

Let's take a random date in the past and compare it with today. Do you remember where you were when David O'Leary sent the Romanian keeper the wrong way in Genoa in 1990? I was in Goggins Pub in Monkstown. That balmy night, our victory was met by a local convoy of rusty Toyota Corollas, bedecked in tricolours, followed by young lads doing wheelies on Choppers.

On that day, 25 June 1990, Ireland was about as developed as modern-day Albania, Cuba, Kazakhstan or Mauritius, according to the UN.[14] Take your pick. If you want to jog the memory, there's a great video on YouTube of the locals in Balbriggan celebrating that night. It's well worth a look. We do a mean emaciated impression – skinny, stone-washed, bad teeth and even worse mullets. Consider how far we have travelled in such a short space of time.

A German friend of mine, visiting Dublin in May 1990, and having never seen girls decked out in their full communion clobber, replete with long white dresses and veils, declared that while she respected our tribal traditions, she thought that, as members of the EU, the persistence of the practice of 'child brides' in a European member state should not be tolerated by Brussels. The fact that someone from Germany, the country whose money kept the lights on and built our roundabouts, still thought it possible that such an atavistic practice could persist here, is indicative of where sophisticated secular Europe thought Ireland was perennially moored.

Further evidence of this seismic change in Irish society can be seen when we compare female labour force participation rates. In the early part of the decade that culminated with Pope John Paul II's visit, just over 20% of Irish women were at work.[15] To put this in perspective, Ireland's female participation rate then was comparable to where Afghanistan (19.5%), Saudi Arabia (22.3%) and the Arab world as a whole (20.9%) are today.[16] For women with ambitions to work and further their career, Ireland was a Catholic Caliphate with ISIS-style levels of female participation.

By the early 1980s, when we had the first abortion referendum, female participation was still exceptionally low at around 30%, where Bangladesh and Oman are now. Today it is 53.6%, in line with both EU and OECD averages.[17] More women are now graduating from university than men.[18] Girls are outperforming boys in secondary school.[19]

We Irish have also become hyper-educated. Fifty years on from the abolition of fees for second-level education, when a third of children concluded their education following primary school and fewer than 36% were still in school at 16,[20] now 97% of students are completing their Junior Cert and over 91% go on to finish the Leaving Cert.[21] Meanwhile, the share of Irish adults with a university degree has also surged from around 15% in 1989 to 43% today, ranking the Irish as some of the most educated people in the world.[22] Those aged 35–39 are more than twice as likely to have a third-level qualification as their parents' generation (aged 65–69).[23]

Irish people are living longer. During the period of the culture war, average life expectancy rose by nine years, from 73 in 1980 to 82 now. The nation's death rate has also fallen by more than a third over the same period, while rates of infant mortality are now a fifth of their 1980 levels. Medical advancements have seen immunisation rates against measles surge from a mere 10% in 1983 to near total coverage today.[24]

While the Pope's Children have had free access to the contraceptives that were banned at the time of the first papal visit, our fertility rate remains amongst the highest in Europe, yet the rate of teenage pregnancies has been cut in half.[25] Babies are among the best indicators of belief in the future in developed countries. Contrast this Irish experience with the story of central and eastern Europe after the fall of communism.[26] Fertility rates from Serbia to Russia collapsed following the economic trauma brought about by the end of the command system. Suddenly impoverished, many people gave up on the future and signalled this by having fewer kids. In Ireland, fertility rates are still high by international standards, indicative of a thumbs-up to the future.

While there is still a considerable way to go, the gender pay gap has fallen dramatically over the generations, from around 33% in the mid-1980s to 23% in 2014.[27] The power of trade unions has been in steady decline over the past forty years, with union membership as a proportion of all those in employment almost halving from 62% in 1980 to 27% today.[28,29] As trade union membership declined, standards of living increased. I'll come back to this later.

Today Ireland ranks eighth amongst advanced economies on the Inclusive Development Index compiled by the World Economic Forum, with the second-highest level of labour productivity.[30]

As we got richer, we became more, not less, equal. This makes Ireland unusual in the western world, where the trend has been towards more, not less, income inequality. (Of course, income inequality is not the same as wealth inequality, and we will come back to that in Chaper 29.)

Still, the question remains: why did the economy take off when it did and not before? My belief is that the economy was driven from the bottom up more than from the top down.

THE BIG MYTH

In trying to examine why the economy took off so dramatically in the early 1990s, we should address a national myth that is often repeated about the economy: the Whitaker/Lemass myth.

The branding department of Leinster House works overtime at creating national myths. This is understandable. That's its job. Some of the best writers in society are political commentators working within that particular bubble. But amongst this talented cadre, there is a tendency, again inherited from those who went before them, to ascribe all economic successes to momentous decisions taken by civil servants and politicians. Because of incessant repetition, we are inclined to believe this Jackanory.

The Lemass/Whitaker fairytale is peddled by writers who spend an inordinate amount of time around Government Buildings. Many of them eventually leave journalism to take up much less risky positions as advisors to the political machine. In the past, this school has been termed the Doheny and Nesbitt School of Economics, but I'd prefer to call it the MacGill Summer School of Economics. The MacGill Summer School is a meeting of the great and good of the Irish political/economic machine, though it got into hot water in 2018 for its embarrassing paucity of women on the bill.

I do not want to have a go at the individuals involved. I organise two festivals myself and know how much hard work goes into getting them up and running. I want to focus on the ideology, not the personality.

Every year at the MacGill School, Ireland's nomenklatura meet. The majority of speakers at this event tend to have extremely high wages paid by other taxpayers. When your wages are paid by the taxpayers and not the market, you really don't have any skin in the game. You do not bear any personal risk. You are going to get paid anyway and can say anything, take any position, safe in the knowledge that your income – or incomes if you choose an advisory gig or six – is underwritten by the state. You live in a world that is without financial downside and, thus, you are entirely free to say what you want without consequence. If you don't believe me, have a look at the website and look at who pays the wages of most of the speakers. It may come as a surprise.

Although great company, well-educated and informed, they might not be the best at running a cornershop – or at least they haven't tried. Thus, when they make great statements on the economy, which actually depends on the hundreds of tiny commercial decisions taken by cornershop owners every day, theirs is the view of the inoculated observer rather than the exposed practitioner.

As a result, they tend to specialise in a pursuit that you might call 'postcasting', which is the opposite of forecasting. A great postcaster will tell you exactly what has happened and precisely why it happened. He will convince you in advance that Brexit couldn't possibly happen, and when it does happen he will tell you exactly why it did. Likewise with the housing market crash. Up until the end he will reassure you that there will be a soft landing, and then, in the middle of the meltdown, he will explain precisely why the meltdown occurred. But whether he is wrong or very wrong, the postcaster still gets paid. There is no downside, so why care?

Typically, postcasters believe in a system whereby a very clever servant pulls a lever and somewhere deep within the bowels of the economy, something happens. Therefore, the bigger the lever, the bigger the impact.

This might explain why MacGill tends to call for more investment in this or that sector. But while these may all be laudable sentiments, we know that's not how the commercial economy works.

As we will see in the next few chapters, innovation, not only investment, is the elixir of economic growth. Tinkering around drives innovation and it's very different from the old-fashioned economist's idea of investment. Investment, like a new building, isn't enough. Sure, if you add all the new buildings up you will get a figure that says the economy has grown, but that's not what creates dynamism and sometimes, for a while, it can even disguise fragility. Having too much capital for investment is often the road to ruin. Easy come, easy go. Think about banks investing in ghost estates here. The banks that financed the tail-end of the Irish property boom went bust and did so because of too much investment, not too little. As many entrepreneurs know to their peril, buckets of money to invest, without a good idea, is a very bad idea.

This is why lots of economists and public-sector fetishists, many of whom are cloistered in universities, misunderstand the link between investment and vigorous growth. Investment is not innovation. Bottom-up ideas, not top-down investment, change the world.

The patron saint of the MacGill School of Economics is T.K. Whitaker, a brilliant civil servant who passed away in 2017 at the wonderful age of 100. Whitaker is credited with persuading then Taoiseach Sean Lemass to open up the closed economy at the end of the calamitous 1950s. I say 'calamitous' because Ireland managed to miss the post-war boom of the 1950s, which saw the European, American and British economies take off. Isolated in our dogmatic fantasy world of inward-looking protectionist economics and an even more inward-looking religious code of beliefs, we missed out on this boom.

The MacGill Summer School of Economics contends that this event was a pivotal moment in Ireland's economic history, from which point on the economy started to motor. This sounds great and, indeed, it is taught in the Leaving Cert history course. These days the Lemass hagiography industry is also alive and well, which is all grand if you like that sort of thing. The only problem is that the story isn't accurate!

Whitaker and Lemass unveiled and began to implement their plan in 1958. In economics, things never happen overnight, but if this really was a seminal moment as the story tells us, we would imagine that the Irish economy took off relatively soon after that. But this didn't happen. Relative to other poor countries, our performance was dire and remained dire. Even if you give the so-called miracle plan thirty years to work, which would be generous, we see continued failure, not success.

The best way to capture this failure is to look at emigration. People move if there are no opportunities or if their creativity is being stultified. Over 1.1 million (excluding those who returned) emigrated between independence and the end of the 1980s.[31]

During the miracle years of the Lemass/Whitaker fable, things don't look too healthy: 409,000 were forced to leave during the 1950s, and from the 1960s to the late 1980s, a further 350,000 left the country.[32]

To help us contextualise, look at Figure 3, which maps Ireland's growth against the rest of Europe from 1950 to 1987.[33] The logic of the chart is that countries that started off poorer should grow more quickly – the poorer you are, the quicker you catch up. You would expect Ireland, particularly with our miracle plan, to grow at the same rate as the likes of Spain and Greece, catching up with Denmark and Belgium, who were already twice as rich as us per head. But that didn't happen. While Greece, Italy and Spain grew strongly as you'd expect, Ireland languished.

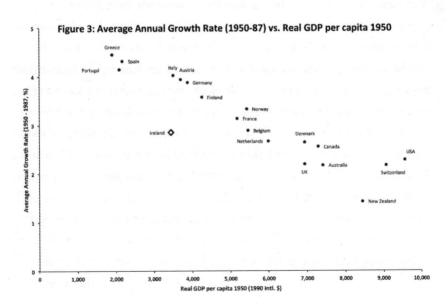

Figure 3: Average Annual Growth Rate (1950-87) vs. Real GDP per capita 1950

From 1950 to 1987, Ireland's performance slumped behind all other European countries. With a starting income per head of around $3,500, we grew at around the same rate, on average, as Belgium, with an income per head of $6,000, and Denmark, with an income per head of $7,000. In contrast, the country with the same income per head as us, Italy, grew much, much faster.[34]

This evidence flies in the face of the accepted narrative of the MacGill Summer School of Economics. It's just not true, or at least this is not what the numbers tell us. The economy continued to underperform despite a change in official policy.

When you think about it, the official ideology of the country – of censure and repression of individual effort and commercial expression – did not change one iota despite a more enlightened worldview from the top of the nomenklatura. Yes, there was glasnost but no perestroika. The value system remained wedded to dogma, not the individual. Mutinies were suppressed, and this suffocation didn't change until the late 1980s. You can have all the signalling you want from the top and indeed this can encourage foreign firms to come in here to create assembly-line industries that may provide a wage, but you need liberation of the mind to create a real productive, creative, self-regenerative economy. For this, you need a free, independent, risk-taking bourgeoisie. You need the Radical Centre.

There is no point changing the guard at the top if you don't liberate the citizen on the ground.

The Lemass/Whitaker line fed to most students also reflects the Irish academic weakness for the 'Great Man' in history approach to economics. I'm less interested in the 'Great Man' in history than the 'Little Woman' in history. But the 'Great Man' approach is favoured by official chroniclers of the state, possibly because they are embedded in the system. They are the deep insiders, the politicians, the advisors, the Leinster House anoraks, the academics, the IBEC bigwigs, the trade union specialists and their journalistic diarists, attributing economic success to some lever pulled by someone big in government which changes the course of events. That someone might even be them.

This line of storytelling might stem from the fact that history is often written by public servants and because the state retains a statist mind-set, consistently wanting to take credit. Whatever the reason, there is not much evidence of the Lemass/Whitaker dream team turnaround during the period when it was supposed to be a reality.

Something else was going on that can't be explained by wise men pulling levers, or pulling anything else for that matter.

THE REAL STORY

Rather than look to the 'top-down' for all the answers, maybe it's better to look to the 'bottom-up'. The story of the past generation's economic take-off has been that the middle class has become much, much bigger and that this happened around 1990. The proportion of people dwelling in this vast middle ground, with incomes between two-thirds and double the national median (ranging from about €24,475 to €73,426 in 2010), has surged to nearly 70% of the whole country. We are a middle-class nation with middle-class values. Fascinating research by the American institute Pew reveals that out of 11 western European countries, Ireland has experienced both the most rapid growth in income over the period from 1991 to 2010 and the biggest expansion of the middle class. While the middle class in Germany, Italy, Spain and Finland shrank, in Ireland it roared ahead between Italia '90 and now.[35]

Sometimes we don't appreciate this. If you read the papers or listen to the radio, you might think that Ireland is some sort of broken, inefficient country with a few extremely wealthy people pulling the strings and a mass underclass disenfranchised and locked out of the system. There are obviously too many people who still feel that opportunity is bypassing them and it is clear that a huge amount of wealth – rather than income – is in the hands of too few people, but the overall story is one of huge societal uplift.

The figures are startling.

This expansion of the middle class predominantly reflects the upward-mobility of Ireland's working class, whose relentless ambition and determined progress has seen them move up in the world. The share of the population in lower-income households dropped from around 27% to 19% over the same period. What's more, as the ranks of the middle class have swelled, they have become richer too, much richer, in fact. Wind the clocks back to 1991, when the Pope's Children were still in school, and your typical middle-class family was taking home an inflation-adjusted paycheque of around €23,600. By 2010, that same family was earning nearly twice that sum.[36]

One other interesting fact of recent Irish experience is that, while most of the social mobility has been upwards, there is a lot of moving up and down, meaning that social class – as measured by income – is quite fluid. The Revenue Commissioners, working with tax returns between 2006 and 2016, covering the crash period, breaks down the income distribution into deciles and focuses on the bottom, middle and top.[37] The data indicated that one in five people are stuck in the bottom but, in contrast, almost four in five (77%) people who were in the bottom group in 2006 had moved up to the middle by 2016.

In the middle, there is more mobility upwards (43%) than downwards (36%). And while over half (57%) of those at the top hold onto their position, 43% have moved from the top to the middle. This means that there is what could be called social churn in Ireland, where the chances of moving up are very significant but the chances of falling back from the top are high too. Social mobility is real in Ireland.

This is the Irish Dream, where hard work pays off. This should be interpreted as the system being reasonably fair – so, yes, you can get on, but once you get there, you can fall back too. This fluidity is much more egalitarian than in other countries where the rich stay rich and the poor remain poor. In Ireland the idea that with hard work and a bit of good fortune you can get out of poverty is crucial to understanding the relative passivity and contentment of the electorate. There's no need to be radical because the rising tide is raising, if not all the boats, at least most of them.

In fact, upward social mobility in Ireland is definitely understated by the numbers. This is because of the influence of immigration. The higher the number of immigrants, the more impressive the upwards social mobility. In Ireland, one in six is foreign-born.[38] Many of these individuals were not here ten or fifteen years ago. Think about it: most immigrants arrive here relatively poor, attracted by higher wages and better opportunities. So, if they stay, almost by definition they have moved up a social class or three. This is not captured in the numbers because they were not here years ago. As Ireland has been receiving more immigrants per head than most European countries in the past few years,[39] the upward social mobility encouraged by our economy is probably substantially more impressive than the figures suggest.

I'll give you just one example of this. Let's look at the experience of Croatians, one of our most recent groups of migrants. A total of 18,621 Croatians have been issued with Irish PPSNs since Croatia joined the EU in 2013.[40] In 2017, 4,908 PPSNs were issued to Croatians, slightly down from the 5,312 issued in 2016. This surge in the number of Croatians coming to Ireland is fairly recent, given that just 86 PPSNs were issued to Croatians as recently as 2012, the year before Croatia gained accession to the EU. What's more, the number of Croatians getting PPSNs in the first four months of 2018, at 1,482, is more than half the total of 2,289 issued over the nine years from 2000 to 2009.

For Croatians, upward social mobility is the reason they are coming to Ireland and money is clearly the biggest draw. The average monthly salary after tax in Zagreb is 5,408.98 kuna or €714.46, and young Croats see that the average monthly salary after tax in Dublin is 18,685.85 kuna or €2,468.19.[41] This is an enormous 245.46% disparity.

This is what I am talking about.

Taken together, the experience of locals and the immigrants implies huge upward mobility, yet it goes largely unreported.

THE COMMENTARIAT

So why aren't these impressive economic achievements getting reported or celebrated? This might, in part, be down to the Irish trait of self-deprecation, and not taking things, particularly ourselves, too seriously. We hate a bragging gobshite more than most, and our mammies always told us that pride is up there as one of the deadliest of the deadly sins.

Another reason might be that bad news sells, and that news is only news when something is wrong – even when there are a lot more 'rights' than 'wrongs'. It could be that the Commentariat, the be-penned aristocracy of leader writers, current affairs producers and columnists, who set the tone of the nation to some extent, tends to be slightly more left-leaning politically. As a result, their sympathies could be more aligned to an imagined protesting class as opposed to the real Contented Class.

In terms of general society, the Contented Class is much, much bigger, but much more silent. For example, a recent survey reveals that only 8% of Irish people regularly protest about anything and over 90% of us have never been on a protest march, ever.[42] You wouldn't think that from the wall-to-wall coverage given to, let's say, the anti-water charge demonstrations.

It could also be because of what behavioural economists call 'the availability heuristic'. Daniel Kanheman explains that our brains play tricks on us and we have highly selective memories. We like shortcuts, such as, 'If you can think of it, it must be true.' And as bad news of some shocking story tends to stay in our brains, we have a tendency to remember bad things, which leads to more generalised anxiety that things are getting worse, even when things are going quite well. Even think of that description, 'quite well': it's not the sort of thing to make you sit up and drop everything. So a headline like, 'Today, four and a half million Irish people became €58.9 million richer' doesn't sell, but it's true and pretty impressive.[43]

Yet when we get bogged down in the relentless churn of finger-pointing, daily political recrimination and incessant media point-scoring, we rarely look up, pause and remind ourselves that Ireland's economic renaissance has been unique in the developed world. Travelling around and working in other countries opens your eyes not just to what is wrong here, but also what is right. In addition, there has been no let-up in commercial dynamism. The recovery from the crash has been much more muscular than many expected. In 2018, for the first time in ten years, more Irish citizens returned home than left the country.[44] The overall effect was an increase of 64,500 residents for the year, bringing the population to 4.857 million. The enfeebled, debt-ravaged economy of ten years ago is no more, as Irish people have paid back more and more debt incurred during the Celtic Bubble phase. Irish debt to disposable income fell by over 50 percentage points in the four years from 2014 to 2018.[45] This implies that today's economic vitality is not fuelled by debt. It is no sugar rush. Unlike the bubble phase between 2000 and 2008, this expansion is hard earned not casually rented.

Most impressively, the period of boom, then bust, followed by growth again is a decade-long subplot in a long, three-decade story of social tolerance and economic growth reinforcing each other. Asian countries and one or two others apart, Ireland is the only developed country on earth to have experienced such prolonged economic effervescence.

If you ever read my newspaper columns, you will know that on occasion I've been called Doctor Doom and Gloom, so the Panglossian sunlit uplands is not my natural habitat. However, when something as fascinating and unique as a thirty-year economic boom, interrupted but not stopped by a property crash, is playing out in front of your eyes, in your own country, in your own lifetime, it is something to write home about.

We are a one-off. We are a growth freak.

CHAPTER 4

DISSENT MAKES THE ECONOMY DANCE

ECONOMICS HAPPENS BETWEEN OUR EARS

I n her fascinating book *Bourgeois Dignity*, the great polymath and professor of economics, history and literature Deirdre McCloskey argues that economic vibrancy depends less on material things like trade, investment, interest rates and taxation, and much more on what people believe in.

She makes the point that the modern world economy started in the 18th century. This is when the world economy began to take off, when civilised societies and their trading, risk-taking merchant caste, not just the kings and knights, began to reap the benefits. This is when the fruits of economic growth began to be shared with the common man. Up to then, only the aristocracy garnered the fruits of the economy in any material sense. We are talking about individual commercial self-expression, about the right to have a go, take a risk, imagine a better financial future and create something commercially, releasing what the great John Maynard Keynes described as 'the animal spirits' of commerce.

McCloskey's critical point is that when a society not only bequeaths the right to take a risk, but also affords dignity and status to that commercial effort, the economy takes off. The way in which the society sees the individual is an extremely important ingredient in the economic mix. As a result, culture matters.

The great Irish culture war of 1979 to 2018 – what could be termed the second civil war – was about the primacy of individuals to make their own choices about their own lives. There is a direct connection between the workings of the economy and such societal factors as the availability of divorce, abortion and contraception, private morality, women being educated, the LGBTQ community being afforded dignity, and belief in science over superstition. In the western world, Enlightenment values and a successful economy go hand in hand. The more tolerant we became, the richer we became. The essence of this is respect for personal choices, individual sovereignty and its economic bedfellow, commercial self-expression.

Economics tends to ignore values like tolerance, dignity, hope and love, which in fact drive commercial activity. Setting up a company is a great adventure of self-expression, hope, endurance and creative resilience. However, economists largely focus on adding up the outputs to tell us how big the economy happens to be at a certain point in time. This only tells you what has happened after the decision is taken to 'have a go'; it doesn't tell you why the decision was made or what the supportive background noise was. So much of economics underestimates the fascinating human ingenuity involved in backing yourself in the commercial world.

Traditional economics rarely explores why some people take risks and others don't, and it is crucial, because, when you think about it, these are the characteristics that really drive us humans on every day.

When I look around, it is human values such as hope, expectation, talk, opinion, imagination and individual grit that power commerce. The essential force that propels the economy is the force of ideas. Critically, for incomes to grow in any society, more people must believe in the possibilities they imagine for themselves. Commercial optimism is the essential chemistry of commercial effort. You must believe in it. The business person must believe that their dreams are achievable and, what's more, that they will get a pat on the back for having a go, rather than be criticised. And if they fail, they must believe they will be encouraged to have a go again. Instead of being sneered at, they ought to be complimented and afforded status amongst their peers.

To achieve this state, we must experience a change in our culture to the point where it becomes supportive of commerce. As the spark of commerce lies in the human mind, we therefore need a change in our culture towards the individual.

It should come as no surprise that the economy here began to take off when the liberal side began to win the culture war, when tolerance began to get the upper hand in the second civil war. There was so much pent up talent in the country that, once liberated, people took the economy into their own hands. So, we need to look not just at material things, like counting the number of cranes, factories or farms, but also to delve deeper into people's personal experiences. When we add up the millions of personal commercial decisions and choices, we have something called the economy.

Therefore, to gauge economic changes we must examine something ephemeral that 'white coat' economists, fascinated with material inputs, tend to ignore: the public mood and the ideology of the country.

EMBRACING OUTSIDERS

When we hear the term ideology, we often think of the growling ideologues who scale some barrier or other, protesting at this outrage or that. But ideology can also be a quiet, private, self-contained set of ethics. It doesn't have to be noisy or driven by a specific battle. It doesn't have to be divisive. It can be silently confident without being bragging or exclusionary.

By the public mood I mean the tone of public debates and public discourse. I am referring to the general change in the national conversation, where things that are now regarded as normal, the opinions that are now regarded as acceptable, are encouraged. I am talking about the general level of tolerance, encouragement and acceptance of diversity, difference and uniqueness. This is what changed Ireland.

A new suite of beliefs drove and is still driving the commercial surge. We don't know what people are thinking unless they say it. Words change the world. Rhetoric and the gradual spread of tolerance gently elbow out extremes and bequeath a sort of dogged confidence to the middle ground, where average people live, not as part of a great group, but as free individuals in their own right.

This is the ideology of the accepting nation. The less dogmatic we have become, the more nuanced and less absolutist, the more sophisticated and richer we have become.

Individual freedom and dignity for people to be who they want to be, to love who they want to love and to control their own lives has been the silent backdrop to the economic fireworks.

At the heart of the ever-changing, constantly evolving carnival of economic life is a society that encourages creative people to experiment and to have a go. These are the people who make the economy dance. These creatures are incompatible with a society of strict moral rules, dogma and control. This is why these people tend to leave such a country if they can, to pursue their dreams elsewhere.

Watching Saoirse Ronan in the film adaptation of Colm Tóibín's *Brooklyn*, it struck me that her character's freedom in New York was not the freedom of the rich, but the freedom of the curious, in a city full of other curious people trying to live a dream of self-improvement, in a country that encouraged such a search. By contrast, Ireland in the early 1950s was cold, stuffy and limiting. The person was the same person, but the environment was not. And the environment is the critical element in the creative dish.

As the Irish culture war raged, each small victory set our everyman hero free just a little bit more.

THE ECONOMIST'S BLINDSPOT

Of all the great questions facing us about the economy, perhaps the most interesting question is why do some people take risks to express themselves commercially and others don't? What sparks innovation and commercial creativity?

This area is often an economist's blindspot. Writing peer-reviewed articles in journals is not commerce. In the main, economists are not innovators in the commercial sense of the word. The vast majority work in universities, cloistered away with their academic work. Others work mainly in government departments and even those who work in the private sector are largely report writers. I know this as I've worked all three jobs. When you think about it, this total lack of real-world commercial experience renders my tribe remarkably unfit to prognosticate on commerce.

Modern economists are like medieval monks, beavering away behind high walls, writing their sacred manuscripts for each other to admire and critique. The congregation back then couldn't read Latin, so the manuscripts weren't written for the people. Similarly, most people can't follow the maths and equations that dominate many economic papers. The noble art of elucidation is not one valued by people whose job should be to elucidate. That said, they are my tribe. They can be great company and intensely curious, but they are rarely adept at explaining what really makes the economy tick.

I am not the first of the tribe to say this. There are plenty of economists trying to reassess the subject and come up with more compelling theories that actually do the job economics is supposed to do. Economics itself is doing a bit of self-analysis, which is no bad thing.

Without a doubt economics can make the connection between taxes and growth or between interest rates and unemployment. Statistics can tell you what the precise impact on each variable is likely to be. I say 'likely', because there are few certainties. But apart from measuring, the question of why a country like Ireland grows rapidly and another like Belgium does not in the same period is often not satisfactorily teased out. The blindspot may explain why no economist in 1988 predicted anything vaguely resembling the great Irish surge. Most missed the great crash of 2007–8 and most missed the resurgence of the economy since 2013.

So where does that leave us?

It leaves us having to look elsewhere to explain the modern world.

WHAT HAVE THE LIBERALS EVER DONE FOR US?

In the modern commercial world people chat, gossip, trade, make money, employ each other, and create new products that we didn't think we wanted until they were created. It's the world of commercial successes and failures, where some things work and some things don't. It's the world of tinkering around, innovating and taking responsibility for failure as well as success. It's the world of people having skin in the game and if they win, they celebrate and get rewarded and if they fail they pay out of their own pocket. Come to think about it, this world of risk and reward, cut and thrust, is about as far from the cloisters of our universities as you can go. This may be why academics are so fond of telling people they are wrong, when those who work in the real world understand that there is rarely a single right answer; there can be many right answers.

In the commercial world things can be right until they are suddenly wrong. In the constant churn of commercial success or failure, there is no right or wrong. What there may be is 'right for now' if a business is doing well or 'wrong for now' if it's doing badly.

In general, we need a score card and profit isn't a bad arbiter. At least it's consistent.

The person who makes the economy tick is the entrepreneur. Profit is the referee. This is the nub of the argument. Societies that encourage people to have a go generate the essential alchemy of commerce. Over the last few years, Ireland has been such a society, encouraging risk-takers, offering them dignity rather than waiting to sneer at their failure.

We see this all over the world. In Germany after the war, the people who rebuilt the country and created the world-beating West German economy were the small family businesses. There is little doubt that Marshall Aid provided the backdrop, but the essential character was the unsung German who travelled the world selling his German wares. Imagine how difficult that must have been. But the urge for self-expression, for personal responsibility, drove these innovators in their dingy hotels in the bad areas of cities, where the very mention of their nationality must have sparked hostility. But they did it.

In modern China too, the system encourages its people to express themselves commercially and the Chinese people have responded in force. Indeed, China may be the exception, being a country that has encouraged self-expression and liberalism in commerce and limited it in politics.

In the majority of countries, or for those of us in the west at least, encouraging business goes together with encouraging other forms of liberalism. Before we explore this development, let's just remind ourselves what liberalism has given us, not least because these days it is common to hear people use the world 'liberal' as some sort of insult.

Liberalism gave us the vote. Liberalism gave us equality. Liberalism gave us our inalienable rights. Liberalism gave us free speech. Liberalism gave us tolerance and allowed people to be curious – sexually, philosophically and commercially. Liberalism encouraged people to experiment.

Liberalism created the modern world based on individual dignity and faith in human progress.

There is, and has always been, a strong correlation between tolerance and wealth. The more open, tolerant and irreverent a society, and the more foreigners and non-mainstream people living in it, the more effervescent the economy. When countries or cities become less tolerant (such as in parts of Eastern Europe and Brexit Britain today, for example), the creative class flees to other much more attractive places, where the arts and culture are flourishing.

This is soft economic power. In the past, hard economic power – such as steel and coal reserves, large populations and political or military might – mattered.

Today, what matters is the essential feel of a place, the culture, the experience, the mix of people, the nightlife, the lifestyle and dignity afforded to those who take a risk, whether with their sexuality, their art or their commercial efforts.

Let's look at one example. Richard Florida points out that in the US there is a strong positive link between the creative class and the 'gay index' (the concentration of gay people and the relative tolerance of legislation in a city or state). The reason for this is that gay people are much more likely to feel comfortable settling in tolerant cities, and these places are also much more likely to display soft economic power. (This is not to say that gay people are more creative, but where you see a significant presence of a creative class, you also see more gay people.)

Until very recently, gay people were social 'outsiders' and it has long been noted that outsiders of one kind or another have the potential to create disproportionate economic wealth. Economic history is full of examples of the link between outsiders and economic vibrancy.

Take, as an older example, the history of a group of medieval outsiders – the Jews. From Babylon and Alexandria to Seville, ancient cities that were tolerant of their Jewish populations prospered. When Jews were later banished, in a matter of years those cities began to flounder commercially.

Imperial Spain and Portugal had sizeable Jewish populations in the 15th century. Jews there were involved in trading, science, the professions and, amongst other things, astronomy. Spanish and Portuguese explorers were successful partly because they had the best navigators – often Jewish astronomers.

These countries flourished until the Inquisition, when Jews were expelled and pursuits such as curiosity, science and inquiry were discouraged – indeed they were regarded as superfluous because the Vatican had all the answers.

Gradually, Portugal and Spain went into centuries of decline, and the Church's intellectual stranglehold on Iberia strengthened. As late as 1746, the Jesuits in Spain banned the teachings of Copernicus, Galileo and Newton. While the expulsion of Jews was bad enough in itself, this expulsion also represented a closing off of Iberia from the rest of the world, in terms of both ideas and trade.

The history of Sicily is even more alarming in terms of the links between commerce, wealth and tolerance. Until the 15th century, Sicily was rich, sophisticated, tolerant, mixed, multilingual and important. He who controlled Sicily controlled the Mediterranean, and he who controlled the Mediterranean controlled the world.

In 1492 a great tragedy befell Sicily. The island was under the control of the crown of Castile, and when Ferdinand and Isabella of Spain ordered the expulsion of all Jews and Moors from Spain, Sicily had to follow suit.

Jews had played a disproportionate role in trade as well as the professions, particularly medicine and pharmacy.

Gradually, a series of orders was passed that compelled Jews to sell their assets and pay all their outstanding debts immediately and, most ominously, barred them from bearing arms.

Within a few years, what was left of Sicilian trade after the devastating first decrees collapsed to almost nothing. Economically, Sicily went into a tailspin. Without the Jewish traders (who had formed only a tiny percentage of the population), no one traded. Without trade, there was no cash and without cash, there were no jobs.

Economic history offers many examples of how countries and cities that are open to new ideas, new ways of thinking and new people thrive. Those that become intolerant go backwards. In the above example, openness to Jewish people underscored the attitude of Sicily not just to Jews but to all sorts of other dissenters from the mainstream.

The economic lessons are straightforward. A society intolerant of outsiders tends not to be curious about other things, tends to stifle debate, lets local bigwigs go unthreatened, and allows a small coterie of insiders stitch up the economy. Think Putin's Russia. When was the last time you went into a shop and bought something with 'Made in Russia' emblazoned on it?

INNOVATION NOT INVENTION

A good addition to economic thought might be the observation that soft innovation, rather than hard invention, makes the economy dance. Innovation is what happens when human commercial ingenuity and invention are fused together. So, when you fly on Ryanair, the biggest airline in Europe, consider whether it was innovation or invention that created this company.

Did Ireland have the right to become home to the biggest airline in Europe? Traditional economics argues that enterprise flourishes when certain advantages are present, like an existing industry to feed off, or a one-off spectacular invention, or a particularly skilled and highly trained workforce in the sector. But none of those factors explain Ryanair's success. We had no invention, no novel technology. No plane has ever been made in Ireland, nor did we have a large domestic landmass and market of passengers – you can fly over the country in 20 minutes. We have no military complex feeding aeronautical talent and technology into the hands of entrepreneurs. When observed through the traditional economic framework of how industry/enterprise works, there was no way that Ireland had the right to play in the airline business. But that's only if you base economic surges on traditional economic ideas like capital and technology alone.

Ryanair exploded because of a small innovation in Michael O'Leary's head. He understood that he could do air travel cheaper, much cheaper, and that he could fly planes to the middle of nowhere and people would willingly travel there as long as fares were as cheap as possible. The industry said he was mad, largely because there was no dramatic invention and it hadn't been done before in Europe. But Ryanair is an example of innovation, not invention. Ryanair built no new planes, no new wings, no Rolls Royce engines, just a little tinkering with the existing business model. That's innovation. It's what goes on in the crucible of economic dynamism, the human mind.

Such a relentless creative process demands that there are always losers when business models are disrupted. Therefore, creativity demands that we accept that others will lose as someone gains. Acceptance of this eventuality is a crucial feature of accepting the dignity of the entrepreneur and innovative effort. A strict government policy that protects existing business, existing producers and, therefore, existing jobs, interrupts the creative process and knocks true innovation backwards.

For Ireland to become properly innovative, we had to reduce barriers to people having a go, opening a business, dreaming that there was a different way of doing things. For this to happen, the national conversation had to change and become more favourable towards the small business person, who dreams of doing things differently. We also had to stop shaming profits and accept that the referee in the innovation game is profit.

For a country to grow, profit has to stop being a bad word.

COMMERCIAL SELF-EXPRESSION

What has happened in Ireland in the past 30 years, the essence of the Radical Centre, has been the encouragement of business and self-expression.

There is more to investment than tax alone. While the multinationals came here initially for tax purposes, Ireland is now an essential part of the global supply chain and, in a sophisticated service economy, people matter as much as taxes. If this was not the case, why have Ireland's multinationals not moved en masse to Estonia, which has lower corporation tax and EU market access? Indeed, the fact that multinationals are not pulling out but still piling in, despite the EU's clear desire to see our corporation taxes raised, underpins the argument that tolerance matters. We will come back to the multinationals and tax later.

Multinational investment is a symptom of the process we're describing, not its counter-argument. We're an attractive location in the first place because of our educated, progressive, adaptable and entrepreneurial workforce. Yes, our corporate tax rate helps, but the adoption of that rate is a further example of Ireland's increasingly global outlook and entrepreneurial bent. This is what 'having a go' means: you make something out of nothing and the country comes up with a commercial idea that can be executed.

But very few high-end service companies would come here if we were stuck with the same austere Moving Statue Catholicism, as opposed to our more fun-loving Bouncy Castle Catholicism, because they wouldn't be able to find the right people.

These days the major investment a company makes, particularly a services company, is in humans, not factories or machines. Fixed capital investment has been falling dramatically, leading to the observation that we are moving into the next phase of capitalism – capitalism without capital. The implication of this is obvious: human ingenuity is driving the economy, and that is sparked not by heavy machinery but by that lightest of devices, the human brain. And the human brain is at its most inventive when the individual is free.

Professor John FitzGerald, a man who has forgotten more about the Irish economy than most of us have ever learnt about it, has tried to put a figure on the impact of the multinationals on the Irish growth story. He suggests that multinational investment explains about 15% of the overall growth rate.[46] Now, 15% is a significant figure and we would miss it if it were to go somewhere else. But explaining 15% of the growth miracle means that the other 85% is unexplained. And it is this 85% that we want to tease out.

The place to look is small businesses, because over 70% of Irish people are employed in SMEs.[47] This is higher than the EU average and far more significant than the multinationals who employ just over 14%.[48] So when it comes to employment, Irish small businesses and Irish entrepreneurs are the main engine of growth and employment.

These are the companies that make something out of nothing. Over half of all Irish people are employed in small or micro companies of under 50 people.[49] The main source of employment growth here is in small, young companies as opposed to large, old companies. These companies are opening all the time and creating new jobs. For example, 62 new companies were formed every day in the first quarter of 2018, while at the same time the rate of insolvencies fell by nearly 40%.[50] A total of 22,354 new companies were registered in Ireland in 2017, up from 21,018 in 2016.[51]

This is flamboyant commercial self-expression. And all the time unemployment is falling, encouraging more people to have a go.

The multinationals are highly productive, but so too are young Irish companies driven by young Irish entrepreneurs. The annual productivity of Irish SMEs averages approximately €71,300, more than one-and-a-half times the EU average.[52] These figures suggest that we are seeing significant numbers of what are called 'intrapreneurs', working within companies. The presence of such commercially savvy self-starters within the Radical Centre's workforce explains why multinationals continue to invest hugely, despite more competitive tax packages and lower costs being available elsewhere.

Attitudes to entrepreneurship have been measured,[53] and provide us with evidence that the national mood matters. Over four out of five Irish people afford 'very high status' to entrepreneurs, as opposed to only 60% in the rest of the EU. Entrepreneurship in Ireland receives the most media attention (72.2%) of all EU member states. The EU average is 53.3%. Ireland also has the second-highest employment share in the EU of 'young high growth enterprises' (19.1%).

These exuberant young companies have catapulted Ireland to the top of the EU in terms of using technology in business. In 2016 Ireland was number one in the EU for: the share of SMEs selling online (29.6% versus an EU average of 17.2%); turnover from e-commerce (21.8% versus an EU average of 9.4%); the percentage of employees with ICT skills (33.9% versus an EU average of 18.8%); and the availability of support to help engineers and scientists to commercialise their ideas through new and growing firms.[54]

In addition, Ireland has the second-highest percentage of SMEs that do in-house R&D, that introduce product/process innovations, and that introduce market or organisational innovations. Ireland records the highest percentage of businesses that submit proposals in a public electronic tender system (30.1%), which is significantly higher than the EU average (12.9%). Ireland has the highest percentage of SMEs that export online within the EU (16.2%) and the second-highest percentage of SMEs that import online within the EU (29.7%).[55]

This is a country in an innovative spurt. And this, as well as the multinational story, explains a lot of the growth dynamic and the general restlessness of the country. This is why immigrants are coming here in droves. The place smells of opportunity.

And this endeavour is being supported by the state. In comparison with other countries, Irish SMEs don't face major administrative or legal burdens. Ireland operates the fastest insolvency resolution process in Europe, which takes just 0.4 years compared to the EU average (1.97 years). Ireland is one of the EU's top three performers when it comes to public administration being responsive to the needs of SMEs, with a score that is well above the EU average and has continuously improved since 2008. Just 39% of Irish SMEs feel the complexity of administrative procedures is a problem for doing business, compared to an average of 62% across the EU. A measure of the ease of paying taxes is the time it takes you, and according to the European Commission, the time it takes to pay taxes in Ireland is the second-lowest in Europe (82 hours), compared to the EU average of 175.6 hours.[56]

Significantly, Ireland is far ahead of the European average when it comes to opening companies and it is considerably ahead when it comes to women setting up new businesses.

The extraordinary appetite for risk and endeavour shows a nation striving constantly for commercial self-improvement. This is a noble struggle and it goes hand-in-hand with social liberalism. We live in an economy that is hyper-dynamic and hyper-productive, we are moving around, commuting, getting up at all hours, switched on, plugged in, trading, buying, selling, innovating and making money like no other country in Europe. Immigrants are coming in and doing the same and the dynamism of the country is unique in Europe. This is the new Ireland and it is very different from the static, beaten-down, traumatised Ireland of only a few years ago.

The Pope's Children were born on a remote island, a chunk of it at war, with queues outside the American embassy, Latin American levels of national debt, run by a banana republic tribal chieftain turned kleptocrat. Just to cap it off, the country had no natural resources. Ireland back then was hardly a typical Harvard Business School case study of a high-potential start-up.

But that's what we became, and not just a high potential start-up. As they say in Silicon Valley, we became a unicorn – a country whose economic performance is so fantastic, a country whose economic accomplishments are so unique, that it stands out from all the others. When you look at the Irish feat of economic advancement over the past 40 years or so, in one generation, we have truly become a unicorn amongst jennets.

Had you suggested in 1979 that to be born in Ireland would turn out to be a great stroke of provenance from an economic point of view, most people in the world would have laughed at you. The first 60 years of independence were an economic calamity characterised by poverty, mass emigration and technological backwardness. As the young people of Ireland, looking thin, pasty and poor, listened to the Pope, drank flagons and fornicated without protection, there was no reason to think the future would be much different to the past. Underachievement beckoned.

But it didn't turn out that way. Ireland followed a different trajectory. This economic combustion was unexpected. Nobody, absolutely nobody, saw this coming.

In the late 1970s, the nations expected to bloom were the euro-centric Belgians, the mercantile Italians, the corporatist French, the relentless Germans (of course) and even the self-congratulating British, under the messianic idealogue Mrs Thatcher. No one placed a bet on the Irish: Europe's poetic, romantic but serially underachieving Hibernians. Even those voracious conquerors the Romans, who rarely missed a mercantile trick, took a quick look at this place two millennia ago and passed.

At independence, Irish incomes were about 60% of those in the UK and about 40% of those of our American cousins. Taking this as a proxy for standard of living, Ireland in the run-up to independence was equivalent to the UK in the year 1863! This gap grew as the society became more closed. Over the 40-year period from independence to 1960, Irish GDP per capita rose by about 70% – nowhere near the 120% in the UK and US; and half the 150% experienced in France and other European countries.[57]

There was no reason to believe that this story of relative poverty, low wages and emigration would change.

Then in the late 1980s, apparently out of nowhere, something erupted; you could almost sense it, the sweet smell of liberty.

CHAPTER 5

THE SOCIAL ANIMAL

WHY CULTURE IS DATA

Now that we've seen why attitudes matter, let's explore how attitudes spread in society and grow from being minority opinion to becoming mainstream ideology. To do this we must examine how public opinion changes.

You rarely hear economists talk about public opinion when discussing the inputs that drive national income. Economists are always looking for data, which is a good thing, but data is not simply the traditional stuff you can count like factories, although factories are part of the picture. Tech is undoubtedly important. While big capital investment programmes help, investment alone is not how countries get rich. Indeed, too much investment in property, not too little, is what dragged Ireland down in 2008. If investment was the answer, the Soviet Union would have been loaded, given all the huge government investment the Soviets undertook. And in recent years, we have also seen capitalism without capital, whereby smart companies are creating enormous value with precious little capital investment – think Spotify. Disruption is the friend of people with more ideas than capital. Countries get rich through smart innovation, not blunt investment.

Possibly because I have spent many years presenting TV and radio shows, I believe that to get the whole economic picture, we should listen to the nation more – what we are saying and how we are talking. In order for commerce to flourish, innovation must be encouraged by public opinion, which is why talk is important. How we talk sets the tone for the country. If the national conversation is supportive of people having a go in commerce, as it is of people having a go in art, sport, music or literature, then we are on our way. Talk is the national conversation. The national conversation is popular culture.

Culture and the norms that we share are as important to economics as cutting taxes or building factories, roads and bridges. Because before we build bridges, cut taxes or throw ourselves into a start-up like setting up a café, we have conversations, and the tone and biases in those conversations frame our worldview. If the bias in society bequeaths dignity in the commercial endeavour, we are more likely to plough ahead with the project than we would in a society that belittles and mocks commerce.

Therefore, talk matters enormously. As talk becomes more supportive of individual choices it becomes more supportive of individual effort.

Our attitudes to anyone who is resplendent in their individuality go hand in hand with our attitude to commercial effort. Countries that are open to diversity are rich. But they are rich because they are open to diversity, not the other way round.

To get the big picture we need to look at newspapers, TV programmes, language on the street and online, including low, high and middle-brow culture, in order to gauge this tolerant, economy-enhancing energy. Our big broad world is not just the cold material data so beloved of narrow statisticians and economists. These things help, but they are not enough.

Albert Einstein said: 'Not everything that counts can be counted, and not everything that can be counted counts.' Just because the Central Statistics Office can't measure or doesn't measure something, doesn't mean it didn't happen. Public opinion is the litmus test for tolerance and not just for tolerance but for acceptance and encouragement of those who once felt uncomfortable here. It's hard to measure, but you can feel it, and you know what it is when you feel it. We felt it on the repeal referendum day.

To name but a few of the key moments over the past few decades: dignity was conferred on poor kids who couldn't afford education; married women didn't have to give up work; contraception became available; homosexuality was decriminalised; divorce was legalised; gay marriage was legalised; racism became unacceptable; immigration accelerated; and now, following the #MeToo movement, women have shouted 'stop' to mistreatment and abuse. Hundreds of thousands of Irish people have been liberated. We have responded to this freedom with levels of commercial effort and innovation unprecedented in our history.

TALK MATTERS

Interestingly, we all play our part in changing the national mood, even if we don't quite understand how. Talk permeates through the economy, affecting everything we do. Once talk percolates, it changes attitudes and beliefs. Let's examine talk in the economy and use this to explain how public opinion changes.

Talk is important because we humans are sociable and highly susceptible to having our minds changed. If our minds can change with the ebb and flow of talk, the direction of the economy can change too. When you think about it, what we call 'the economy' is only the aggregation of the small decisions we all take every day. Every time you make a small decision – to buy something, to invest, to sell, to save – you are affecting the economy and affecting the mood of those around you. It all matters.

When you add up all these millions of tiny individual economic decisions, you get something big, and that's the economy. And if talk can change the economy by changing the mood, talk can change the national conversation and alter the national set of values.

If you stand back, at its core economics is only the study of us, this weird, wonderful and complicated animal, the human being. This is why it's difficult to stand over the notion that economics is a hard science in the same way as, let's say, physics. In physics, there are hard and fast rules, direct causes and effects. Economics, by contrast, is much more wishy-washy (to use a technical term), much more liable to change, to have mood swings.

There's a sneaking feeling that the reason economists are so intent on models, equations and elegant mathematics is because they want to be thought of as very smart. And everyone knows that, in the hierarchy of school-smart, maths and science subjects were always thought of as being harder and, therefore, smarter than other pursuits.

There is a type of 'physics envy' going on, where only really smart people understand complex equations, so we will wrap up the observational study of humans in the straitjacket of rigid relationships, which in many instances don't exist.

Economics is not a branch of engineering like building a bridge or a plane, where you know that if you apply a certain pressure the thing will collapse or fall out of the sky. Economics is much more difficult and far more esoteric because it's about us and we are emotional beings. In addition, we can't predict what is going to be profitable or not, precisely because we, the unpredictable humans, are the essential arbiter of whether a thing is successful or not, and we have no idea – because we are unpredictable! This is why most economists are not rich, because if we really understood and could forecast, we would be miles ahead. But this lack of predictability also keeps humans trying, which provides the kinetic energy of the commercial drama.

Therefore, we can't understand the economy without understanding humanity and what drives us, what makes us tick. There are no real laws and unfortunately the profession of economics clings hard and fast to rules, even when a cursory glance at human behaviour casts doubt on them.

Here's a good everyday example.

THE HERD

Each year at the beginning of my course at Trinity College Dublin, I ask the students, who have all studied economics for a while, what they know about economics. What are the main ideas? What sort of rules exist?

Typically a few hands go up and one of the responses usually includes: we assume that humans are rational. The reason for this is so that the mathematical models will work. Remember, hard and fast rules demand rational, predictable people. So the economics profession has invented a human that is cold, rational, and utility-maximising, unencumbered by biases and prejudices. 'Economics Man' or 'Homo Economicus' is scientific, unemotional and calculating. When making economic decisions, Homo Economicus takes in all the information, weighs up all the options, and calmly, logically makes a measured decision.

My first question to you dear reader is: have you ever met a human being like this? More importantly, would you go out on a Friday night for a pint with someone like this?

We humans are not like this. In reality, we are the opposite. We are emotional, suggestible, irrational. We move with the herd. We tend to be irrationally optimistic. Why do you think we fall in love, support useless football teams and always think, 'This time it's different'? I've a few friends on their second marriages – the triumph of hope over experience. Like all humans, they are irrepressibly hardwired for optimism. Bad things only happen to others.

We are not rational at all; in fact, we are highly irrational. We don't really know our own minds and are extraordinarily impressionable.

We are suggestible because we are profoundly social animals. Real economics is all about the social. Think about pets. Sometimes when I walk our family labrador Sasha, I wonder about how much time she spends on her own. Sure, on the pier, she gets all excited with other dogs, and wanders away to Scrumdiddly's ice cream counter, but in general she loves company. She gets excited when we are around. Dogs are social. (Cats, on the other hand, are a different kettle of fish.)

Now, think about us humans.

Why do you think humans have become the most dominant animal on earth? How did we come to rule the place? If you had been asked to place a bet, 10 million years ago when we decided to come down out of the trees, or even 100,000 years ago when we decided to go for a walk out of Africa, on which animal would emerge as dominant, would you have backed us? We were not dominant then. We were one of thousands of competing animals trying to survive.

Why not the lion or the tiger, something dangerous, a vicious predator rather than the human, which had little intrinsic strength and couldn't naturally defend itself against bigger predators?

What distinguishes us?

One of the key differences is that we can talk. When you can talk, you can create memories, stories, identities and ideas behind which you can mobilise enormous groups of humans moving in one direction. This is an extremely powerful force. This is how values are created. Values are simply the stories we tell each other about the type of people we think we are and the type of people we think our tribe should be.

Talking allowed us to herd together around something more than food. It allowed us to entertain big ideas, to influence and convince ourselves that we are in one distinct group. Once you can create memories and stories, you can create incredibly powerful forces like religion, nations, money, advertising and ideologies. And in the post-religious, consumerist world, of which Ireland is a full participant, advertising is based on this tribal sense of identity. Billions of euros are spent every year to convince us that we are part of something bigger.

We can also coalesce around accepted norms. And if these norms change from preventing people being commercially creative to encouraging people to have a go, an enormous dynamism is released.

Talk allows this energy to be released.

Suggestibility is the key to understanding these collective human herding instincts and at the root of this is gossip. I don't know about you, but when I'm not working, I'm usually gossiping. I love an auld chinwag. And when we gossip and chat to each other, we influence each other, pushing deep buttons, changing each other's minds and sending us off on tangents, often driven by elemental sensory concepts like fear, panic, greed or, more normally, jealousy or gratitude. This is the basis of the virtues like hope. The hope that today's effort will pay off tomorrow.

Without appreciating how group psychology affects human behaviour, we won't understand how ideas are formed, how the national mood changes and how the economy operates. When Ireland was censorious, the national conversation was against things: against small indiscretions, against small business, against all sorts of expressions of freedom.

When that changed – and it was changed by talk, by examples of success and by all of us influencing each other – we embraced the have-a-go culture.

FAITH AND HOPE AND SUCCESS

One way to look at modern culture wars is to frame them not so much as a battle between the traditional and the modern, but as a battle between faith and hope. Faith is a backward-looking concept. 'Keep the faith' means to hold onto something. Hope, on the other hand, is forward-looking. Hope is the patron saint of individual self-improvement and hope is the catalyst for change.

Faith, when seen as identity, is the enemy of change. Identity can be rigid and inimical to change. If a country changes its core identity, then it's probably because of the little mutinies in the minds of many. One consequence of the mutiny against the old shibboleths, against the excessive moralising of the Church, was a diminishment of that other core identity in Ireland: nationalism. This sacred cow was slain when the people voted overwhelmingly to amend Articles 2 and 3 of the constitution, which laid claim to Northern Ireland. This was a big change and was part of the revolution of the Irish imagination. Interestingly, contrary to what was imagined at the time, the peace dividend from the north actually went south.

The peace process is 20 years old now and one question which perplexes many is why the economy in Northern Ireland has not performed like the economy in the Republic. The obvious but rarely cited answer lies in attitudes and talk. In the North, economic dynamism is stifled by an oversized public sector. There is no business appetite because it's not needed; the state still provides. An excessive state sector smothers the creative individual and reduces the need to encourage commercial effort. In addition, because everything is seen through the sectarian prism of 'you win, therefore I lose', there has been no independent business culture to avail of the opportunities that peace afforded, particularly the international business dimension. That business came south. The peace dividend came to the place that was never at war but that had a culture war which resulted in the victory for the common man. We will go back up North later on; in fact we will end up there.

Over the past 40 years, the story of Ireland has been the victory of individual hope over collective faith. Better still, this hope has been enshrined in laws that have fostered and encouraged innovation. The cultural revolution was a victory of personal hope over collective identity. And the national language and national discourse over those intervening years altered, and was transformed by, that most ephemeral of things called talk, which changed public opinion. Public opinion increasingly bestowed dignity on lots of people who had been excluded in the past.

As an example, here is a tiny gesture which means a hell of a lot to those affected and costs nothing. On 2 June 2018, footballer John O'Shea had his testimonial, following 108 caps. I've travelled all over the world watching this football team over 30 years. In fact, I was there in Gelsenkirchen with my son, away to the left above the German goal with the travelling fans, when O'Shea poked home from three yards to draw level with the world champions. One of the better nights in green. Away games are a hoot and the people who follow the teams are from all backgrounds, all classes and all parts of the country. In the Aviva on 2 June 2018, Ireland wore a kit emblazoned with the rainbow flag colours of the LGBTQ community. This is what I mean by the changing national mood. This is public opinion. This is the national conversation and this is what tolerance looks like when it is embedded. Can you imagine that happening in Italia '90?

Liberal values and the triumph of all the little-by-little, trial-and-error victories push us on every day. These are not heroic, over-the-barricade, revolutionary virtues but more the tiny signs and signals that we send out every day to family, colleagues and neighbours respecting their dignity, applauding their efforts and encouraging commerce that may eventually lead to collective innovations and movements forward in society.

Economic take-off came late in Ireland – not in the 1950s, 1960s or 1970s, as happened in other European countries – because the Church, as well as the post-colonial revolutionary idealists of the Republic, ever present in art and the intelligentsia, disliked what they saw as the mediocrity of the curious bourgeoisie. We see a similar pattern in post-colonial Africa and India, where a generation of liberators were Marxist. They replaced imperialist dogma with communist dogma and in so doing, squeezed the creative middle. Interestingly, now that that generation is largely gone, Indian and African economies are growing rapidly.

In Ireland, the fact is that the economy grew impressively, year-in, year-out, not just in the so-called Celtic Tiger sugar-rush, but over the course of more than 30 years, trumping the rest of Europe. Traditional economics alone cannot explain this. Business-friendly, civilised values do.

The emergence of the Radical Centre has been the great victory for the common man and common woman, trying things out for themselves, taking a risk and having a go.

CHAPTER 6

JOYCE VERSUS YEATS

THE ENTREPRENEUR AS ARTIST

One of the most striking and laudable attributes of modern Ireland is the way we celebrate our artists, writers, musicians and creative people. Sometimes this goes over the top with, for example, an Oscar Wilde tea towel collection, but, in general, offering dignity to artistic self-expression must embolden new writers to also have a go. They feel valued by a society that celebrates their success and appreciates their contribution. Unfashionable as it seems, I've always thought that artists and entrepreneurs are quite similar characters. If we think of the entrepreneur as a creative individual, driven to express themselves, then we can begin to appreciate that the entrepreneur could occupy the same space in our world as the artist. They are the same type of person, cut from the same cloth.

Typically, neither the artist nor the entrepreneur places the same kind of value as most of us on a regular wage, a job working for someone else, insurance policies or a nine-to-five existence. They want to be free. They are both, to use the words of Professor Declan Kiberd, 'brokers in risk'. As philosopher Nassim Taleb might say, they both have 'skin in the game'.

They are both individualists, neither wants a boss and both understand that they live in a world of risk, where the individual shoulders the responsibility and that they are only as good as their last gig. If a changed national conversation offers these types of people the dignity they deserve, they flourish, and so as a result do the rest of us.

All innovation is based on constant churn, this constant disruption.

As we have been talking about a late-1980s economic rocket about to launch, let's consider an example from the music business at the time. U2 released *The Joshua Tree* in 1987, the same year that Michael O'Leary was asked to take a look at Ryanair's books. The album broke new ground, sold shedloads and catapulted Bono and the lads to superstardom. Yet their success also disrupted other bands who were just there on the cusp with them. In the battle for global domination, U2 pulled away largely because of innovations in Bono's head. This is creative disruption.

Great books or great movies are also forms of creative disruption. When Anne Enright pens a novel, it may engender envy in other novelists (although they might not say it), precisely because they think it might put their work in the shade. That incentivises and spurs them on to greater imaginative feats.

Lenny Abrahamson wrote a letter to Emma Donoghue, convincing her that he was the right director to adapt her novel *Room*. The movie went on to win an Oscar for Bree Larson and a best director nomination for Abrahamson. The letter was also an act of creative disruption because it began the artistic, creative, entrepreneurial process that generated something new and valuable where nothing existed before. The economic implement that creates something from nothing is the human brain and the creative process has to be given dignity in order to flourish.

The creative process is the same for the artist and for the entrepreneur. Both back themselves in a world of probability and improbability. Innovation doesn't always have to be heroic. For example, I am writing these lines on the back of a bus from Galway. It is one of the 57 buses on this route, 19 are operated by GoBus and 25 by Citylink. Dublin and

Galway are well served with lots of buses travelling between the two cities each day.[58] When CIÉ had the monopoly on this route, there was only one per day. Now there are 11 or so on Bus Éireann's timetable alone. Once the society allowed and encouraged others to come in to compete, the services became more regular, the prices went down, and the quality of the buses improved dramatically. The wifi down here at the back is pretty good too.

When the guy who runs these new buses sat down to think about how he could make it work, he must have considered lots of smaller questions. How could he make the buses run better? How many people did he need to employ? Where could he get the money? How much profit could he make? All these questions led to small, unheroic creative decisions, sharpened by the knowledge that there was a risk that needed to be negotiated. It may not seem heroic, but for the passengers it's a good deal, and for the families employed in this endeavour, it's pretty significant.

This is innovation. As in the arts, one commercial disruption leads to another, begetting another. The real winners in the great Irish innovation game are the long-distance commuters, music listeners, film goers, readers and punters beside me as we whizz down the motorway towards Athlone. We are all collectively better off, even if some competitors lose out. Sometimes there are no losers.

Take a venture I am involved with, the Dalkey Book Festival. My wife Sian and I decided to set it up during the recession following a chat with the local traders in Dalkey. The traders complained that the town was dying on its feet commercially. We went home from a rather depressing meeting in the town hall and decided to create a small book festival. There is no unique invention here. Lots of towns and cities have these festivals. We simply thought we could do something similar.

In 2010, we opened up and sold 800 tickets, which we thought was great. Today we sell 14,000 tickets, employ lots of people – including producers, designers and website creators – help generate money for the businesses in the town, generate tax revenue for the state and host 76 events over four days with over one hundred writers selling thousands of books, and meanwhile thousands of happy punters seem to have a great time.

I am not bragging here; I just want to show how innovation creates something out of nothing. This is a small business; sustainable and valuable. This is entrepreneurial innovation and it is part of what makes the economy tick.

The wheels of commerce drive growth and enhance spending. Income begets spending, which begets more income and this circular flow of money is precisely what generates higher living standards.

If you have a society that positions itself against these entrepreneurial innovations, you dissuade people from taking that initial step, the initial urge to have a go.

Part of the spark of innovation is this general encouragement that society gives the innovators. In Michael O'Leary's case, the personal motive may be money or the satisfaction of knowing that he broke the mould out of nowhere. In Bono's case, the incentive may be a full stadium or a Grammy. In Anne Enright's case, it could be the Man Booker Prize, while for Lenny Abrahamson it could be the Oscar. Who knows – and, actually, who cares – what their motivation is? The point is that society encourages them to innovate, making us all better off.

This is why, although it is rarely pointed out, cultural isolationism and stifling dogma, whether religious or political, go hand in hand with economic stagnation. Censorship stifles innovation. If we don't support innovators, we get no disruption and we get no progress.

An interesting way of looking at this notion of dogma versus development is to think about excessively religious or politically dogmatic countries. For example, people in the ridiculously well-endowed Venezuela, a country with more oil reserves than anywhere else,[59] are going hungry, largely because the dull Marxist dogma of the Chavistas has choked innovation. Or consider the enslaving ideology of communism as practised by Mao or any of his devotees. It's not that the goals of the 'isms' are necessarily wrong; it is just that if you take out the dynamic of innovation, the creative urge to try something new, you tend to stifle the very innovation that creates wealth and drives the economy, which you can then redistribute, if that's what you want to do.

Such political experiments, and dozens before them, involved great rhetorical leaps forward which only drove the people ever backwards.

This repetitive playbook has followed all countries that take doctrine too seriously.

ODD BEDFELLOWS

We in Ireland never had the more extreme Marxist stuff but we had an extremely powerful coalition against the constructive businessperson. From independence in 1921 until the start of the culture war in 1979, our national conversation was dominated by the dogma of fundamentalist Catholicism, whipped up by biblical references to rich men, camels and eyes of needles. In the Church's view, a commercial life could not be an ethical life, despite the Catholic Church being one of the wealthiest multinational corporations on the planet. However, by associating the small businessperson with the uber-wealthy, the Church hinted that commerce was undignified. Hints were all you needed back then. The eye of the needle did the rest.

Extreme Irish nationalism, meanwhile, fetishised the colonised worker/peasant and created a false enemy in the small businessperson. The James Connolly wing of the national liberation struggle was steeped in its distaste for the civic bourgeoisie, who were armed to the teeth with their weapon of class oppression, the relatively innocuous limited company.

On top of this was de Valera's isolationist economics with its mantra of protection from competition, the anti-commercial cult of the civil service combined with an intellectual and classist haughtiness towards the mundane but noble daily toil of business. This was an almost perfect storm of disparate dogmas, structures and prejudices that strangled economic innovation, sending the economy backwards and propelling hundreds of thousands of emigrants from these shores to follow their dreams elsewhere.

The anti-commercial bias in post-independence Ireland came from so many powerful sources, it's a wonder that the economy worked at all. Indeed, it didn't just come from a High Church suspicion of the mercantile freedom of the entrepreneur nor from the warped nationalism of the soldier of destiny; nor was it exclusively the target of the extreme Larkin left or the civil service bureaucracy who laid down the law. It also came from our most celebrated, unimpugnable sources: the artistic aristocracy that gave romantic legitimacy to the entire national project.

It's worth bearing in mind what we have been talking about in previous chapters – how important it is that society allows commercial self-expression and confers dignity on those who back themselves. If a society and its chief scriptwriters sneer at commercial effort, then it's highly likely that those people who are willing to take risks will take themselves, their ideas and their energies off somewhere where they are welcomed and encouraged – and this is exactly what happened.

In school, I never really understood the thinking of our great poet W.B. Yeats, in his immortal line from his poem 'September 1913': 'fumble in a greasy till'. Why did Yeats set his sights on the lowly commercial trader? How did the small businessperson become an enemy of the state to be exorcised by our national poet? And more perplexing for me in the 1980s, I couldn't understand why not one of our English teachers would stand up for the small group in society that was possibly preventing this country from going bankrupt. Why, given the pantheon of other malcontents out there, did Yeats target the entrepreneur as the enemy and the ultimate anti-patriot?

The arch-poet's sneering is astonishing when you examine the social class from which the 1916 rebels – the people who did the fighting – came. The vast majority of the rebels in the GPO during Easter week were employed, which, in a city with very high levels of unemployment, tells its own story. However, what is more interesting is the fact that most were from the class that Marx would describe as the hated petite bourgeoisie. These were the last people a traditional, early-20th-century revolutionary liberation movement would have expected to draw from.

They were clerks, drapers, drapers' assistants, confectioners, druggists, furniture salesmen, lots of grocers and insurance clerks and even a pair of silk weavers and a pawnbroker. These are the very people that Yeats was accusing of fumbling in the greasy till. The employment list is fascinating and what it reveals is not a proletarian revolution – romanticised by Connolly and Yeats – but a rising of the petite bourgeoisie or the struggling commercial lower middle class. They were Christian Brothers revolutionaries.

'September 1913', a poem drummed into hundreds of thousands of Leaving Cert students, pits the struggling entrepreneur – the class who did lots of the fighting – against all the greats of Irish history like Wolfe Tone, despite the fact that Tone's revolutionaries also came from precisely the same entrepreneurial class. Tone's people were Dublin's non-conformist Presbyterians who had to go to work for a living. They were the entrepreneurs, but they were revolutionary entrepreneurs driven by 18th-century Enlightenment values of liberty, fraternity, and equality. They were the original Radical Centre in the anti-colonial, American revolutionary tradition.

These commercial radicals are a stark contrast to Yeats's sneering Anglo-Irish landed gentry class, Cromwell's NCOs who got lucky. Sitting around collecting rents from labouring tenants is a much nicer way of making a living than working, but it makes you slightly elevated from the reality of the daily toil. Such louche drones and their rentier behaviour never leads to innovation, except possibly in poetry, but it absolutely does lead to haughtiness.

This haughtiness and contempt for trade and the honourable daily commercial struggle can also be sensed amongst academics, artists, political thinkers and journalists. Deirdre McCloskey terms this class the 'Clerisy'. She contends, and I agree with her, that this class decided that commercial innovation was in some way undignified and base. For the Clerisy, the true romantic could never be mercantile and the true romantic vision for society couldn't rest on something as inoffensive as the free-thinking individual, tinkering away, making things work better, selling in the open market, employing others for their brains and brawn, and doing all this peacefully, being respected and respecting others.

How could towering intellectuals accept such ordinary people and their ordinary lifestyles as being heroic, let alone ethical?

So romantic Ireland ends up being located in this slightly depraved sweet-spot, where de Valera's comely maidens meet Yeats's imaginary revolutionaries, setting their sights on the creative Radical Centre, with obvious economic consequences for the million people who ran away from this state in its first 70 years.

The Clerisy argued, with unfortunate success, that these tolerant, free-thinking individuals were the enemy of the people, leading ultimately to the ant-colony vision of society favoured by the extreme left and extreme right, from Pol Pot to Mao, Hitler and his cronies, and lots of other two-bit, tin-pot imitators in between.

When I sat in school reading Yeats – and believe me, I loved the words – something jarred. To me, he was guilty of an aristocratic, quasi-feudal dislike of the merchant who was 'in trade'. You used to hear the same shtick amongst the English upper class. The Clerisy sets the tone for the society, and if a disparaging message is constantly repeated – by the Church via the eye of the needle, by the romantic scriptwriters of the revolution via revered poetry and the high arts, by academia and by the newspapers – it begins to form a national narrative with enough common ground in disparaging commerce to turn it into the soundtrack of the country.

Then it trickles down.

THE POINTS RACE TO THE BOTTOM

Such prejudice also appears lower down the pecking order in Ireland, where sniggering at commerce and trading effort is common among accredited professions. A good place to see this is in the annual CAO points race, which is little more than a list of the career preferences of respectable Ireland. The highest points go to courses that lead directly to the professions, reflecting paternal bias probably far more than the teenagers' own aspirations. What teenager ever looked in the mirror and said to herself, 'I really want to be a dentist. I want to look into people's mouths for the rest of my life'?

Professional bias might explain why clever boys in Ireland were told by their mothers to become lawyers or some other professional. Being a professional confers societal status that mere commerce can't attain, and the Irish mammy's social antennae are a highly sensitive ranking instrument, as we all know.

Lower down the food chain, when I was young, lads were urged to get 'good' jobs in the bank or the civil service. What made these jobs good was that they were permanent. Obviously in a society with high recurring levels of unemployment and emigration, it's not hard to see why parents would urge their kids to opt for security. However, one of the unintended consequences of this was to snuff out potential commercial creative talent in a great societal game of risk-avoidance. The more kids were urged towards non-commercial security, the fewer risks were taken and the fewer jobs were created. This obviously reinforces economic inertia, reinforcing the stultifying cycle.

From the vantage point of the 21st century, the story of how the commercial small businessperson became an enemy of the Irish state is odd. And it had lamentable economic consequences. When business and enterprise were not afforded dignity, these crucial individual dynamos of the economy went into retreat. The country went into a tailspin. Ireland from 1920 to 1990 failed economically relative to all our neighbours. A litmus test for this failure is emigration. People don't leave successful countries; they leave failed states. Over one million people, with their own dreams, gifts and talents, left this suffocating place between 1922 and 1990.[60]

BLOOM'S PEOPLE

Amongst the greats of Irish literature, only James Joyce saw fit to place the small-time businessperson front and centre as hero. After all, what was Leopold Bloom but an advertising copywriter? For Marxists, aristocrats and bishops, the advertising copywriter was amongst the lowest forms of life in the capitalist swamp. Until Joyce made him his star.

But it wasn't just Bloom, the member of the civic bourgeoisie, but also Bloom's mundane, everyday thoughts that Joyce elevated. As Declan Kiberd points out in *Ulysses and Us*, Joyce considers Bloom's inner thoughts worthy of dignity and reverence. Up until Joyce, the inner thoughts of the hero were reserved for big men considering some romantic, heroic act, such as Hamlet contemplating suicide. Joyce smashes all this up and regards Bloom's small, ordinary thoughts, such as his musings on having a cup of tea, as worthy of elucidation. These are the inner workings of the everyday man, not some romantic demi-god.

With Bloom, the ordinary is heroic, and the hero is ordinary.

In the character of Bloom, with his bourgeois, entrepreneurial obsessions about making the Dublin trams work better or the sewage system more efficient, we see trial and error, the incessant tinkering of the entrepreneur. And we also see the other trait of the questioning entrepreneurial mind – the underlying value of tolerance. Bloom inhabited the bourgeois world of cafés, public parks, safe streets and public museums. Strolling around was his thing. Bloom's walks in what Kiberd describes as 'the public zone which was warm, nurturing and affirmative' are central to his everyday story. Joyce's streets were the democratic spaces where the tolerant shopkeeper was going about the business of commerce. The city was the stage.

And, for Bloom, the city street is where it all happens, with free-thinking independent citizens going about their business, tolerantly. This was Joyce's world, the real modern world as it was, with dignity conferred on ordinary people. His world was not some imaginary, Celtic twilight populated by fictitious Yeatsian inventions.

For Joyce, the modern world was pretty good and should not be endangered by the sneering of an invented, perfect world. This brings us back again to the battle between the pretty good and the perfect. Joyce was not on the Leaving Cert; I suspect he was regarded as being too radical by the established educational Clerisy.

Bloom's modern world was more fragile than anyone understood. Not 20 short years after the original Bloomsday, 16 June 1904, that tolerant, striving, tinkering world was gone. The Radical Centre was sacrificed, crushed by the radical left and right, both driven by their ant-hill view of humanity.

Despots, extremists and faith-based religious leaders, drunk on an irrational hatred of the independent, free-thinking, inventive commercial citizen who pays her taxes, finances public libraries, goes to work and, in some cases, fights in the GPO for a better future, brought the curtain down on Bloom's world, and in an act of ethnic lunacy, on Bloom's people, the Jews.

RULE BREAKERS

The alliance against the questioning entrepreneur, the small employer, the dynamo of economic innovation, commerce and vitality, came in so many forms, it is difficult to calculate what so much negativity did to the commercial culture of the country. We can look at the result: the post-independence economy, steeped in protectionism and censure, drove the country backwards as the rhetoric of Irish exceptionalism soared ever higher.

Such is the iron rule of modern economics. If you choose strict dogmas, whether of the modernist left or of the traditionalist right, you also get an unhealthy dose of intellectual censorship and a fear of new ideas. That country tends to go into an economic tailspin.

Modern economics needs rule breakers. Rule breakers are not normally encouraged in dogmatic societies. Rule breakers have been pushing us forward since we first sat in a cave messing around with flint. Who thought to make fire but the most creative of all the humans in the cave?

Innovation is driven by creative people, often but not exclusively the oddballs and misfits, who question authority, who break rules and who embrace change. It is then communicated by open societies that are unafraid of ideas and encourage open exchange. In all societies, of course, there also have to be rule-followers, systems and conventions, but the rule-breakers are crucial for the initial spark. Every society has them, but not every society in every era encourages them. When they are encouraged, markets flourish, wealth is created that can be used to improve the lot of everyone.

If you suffocate these people, you suffocate innovation and ultimately economic prosperity. Nobody ever got rich by doing the same thing over and over again when those around them were tinkering away at the machine, trying to make things a bit better – whether this is coming up with a new business model for an existing industry, like Ryanair, or opening a coffee shop. Nassim Taleb points out that innovation can take a long time. For example, it took thousands of years after the invention of the wheel for someone to think that putting tiny wheels on suitcases might be quite a good idea. This simple innovation transformed many travellers from looking like human oxen, sweating, hauling heavy bags all over airports, into well-turned-out adventurers, gliding effortlessly through sleek airports, trailing little trollies behind them.

Good ideas stem from the great human process of trial and error and ultimately coming up with a better way of doing things. When Sharon Horgan came up with *Catastrophe*, the story wasn't new: boy meets girl, she gets pregnant and away we go. The creative innovation wasn't the cameras, the studios, the mechanical inventions that people in the TV business talk about. The innovation was between Sharon Horgan's ears, that beautifully creative, funny, irreverent mind. Could she have made that in the Ireland of three or four decades ago? Are you having a laugh?

CHAPTER 7

THE RADICAL CENTRE TRIUMPHS

O f the 6.3 million people born in this country in the past one hundred years, the first 3.9 million babies were born into a country dominated by statist dogma and religious extremism, where people were bullied by both Church and state.[61] Close to 4 million individuals – you may be one of them – were born into that Ireland with a crippled economy and an ideological straitjacket of a top-down state, suspicious of entrepreneurial effort and free trade. The landscape was extremely censored, policed by bishops, priests and nuns, and enthusiastically aided by a veritable Stasi of sanctimonious informants.

The second Ireland, the one that was conceived in and around the time the Pope arrived, is an Ireland that has replaced the ideology of tradition with a new-found respect for the individual. This is the modern Ireland of the tolerant, ambitious Radical Centre.

The transformation of social attitudes was confirmed on 25 May 2018 with the overwhelming Yes vote in the repeal referendum. A massive youthquake shook the old order. While this mass social and cultural upheaval driven by the young Repealers was facilitated by social media, possibly more interesting is the fact that all the way up to the age of 65, the vote was overwhelmingly Yes. Across the board, attitudes that were expected to be much harder had softened dramatically. Maybe people were not prepared to admit it publicly in case their own personal mutiny wasn't shared by others, but this was the beauty of it. They were shared, and when these millions of personal uprisings came together the force was unstoppable.

Yet up until the final hours, each side believed it would be neck and neck. The revolution was private, silent and definitive. This national makeover has not been strident, vocal or clamorous, rather it's been the progressive accumulation of hundreds of little mutinies inside the heads of millions of Irish people, triggered by private humiliations and personal stories against ideologies that sought to dominate.

The change in the value system of the country has been dramatic and this transition, from the tyranny of tradition to the liberation of the individual, began around the time Pope John Paul II told the young people of Ireland he loved them and ended when Pope Francis apologised to them.

In 1981, just after the papal visit and just ahead of the 1983 abortion referendum, the European Social Survey conducted a wide-ranging survey of Ireland, interviewing thousands of people.[62] The results expose an extraordinarily conservative country, with deep-rooted animosity to people outside the mainstream, a level of moral and sexual conformity that is quite startling.

When asked whether people should be allowed to enjoy sexual freedom, 70% of people said no; with only 19% saying yes. This is a shocking level of public support for private sexual repression. When asked whether sexuality should be left to individual choice, a huge 61% of Irish people disagreed. This implies that people believed that their own sexuality should be determined by someone else, by society's general conservative norms and not by themselves.

Nearly six out of ten people believed that being gay was unacceptable. To give you a sense of the nation's value system, more people (58%)

believed that being gay was unacceptable than believed that tax evasion was unacceptable (44%). Almost half of the adult population (45%) maintained that divorce was never justified, under any circumstance.

Four out of ten contended that four children was the ideal family size. And 17% – that's more than one in six – believed women should ideally have six children or more. Capturing the moral censoriousness of the time, the survey shows that six out of ten disapproved of single mothers who didn't appear to want a stable relationship with a man.

When asked about what values we should emphasise in children, over 80% believed that we should place more value on authority and family. When asked what qualities we should instill in our children, only 8% of parents identified encouraging imagination while 65% maintained that good table manners were crucial.

Religious observation was almost total. An extraordinary 82% of Irish people claimed to go to church at least once a week and only 5%, or one in twenty, said they never went. Over half of people surveyed contended that the church provided the answers to family problems. Nine out of ten people believed in heaven and one in three said scientific advances would harm humanity and shouldn't be embraced. The survey does throw up strange anomalies such as 97% of people believed in God, which is astounding, but one in three also believed in reincarnation, which is kind of reassuring.

In contrast to how much we value individual rights today, in 1981 less than one in four people thought that giving people more say in their lives was important. Reflecting the groupthink of the day, less than one in ten thought free speech was a vital issue. This was in a country that had just banned Monty Python's *Life of Brian* because, although free speech was not important, religious satire threatened the soul of the nation.

Over half of Irish people identified not with Ireland, but first and foremost with the town or locality from which they hailed. Less than 3% said they were European and only 20% suggested Irish was their preferred identity above their county or village. Yet it was also a time of rampant nationalism and atrocities in the North. Despite violence being visited upon innocents on almost a weekly basis, one in three people professed that they supported the notion of terrorism, which – again seen from today's vantage point – is disturbingly high.

When looking back, it is helpful to dig deep beyond the headlines. In terms of how far this nation has travelled, how did a nation where close to 60% believed that being gay was unacceptable in 1981 become a nation led by a gay, half-Hindu Taoiseach who is the son of an immigrant – in one generation?

The transformation wasn't limited to social norms; critically, attitudes to commercial self-expression have also experienced a quiet revolution.

But the transformation wasn't limited to social norms. The end of dependency has extended into many aspects of society and the Irish national ideology. In the lifetime of the Pope's Children, narrow-gauge nationalism was also rejected, immigration embraced, the trade unions' grip on the economy was loosened dramatically, many of the old regulations and barriers to business have altered dramatically. The entrepreneur, the enemy of Yeats, McQuaid, Larkin and Connolly, but hero to the cosmopolitan outsider Joyce, is now a celebrated figure in the Irish social savannah.

Today 82% of Irish people say that they respect and admire successful entrepreneurs.[63] This is the highest figure in the world, higher than the US or the UK where the official ideology of the Republican and Conservative governments is the deification of business. The Irish Radical Centre in Ireland cheers on quietly, not obstreperously. Only 14% of Polish people, a country still mired by authoritarian dogma on marriage inequality, anti-feminism, anti-immigration and anti-abortion, say they look up to business innovators, whereas a massive 42% of Irish people laud the innovator. That's the fourth highest in the world and again underscores that tolerance and economic vigour go hand in hand.

We are now a broad church of liberal values where the thoughtful, dissenting individual, no matter how she expresses herself, is encouraged. These are the 'live and let live' values that posed such a threat to authority in the past. Today they are the essential life-blood of our vibrant democracy and our dynamic economy.

The Radical Centre is radical enough to know that the constitution is not the best referee of personal morality. It is radical enough to know that bits of Karl Marx can be combined with bits of Edmund Burke. It is not the anti-government, small state movement like the American Tea Party or the more nostalgic bits of the Brexit spectrum. The Radical Centre appreciates the crucial role of the state in providing a launch pad for personal effort. It understands that a strong state is essential. As a result, the Radical Centre doesn't really take hard positions on anything. These everyman heroes want to be left alone to look after their own family and friends, rarely campaigning and happy to celebrate other people getting on and doing well.

They are the solid majority who vote for the centre ground in every election, who pay their taxes and who work hard so that their children will have a better life than they have. The Radical Centre believes in the future, not the past. And while they voted Yes, many of them will have queued up to see Pope Francis. Indeed, over one million tuned in to watch Pope Francis say mass at the Phoenix Park. And, as befits Bouncy Castle Catholicism, as recently as 2013, 73% of all babies born were baptised,[64] while over half of all weddings took place in a Catholic church in 2017.[65] Culturally, Catholicism still resonates.

Those liberated from the religious right and the atheist left, the common people, are the backbone of this society. These are the people known in 'fancy dan' circles as the bourgeoisie, but more commonly known as 'decent skins'. The success of Ireland in the past three decades is grounded in the victory of the value system that underpins decent skins, the ethics of quiet, gradual self-improvement, moving up slowly, without much fuss and, over time, achieving the ultimate aim of being better off.

As the 40-year culture war ground on year after year, referendum after referendum, the Commentariat took sides, editorialising and opining. The liberal left, some driven by Scandinavian envy, longed for this place to turn into a Celtic Sweden: tolerant, multi-cultural and socially democratic with a weakness for high taxes and criss-crossed by cycle lanes. Pitting against these idealists was the old guard: Catholic and nationalist. There was also the harder Left, the ones who had beards before we ever heard of hipsters.

In the end, the extremes were outflanked by the Radical Centre, the Bouncy Castle Catholics. The story of Ireland is the story of the victory of the ordinary person. It's not too romantic, intoxicating or dramatic, but it is real, worthwhile and honourable. It is the Renaissance Nation, a country that has grown twice as fast as our neighbours and can look to the future with guarded confidence.

Now armed with this knowledge, let's go out and have a look at ourselves.

PART 2

THE CENTRE GROUND

CHAPTER 8

OUT AND ABOUT

HOW DO WE LOOK?

The citizens of the Renaissance Nation come in all shapes and sizes. To see the country, I took a little mooch around, a walk here, a jump on the bus or train there, a rush-hour drive and a Saturday afternoon meander through towns and suburbs. My mates think my strolling around with a notebook is odd, as do my family, but I find it therapeutic as well as fascinating. Along the way, I jot down observations, and these are fleshed out and given an economic context in this part of the book.

David Brooks calls this process comic sociology. I'd prefer to call my wanderings 'walkabout economics'. On a walkabout, you might find yourself in a bar, a café or just on the street watching the great waltz of human life as we go about our business, passing each other, stuck in traffic, on the side-line of sports matches, sometimes locked in our own thoughts, sometimes in full gossip, changing each other's minds and having our assumptions questioned. You could find yourself in West Cork listening to posh yachties or in West Belfast observing Irish-speaking Provos, Gaeilge learnt in the Jailteacht. Or you could be in the real Gaeltacht, amongst the locals on the Aran Islands, talking Aer Arann flights, or up in Donegal talking Brexit to farmers. You could be at the cheese counter in Avoca or the hot food counter in Applegreen, on a bike on the Beara Peninsula or in the back of a van delivering kiln-dried logs. All these experiences provide clues, data points for walkabout economics.

Let's take a look at ourselves, what we think about and how we behave. The stories in this section of the book are from the perspective of the curious onlooker, the interested bystander. What drives the walkabout is a fascination with 'us' – the Radical Centre – and what we have collectively achieved over the past generation.

There might be a bit of gentle slagging along the way, but only to shed light on something, to find a way of telling the story, never to sneer or condescend; in almost every case, it is to marvel and celebrate.

One thing that has struck me is how much we've changed our look, not just our talk, over the years. Des Bishop, musing about a transformed Ireland, noted that when he first came to Ireland girls had orange hair and white faces; now they have white hair and orange faces. The nation we see on our walkabout looks different to the nation we would have encountered only a few years ago. It is interesting how vain we have become and how much we are willing to spend on our appearance.

The formerly prudish Paddies have changed.[66] About 60% of us claim we would consider cosmetic surgery, with brow-lifts and lipo being the top procedures of choice. And, reflective of our growing openness and live-and-let-live attitudes, 89% would not judge another woman negatively for having cosmetic surgery. Nearly nine out of 10 admit to wearing fake tan and over half admit to feeling less confident without it. Just 13% admitted to trying injectables like Botox and fillers, with 54% of those opting for Botox and 38% for lip fillers. Perhaps reassuringly, almost 80% said the Kardashian/Jenner family had no influence on their decision. The Renaissance Nation is more Tallafornication than Californication.

This obsession with body image could be linked to our smartphones and the massive increase in consumption of pornography. Of 1,000 people surveyed in a Newstalk-commissioned RED C poll,[67] 67% of Irish people claim to have consumed porn at some time, and 35% hardcore porn. Almost one in 10 adults claims to consume porn at least weekly, while 14% claim to consume monthly. A total of 72% believe that porn gives false expectations in sexual relationships, with women (75%) and those in younger age groups most likely to feel this way.

Armed with these interesting but also skin-deep observations, let's go out on the walkabout, safe in the knowledge that, in the Renaissance Nation, appearances matter. We are going to start in the inner cities and new towns before we get to the countryside and then, by train, bus, bike or car, head out to the burgeoning new suburbs. I'll tell you about the people we meet along the way. You might recognise one or two, but you might see a few unfamiliar faces to add to the mix.

Come with me as we observe the Renaissance Nation in all its splendour.

CHAPTER 9

WHERE HIPSTER MEETS HOWAYA

Skin Fade stares out the window of the crawling Luas at the cut stone walls of Grangegorman. This is his manor. He's heading home to Phibsboro in his baby-blue Adidas and Kenzo combo, Moncler Polo shirt (top button closed) and trackie shorts (light grey, knee-length, towelling). Week-old stubble, fresh skin-fade, double-swallow tattoo on the calf, no socks. It's a bright Saturday, nearly as bright as his pristine Nikes. Hardly tropical, but almost hot enough to head out to Sandycove with a few cans, blaring Stormzy on chrome Beats. You could pick up Voyager 1's signals from his satellite-sized sovereign ring.

This JD Sports mannequin, with the fuck-you pimp-roll of the up-and-coming MMA fighter, still has the bang of a chip-shop spice-bag scrapper off him. But that was then. Now, alone in his thoughts as we snake northwards, clutching his personally engraved snooker cue, Skin Fade is a man going places. Scaffolding is back, business is flying. The PCP deals on vans look good too. He's no gobshite and appreciates that he'll pay over the long term, but fuck it, a man needs wheels to push on. Take your chances, as McGregor would say. The vote yesterday felt good. Skin Fade doesn't do elections; but this referendum was different. He'd had enough and it's nice to get a win from time to time. Feels like you have a stake in the kip. At least it's something.

Opposite him sit a couple. She, Ballet Blonde, he, Flat White Man, all urban lumberjack, brandish a Sherry Fitzgerald brochure. Flat White Man googles square footage conversions to metric. She Instas a shot of her significant other flipping through the brochure and scrawls 'Adulting' over the boomerang loop.

'Can you do that again?' she asks.

'Do what?' he responds, surveying his new manor through the window. Anything past Cat Café in Smithfield is new to him.

She frowns and sighs, lowering the pink iPhone 7, resplendent in its glitter cover.

'Never mind.'

She nervously assesses for the dozenth time. Do they look like 'good people'? The type of person you'd let buy a house?!

The house hunting of the last eight months has completely knocked the book club – her chance to drink buckets of Gavi while pretending to read Sally Rooney – out the window. The tag rugby's gone too. The iCouple, surgically attached to their devices, have already made offers on three other places, only to be priced out of the scramble within 24 hours. Prices keep going up. Even their 35-year mortgage approval time is running out.

This one has to be it.

Naturally, Ballet Blonde has gone for option two of her wardrobe staple, option one – cut-out leggings from ASOS and neon gym gear – not being suitable for the occasion. She's all grey Michael Kors dress with a pop of millennial pink and her signature ballet flats (the stilettoes being reserved for client meetings and nights 'out out'). Only the tell-tale corner swish of her Charlotte Tilbury eyeliner and her Maria Tash piercings hint at her former rebellious college days, before the call of a big four firm threw her into the world of clacking heels and lunchtime boxercise.

Flat White Man thinks her stress level is 'cute', which worries more than annoys. This level of misunderstanding means the marriage might actually last, if they can just find a nest. At the same time, though ... he runs a hand swiftly through his new *Peaky Blinders* haircut, more shot-down Luftwaffe pilot than coked-up Brummie gangster, and sighs. He's nervous too.

He has made a serious effort today. His go-to look is not unlike someone with mild learning disabilities who shops in Barnardo's. Everything above the waist is oversized, everything below is undersized – and that's before he rolls up the strides. There was a time when people who wore glasses generally couldn't see too well. No more. When did people with perfectly good sight start wearing glasses? The thicker the frames, the better the eyesight.

PRICED OUT OF PORTOBELLO?

These displaced professional refugees, priced out of Portobello by the double-income careerist pink pound, contemplate a new life north of the river. At least they've heard there's a decent brunch at Two Boys Brew Café. It's not quite Fumbally on Clanbrassil, but it's an early sign of things to come. And being first, being there before the rest, is critical, not just for bragging rights.

In the chaos of another Irish property mania, this newly coveted part of the Dublin 7 house market has a pioneer, settler feel to it. Speed and vision are of the essence. You have to trust Houzz on this one. Who couldn't bank on a website whose strapline is 'Create the home you've always wanted'? Such a declaration brings out the Johnny Sexton in Ballet Blonde. She's an intense competitor, addicted to interiors porn for years.

The iCouple have a shared Pinterest folder for 'Dream Home'. Flat White's contribution: bar stools and pictures of 'man caves' replete with HD curve TV, PlayStation and American-style lazy boys. Sure, what else would they need a spare room for right now? Kids? Who could afford them?

The great Irish property clock is ticking. Time is literally money. Prices in some upmarket areas are going up by almost €4,000 a month. That's 30% more than the average monthly earnings. To hesitate is to lose. This pair better move quickly or they could end up in Ballyfermot.

We are in the Lower Redbrick Zone. Phibsboro is a key cultural frontline in the capital, a commercial battleground driven by rampant gentrification, redbrick envy and young points-race professionals' terror of living in the unknown savannah that lies beyond the M50 in Nissan Qashqai country.

Like other rapidly gentrifying inner suburbs such as Rialto, Ringsend, Portobello and Kilmainham in Dublin, Sunday's Well or the Lough in Cork, Claddagh or the West End in Galway, the Holylands in Belfast, or indeed around the Milk Market in Limerick, Phibsboro holds to the iron rule of upwardly mobile Ireland. This is the law of 'ancient signalling', most acute on the front lines where hipster on the way up meets howaya on the way out.

Today, those looking to get their hands on a coveted Dublin 7 postcode will need to be earning in excess of €105K[68] – no mean feat when just 1.5% of the population are taking home more than €120K.[69] The Upper Redbrick Zone, the Dublin 6 strongholds of Rathmines and Ranelagh are off limits to all but the top 1% of the country, those earning over €140K.

Interestingly, 87% of Ireland's total wealth is held in property and land,[70] and when this changes hands it's usually a seller's market.

In the Renaissance Nation, with everyone on the move, trading up, knocking down or extending out, we are witnessing 'social grating'. When two tribes grate up against each other in a gentrifying location it causes dislocation and splintering. Ultimately, the old tribe is not so much pushed out as priced out. It's a war of attrition and it may go on for a while. It may even take three property cycles to finish, but once social grating begins, only one tribe wins and that's the tribe with the most money.

As a result, property booms create their own self-reinforcing social revolutions, which are not always pretty. As house prices rise, the complexions of neighbourhoods change, driven by money and, these days, how rich your parents are. Some locals cash in and, once flush, move on to the outer suburbs, around Navan, Portlaoise or farther out past the Applegreen motorway stations. Others stay put and keep schtum, biding their time.

Newbies move in and set about doing up with gusto. If there was a renovation Olympics, Ireland would win gold. In the rapidly changing social mosaic of Ireland, as soon as property prices start to rise, the metamorphosis begins, at least in the minds of both buyers and sellers. Like bankruptcy, gentrification happens in two stages; slowly at first and then very quickly.

Be under no illusion, gentrification is a land-grab.

As long as there are not enough new builds, the property battleground shifts to existing districts, because that's where the houses are. In Ireland, social grating is particularly acute now. In no time, the run-down gets tarted up, the empty becomes full, the derelict is renovated and what were once country towns become dormitory settlements, all revolving around the gravitational pull of the cities.

On the frontline of the Lower Redbrick Zone, the law of ancient signalling demands that anything old is posh and the older it is, the posher it is. Unless, of course, it's Scandinavian, in which case brand-new clean lines can beat archaic texture. Mind you, extreme Danish operating-theatre design is made to look at, not live in; only high-camp architects partial to hand-sanitiser, like the creepy lads in a Jo Nesbo thriller, can live in a place like this.

HIPSTER CREEP

Phibsboro, awash with redbrick Victorian terraces and cottages, is ground zero for upwardly mobile house hunters, like Ballet Blonde, who have pebble-dash allergies.

The first salvoes of the phoney war with older residents are friendly, but soon there'll be a full-frontal commercial assault. When hipster meets howaya, pubs often bear the initial collateral damage. You might call this process 'hipster creep'.

The hipsters profess to love the old boozer, full of lippy Dubs called Git who gargle stout and Harp, placing old-fashioned bets all day. But in truth these lads are on their way out. In the history of occupations, only the Palestinians of Haifa stood less chance. Behind the luxuriant beard and Fairtrade coffee, the hipster is a ruthless urban imperialist. As soon as you can say Metalman Pale Ale, the son of some resurrected property developer has swooped in and bought the place. The renovation starts. Slowly. The key to renovation is not to renovate anything. Initially. Remember the iron rule: the shabbier the gaff, the more amazing it is. At first. But once you see the bikes, you know the hipster artillery is imminent.

Git doesn't even notice. He's too busy accepting pints from his new neighbours, who seem to find his stories of Martin Cahill endlessly fascinating. At the beginning, it's just a couple of bike-and-beard combos, but soon there are dozens of new old-looking fixies, attached like magnets to any available bits of metal. Hipsters never come in ones. They hunt in identikit packs. If IKEA were a person, it would be a hipster: mass-produced and indistinguishable.

Before you know it, the pub is holding an 'open mic' on a Wednesday night, there are Bloody Marys on a 'menu' and then, finally, the place opens for 'brunch' on a Sunday. By then the takeover is total. All it needs for the Anschluss is a new name – usually something from a 1950s B-Western.

You know the occupation is underway when the pug in tartan makes its entrance. At the forefront of all hipster colonisation is the ugly, snorting, inbred dog. If Gregor Mendel had a dog, this would be it. The closer it looks to a four-legged walking scrotum, the better. This genetic mutation, this ET of dogs, this pocket GMO, is small enough to fit in a handbag, little eyes bulging from its crumpled face. Poor things don't live long but while they do, these pugs are on a strict vegan diet. They take a great selfie and look fab in a beanie.

The residential war rumbles on. One tribe moves in, another moves out.

A lot of houses are at the probate stage as an older generation of Dubliner dies out. Many of their families, tempted by easy tracker mortgages during the Tiger years, headed up one of the motorways to Applegreen Land, a vast new suburb which stretches in a giant arc from Drogheda, through Kells to Mullingar and on to Portlaoise, sweeping south to Carlow and meeting the sea again in Gorey. The lucky ones avoided ghost estates, but most suffered in negative equity for at least a decade. Now they need to get the best price for Nan's house to stay afloat. In this latest transfer of wealth, which the property market in Ireland constantly orchestrates, the sons and daughters of Phibsboro hold out for the best price from the sons and daughters of Donnybrook.

Not surprisingly, this gaff, the one Ballet Blonde has her eye on, is on the market to the highest bidder. Tattooed elbows are sharpened.

CHAPTER 10

THE PROPERTY TRAP

PHIZZFEST

This morning there's a queue for the viewing on Victorian Munster Street. The cat-who-got-the-cream estate agent, Pro 14 Peter – good school, bad Leaving – is handing out his business cards, taking names and numbers. He knows we are moving way above the asking price. Judging by their accents and the soft 's' on their plurals, today's hopefuls are his people, more RDS than Hill 16, more Jordi Murphy than Robbie Brady. Ballet Blonde surveys the competition.

Flat White Man feigns interest when Pro 14 Peter mentions that Croke Park is only a few minutes away (you never know – culchies have learnt the art of camouflage these days and it's harder to spot them). Like most of Gonzaga, this urban lumberjack has to pretend to be interested in hurling, but in truth he glazes over. Bar the Kendrick Lamar concert, he's never set foot in the place. But talk of the impending conversion of Mountjoy Prison into an eco-village in the city – that's right up his street. So too are the flyers agitating for more cycle lanes, organised by Phizzfest, the local arts festival turned environmental lobby group. Nothing like an arts, ideas, literary or, better still, food festival to lift the tone of an area.

Ballet Blonde likes the sound of a lobby group. It's something local she can join, infiltrate and ultimately dominate. She wasn't a mover in UCD's L&H by accident. Agitation is her thing, one of her many things. She loved the repeal campaign, leaflet drops, knocking on doors, executing the online campaign in her home constituency of Rathgar. She quite fancies curating an arts festival. Imagine, a little bit of Borris on your own doorstep? Think of the possibilities – writing and all that D7 salt-of-the-earth stuff. The Blonde has always been a little partial to a bit of rough.

But now she has to focus. No room for mistakes.

As Ballet Blonde indulges her momentary skanger fetish, Flat White Man is getting aroused. Renovation porn. Nothing gets him up like something falling down. If interiors porn is foreplay, renovation porn is the dark web. This house is a perfect candidate, smelling as it does of Granny, oxtail soup, and budgie. Nothing betokens renovation potential more than an abandoned budgie cage.

Flat White Man's inner Kevin McCloud is stirring. The grand designer alter ego lying dormant under every conditioned beard doesn't take much coaxing. The more luxuriant the beard, the more the Williamsburg envy. No project is too daunting, no cantilevered mezzanine too formidable. A wall knocked here, a kitchen island there, a few strategic Tom Dixon lights and you'd never know you're not in Ranelagh.

Inside the head of every hopeful house hunter is a tableau of their first showy-offy dinner party. Lebanese or Iranian? Ballet Blonde might do Lebanese, something with coriander from Ottolenghi, obviously. But before that, she has to get the place. She is quite desperate. What could possibly go wrong now?

THE HEIST

Around the iCouple, a legion of tasteful builders, each with their own website and Instagram page, are looking at an exposed brick-'n'-timber Tribeca bonanza. The hopeful hipsters queue up, letting their SoHo loft imaginations run wild. In the hands of the estate agent's copywriter, this slightly shabby, modest but decent Dublin terraced house has become a tabernacle of potential.

The brochure's vocabulary is worth noting. Remember, from now on, once you are seduced, you are not buying the down-at-heel house you see in front of you, you are buying the once-in-a lifetime opportunity that lives in your imagination. The house is not merely a house – you know, four walls, that sort of thing. It is a property. A property is old and lived in, with history and heritage.

Of course, this property is labelled 'period'. Period means many things to many people, but one thing is for sure: period is not new. And older is better. It locates the potential buyer in a bygone, more genteel time, when the day moved more slowly, and people were more civilised. In the taste hierarchy, appreciating period gives the buyer a sense of style and stamps a veneer of tradition on the otherwise grubby commercial transaction.

This signalling is evident not only when wooing the buyer; it defines the seller too. Since time immemorial, the cardinal rule of selling is to appear not to be selling at all. Instead, the seller lets on that he is generously giving the potential buyer an opportunity to avail of something unique. Therefore, when you are selling something with heritage, like a period property, it can be dressed up not as selling, but as passing something on. The estate agent is carefully curating an heirloom.

As with buyers, in the hierarchy of sellers, people who sell old things like to position themselves on a much higher rung of the commercial ladder than those selling new things. Think about the type of people who sell classic cars. You, the buyer, need an appointment to see them, even though they are looking for your money, not the other way round. The same goes for people who sell vintage wine. They wrap themselves in the veil of history and authenticity, which disguises the fact that they are an off-licence shop assistant in a cravat.

And as we are seeing in Dublin 7 this morning, the same goes with houses. It's not a house, it's a property; and it's not only a property, it's a home. In the estate agent's weird patois, a house morphs miraculously into a home.

The word 'home' conveys an image of something special, loved, safe, nurturing – more like a womb than a gaff. The cops never raid a 'crack home', they always raid a crack house. Nothing bad happens in a home, whereas in a house, anything can happen.

The house in Phibsboro has a tiny front garden, with enough space for a few daffodils, but in the brochure the home is 'recessed from the road' as if it were some Palladian mansion. And consider this:

'On entering the property, one comes into an impressive entrance hallway off which the two self-contained reception rooms radiate.'

Read this again. Now say it aloud in the accent your granny used to put on when she answered the phone. You know, that strange sound that country people made in the 1970s when they wanted to sound swanky? In our family, the ringing phone set off status anxiety, as if only aristocrats used the phone. Or at least that was the case for my lovely granny. On picking up the phone, her rich, lush, West Cork accent mutated into some weird hybrid, a cross between the Queen Mother at Ascot and Marty Morrissey at Citywest.

Note the use in the estate agent's patter of the word 'one' instead of 'you'. Somewhere in the back of our heads, this is how we imagine upper-crust Edwardians, like Lady Mary in *Downton Abbey*, spoke to each other.

Sticking with the *Downton Abbey* theme, there is the description of a 'stairwell' as opposed to the stairs, giving the sense of a grand, sweeping staircase curving its way down to the giant open ballroom. If you let your mind go, the uniformed staff could even now be peeking out subserviently from the basement as their betters imbibe Fever-Tree G&Ts.

The mid-terrace house is 130 square metres of Dublin 7 aspiration. It needs total refurbishment, but that will allow Ballet Blonde to stamp her own unique style on the place. The asking price is €500,000, or €3,600 per square metre. Who said we would never repeat the mistakes of the past? Let the bidding begin.

Locals need not apply. Dublin 7 is now officially being gentrified, as will happen to all the city's postcodes with odd as opposed to even numbers. Peaceful ethnic cleansing, population transfers brought to you by AIB.

CHILD OF PRAGUE

A clutch of nans totter past, shaking their heads at the queue of potential buyers, gossiping under the watchful, one-armed Child of Prague. Fine day, a bit nippy but. Pro 14 Peter spots them. In his head, a 'flipping' opportunity presents itself. Bingo.

He can't wait to get home to The Bridge off Shelbourne Road for the late Leinster kick-off. He has a simple game plan. Buy low from the grannies now. Give them what they feel is a fortune in a quiet private sale. Then wait. Segment your market. Then gradually release these properties back on the market. A glossy brochure, hinting at elderflower and wisteria potential, and we are off. Once he has the house, he will change tactic.

In previous years, it was essential to keep the asking price low to get people in the door and then watch them bid the property up to crazy levels, trousering the difference. But now he's doing the opposite. Now, with all this demand, he has set the price ridiculously high. This weeds out the 'mortgage only' people, the sorts who have borrowed to the max even to get into the race. The maths is simple. No one has that income and the Central Bank's rules are sticking. Only those who can make up the difference with Daddy's money are still in at this ridiculous price. Once he gets two or three, he waits. Then he drops the price and waits for the first one to bite.

We tend to form their views of value from the first price asked. So, if a seller asks €700,000 and cuts the price to €600,000, it feels much better than if he had asked €400,000 initially and then bid prices up to €600,000. The first €600,000 feels like a bargain; the second €600,000 feels like a rip-off. Our mind plays tricks on us. Economists call this 'anchoring' and make a big deal of it. Good salespeople call it experience and do it every day. Pro 14 Peter is more street-smart than his gold-button blazer, the international uniform of the eejit, suggests.

THE NEW BRUTALISM

Skin Fade shapes up the street, pigeon-cocky, brushing past a few swaggering Bohs gypsies heading towards Dalymount Park, oblivious to the sweating gym bunnies working out above him in a grotesque tower that some brutalist architect once thought beautiful. What other profession could foist a style called 'brutalism' on the world without the remotest feeling for human sensibilities?

Skin Fade clutches his cue, mystified by something called a 'pop-up restaurant' that is apparently opening but won't announce when exactly. His new neighbours are an odd bunch. It is time to get away from all this insanity, into the sanctuary of Cross Guns snooker club for a few frames with the boys.

The inner suburbs are changing. In the words of Ringsend's finest rap duo, Versatile: 'Too many restaurants, fuck all chippers; fuck all scumbags, too many hipsters … fuck all blokes getting jobs as builders … Haven't seen a ronnie in about three year.'

People are moving in, moving out, moving on. Property is hot again. Old lines are blurring and new ones are being drawn. We see this blurring and economic change everywhere.

The old caste system is being revolutionised, driven by economics, demographics, poor planning and insane property prices – yet again. Ballet Blonde and Skin Fade, sorts who would never have crossed paths a few years ago, are about to become neighbours in our New Ireland.

And yesterday they both voted 'Yes' – one here in Dublin 7, the other in its cultural opposite, her family home in Dublin 6. The things that divided us are still there, but increasingly we have more and more in common.

Attitudes in the Renaissance Nation have blended into the Radical Centre.

CHAPTER 11

BETWEEN THE CANALS

A few miles south, a big Irish family beams down at the coolest man in the city from their box at the Olympia. The closest thing Ireland has to hip-hop aristocracy couldn't be more proud – all three generations of Dublin rap royalty. Their little boy is in the zone, hundreds of fans screaming his name. Who would've thought? At the apex, the matriarch looks upon her swaggering grandson. He's the first of his kind, signed to a big hip-hop label and splashed across the front pages of the newspaper culture sections. Now he is coming home.

She remembers him as a baby and toddler arriving in Artane every morning, sleep in his eyes, all grumpy and early morning crumpled, driven through the city by his mother.

An Irish nana's job is never done. Given the cost of childcare, a willing grandmother can be the difference between solvency and the breadline. A nana is as good as a deposit these days. The matriarch was already minding seven other grandchildren, including the future rapper's older sister. Two little black children in a big Irish family. As the rapper's mum and dad both worked full time, the matriarch effectively raised him and his sister until they were in secondary school. Today, she has 25 grandchildren and 13 great-grandchildren. Now that is a proper Irish matriarch.

The rapper remembers Nana coming to see him playing football all around the city. As a kid, he'd been given a soccer scholarship to the US. Squashed into his mother's car, they'd travel across the city to the likes of Brickfields Park in Crumlin, the San Siro of Dublin schoolboy football. In the car, chatting to his nana, the future rapper felt safe, passing Dublin's dilapidated splendour, northside to southside, hemmed in by the canals – those definitive limits of the city set by the Georgians. When wasn't Dublin about limits set by others? In time, the Victorians edged out towards Rathgar to the south and Glasnevin north of the river, pushing the city out past Phoenix Park and Inchicore to the west and out past East Wall, where the rapper's mum lived as a little kid, towards the sea, places now hosting the gentrifying clash of tribes.

They'd drive down past Kennedy's on the right and St Luke's on the left – 'Bertie's HQ', his mother used to say. The rapper went to the local school, St Pat's Drumcondra, whose most famous past pupil was … that's right, Bertie Ahern! He was the only black kid in national school and only one of two in secondary school. Nana was the only white adult who never made him feel different because of his skin colour.

He loved this area in September when the Dubs flags were out. Right on the North Circular, past the shabby bedsits where he first saw other black faces that weren't related to him. Or at least didn't appear to be. The bedsits are nearly all gone. There's a skip outside every house as these terraces are being 'restored to their former glory' according to the property supplements.

As she looks down at the rapper, strutting his thing, the matriarch remembers it wasn't easy having a black daughter in East Wall in the 1970s and 1980s. Of course, everybody knew Paul McGrath and Phil Lynott, but Paul and Phil were famous, while her daughter was just a normal little girl. She was born in the late 1960s, her father Jamaican. She was about to be adopted when a close relative came to visit the young mother in a Dublin hospital and decided the little baby wasn't going for any adoption. The matriarch, already with five kids of her own under the age of six, took her five-day-old daughter home.

Later, when they moved to Artane, she was the only black girl at secondary school, maybe the only black girl on the northside. 'Half-caste', her beautiful daughter was called. She remembered the Pope coming and all the bunting out. It certainly wasn't easy with the gossip, the rumours and all the bitching behind her back. And, of course, the holier the person, the bigger the bigot.

Now look at him. Her little daughter's little boy, her shy grandson, Alex Anyaegbunam, aka Rejjie Snow, with a full Olympia, a sell-out world tour, American record deal in his hand, the world at his feet.

Skin Fade is here tonight too. He has no idea that the North Cir' used to be Rejjie Snow's stomping ground, but in the pit at the Olympia, nothing matters. Hip-hop is his music. It's the music of the oppressed, the marginalised, the angry. It's Afro-punk for white boys. At that moment, all he cares about is that there is a black Irish Drumcondra rapper, cool as fuck, taking the US hip-hop world by storm. Ireland is certainly blurring. The fact that his manor is being colonised by over-educated hipsters with a weakness for interiors matters little to him now. He's lost in the music.

Rejjie takes the crowd in his palm and moves them. His Nigerian dad and Irish-Jamaican mum are in the box, beaming down at their boy. His nana, the 85-year-old matriarch, loves it. Chuckling to herself, she remembers the last time she was in the Olympia with Alex, at the Christmas panto years ago. She remembers him having to put up with all the snide comments as he waltzed his way through schoolboy defences. It wasn't that long ago, the early 2000s, and Rejjie was still the only black kid in his team and in his class.

Now this; a vindication of sorts. She gazes down at the hundreds of white youngsters, idolising her black Irish grandson. It's a far cry from the 'black babies' of the 1970s, when grannies would touch her black kid for luck.

THE MULTICULTURAL TOUCHLINE WARRIORS

There are few better ways to see what the country is going to look like in a generation than from the side-line of an underage football, GAA or rugby match. Children's sports, alive and well across all codes in this country, give a wonderful snapshot of the different ethnicities living in the Renaissance Nation.

Just before the summer holidays, many clubs organise mini-World Cups or mini-All-Irelands, bringing together hundreds of kids from the hinterland. The blend of languages, colours and cultures on the side-lines is truly astonishing.

My own son's football team has come across an outfit made up of well-drilled Lithuanians. They have played against a squad of all-African boys, save for the solitary white goalie – a boy from a Serbian family. And they have togged out against a predominantly Arabic club where the back four were all called Muhammad. (The name Muhammad has seen the biggest rise in popularity in Ireland in 2016, jumping 36 places in the list of most popular baby names registered.[71])

In this maelstrom of social change, it is reassuring that the one constant – across several cultures – is the touchline warrior. You might recognise the Demented Dads and Motivational Moms who roar instructions, half-encouraging, half-threatening, at their little Ronaldos. One officious-looking mother might be armed with a clipboard. You just know she is in charge by looking at her. Others, equipped with their own personal VARs (video-assisted referees), film every move, every tackle and – pity the actual referees – every decision, only too ready to give their educated, unbiased interpretations of the rules.

Because sport is so popular in Ireland, particularly from age 16 down, the football experience also provides a map of who is settling where in the country. In the same way as Rejjie's nana watched him play all over the country, every weekend parents criss-cross the Renaissance Nation, going to parts they'd never normally go, meeting people they'd never normally meet, seeing bits they'd never normally see – all in the pursuit of schoolboy and schoolgirl sporting endeavour. You can see the changing face of Ireland in the complexions and names of the players. Soon you realise that the settling patterns of immigrants in Ireland are unusual, reflecting the uniquely Irish intersection of property prices, the planning process and suburban development.

There are three main zones. The first is the inner cities, particularly in Dublin. This is where the immigrant population is highest.[72] In the Dublin City North electoral ward, 55% are not categorised as white Irish. In Dublin Mountjoy, that figure goes up to 62%. In Cork district centre B, over 50% are not white Irish, while in Limerick Shannon A polling area, 54% are not white Irish. This mirrors patterns in other countries.

However, when we head out from the multicultural epicentre, we start to see settlement patterns changing, and these patterns are unusual internationally.

As we leave Dublin city centre and move out to the older suburbs, those within the M50, immigrant families disappear almost completely. These estates, built between the 1950s and 1970s, are overwhelmingly Irish and have changed comparatively little in a generation.

Once we cross the M50, the immigrant population begins to rise again. In formerly provincial towns such as Portlaoise and Navan, the immigrant population is significant and rising. But as we go out farther, we see that Ireland becomes more, not less, diverse ethnically. Traditionally, Longford is a place where diversity and tolerance would not be the first descriptions to come to mind. Yet it is the most diverse town in Ireland, with the lowest proportion of white Irish in any municipal district. In the old days, Longford – the home county of Ann Lovett – was dominated physically by St Mel's Cathedral and psychologically by the Catholic Church. Today it has changed completely; 58% voted 'Yes' for repeal in 2018, the same percentage that voted in 1983 against the introduction of the eighth amendment in Dún Laoghaire. Tragically, such attitude changes came too late for Ann Lovett.

After Longford, the most ethnically diverse towns in Ireland are Portlaoise, Navan, Belturbet and Drogheda, which also happens to be the fastest-growing town in the country. Interestingly, immigration in Ireland is either an inner city or provincial town affair.

In assessing the impact of immigration, while the absolute numbers tell one story, the number of newly arrived immigrants per head is the litmus test for how quickly society is changing. In 2016 Ireland accepted one of the highest proportions of new immigrants per head of the population of any country in Europe. In that year alone, 53,708 non-Irish nationals arrived here – 1.14% of the population[73] Brexit Britain took in 26% less than that as a proportion of its population, while Italy, led by an anti-immigrant government, accepted in 0.5% of its population, less than half of the proportion in Ireland.[74]

From having almost no immigration and being almost 100% white Irish – apart from Rejjie's mum and a few others – Ireland is fast becoming one of the most diverse countries in Europe. We are now fourth in the European Union league of immigrants as a proportion of total population, behind Luxembourg, Malta and Cyprus.[75] As a percentage of the population, Ireland today has more immigrants than Sweden, UK, Germany, France and Italy – all countries with significant anti-immigrant political movements.[76] Not to mention Austria and the countries farther east, which have effectively closed their doors.

Immigration is the litmus test of a dynamic country. As did generations of Irish people, immigrants go to countries that offer opportunity. They don't go to places that are faltering. Here again, talk is important. If a society is broadly accepting of difference and diversity, people will come. While they may not necessarily be welcomed with open arms, they know that, when they get here, they will be encouraged to have a go, like the rest of us.

Years ago, at the beginning of the culture war, had you suggested that Ireland would one day be accepting in more foreigners per head than almost any other country in Europe, and that there would be no anti-immigrant nativist movements, most people would have laughed. It was taken for granted that the Irish had the potential to be racist, not least because we had no previous exposure. But as it turns out, the Renaissance Nation now has tolerance hardwired into its DNA.

You may say I am being a bit premature and that there are many individual incidents of racial attacks, and I agree. However, there doesn't appear to be a significant constituency for the development of a nativist movement directed against immigrants. This is a function of the fact that the economy has been growing so quickly because it is tolerant. One dynamic material growth reinforces the other.

Typically, immigrants will come from poorer countries and therefore the chances are the people will have low skills. They start at the bottom and work their way up. However, Ireland has the highest proportion of immigrants coming from countries outside Europe that are ranked 'very high' on the UN's Human Development Index.[77] In fact, 16% of all our migrants come from countries that are at a similar level of development as us. These would therefore be highly educated, highly skilled workers. This compares with 3% of immigrants to Italy coming from countries with very high levels of development, 7% in Germany and 4% in Sweden.[78]

This tells its own story, which is that Ireland is an attractive place to live, not just for poorer migrants, but for rich ones too. This obviously comes down to tolerance, attitudes and opportunity. Rich people don't come to live in countries with atavistic, chauvinistic attitudes.

The matriarch looks down again at the rapper, strutting his stuff on the Olympia stage. Such swagger, such confidence, such a future. She pictures him, just a few years ago, in the back of his mother's car, heading out to the Fifteen Acres in the Phoenix Park, where Dubliners have played soccer for generations, just beside where the Pope had said Mass to a very different nation in 1979. Then he was the self-doubting little black boy from Drumcondra. Today he is Rejjie Snow, hip-hop's up-and-coming superstar. Alex Anyaegbunam has reinvented himself, but so too has his country, Ireland.

CHAPTER 12

THE IN-BETWEENERS

THE SLEEVE

On our economic walkabout we can see the social consequences of our dysfunctional property market. One that I find particularly interesting is that the 'milestones' that constitute being an adult are being pushed out by a decade or so. These milestones are events like moving out from your parents, moving in with your partner or having children and buying a house.

These used to be attainable by Irish people in their late twenties, but now these milestones are being pushed out, largely due to expensive housing. The best indicator of this social change is the massive rise in the number of people who are single in their thirties. The Renaissance Nation is a much more independent and single country than ever before. For example, the number of single women in both the 30–34 and 35–39 age brackets have increased more than threefold since 1980. The change has been dramatic. While fewer than 15% of 30–35-year-old Irish women were single in 1981, today over 52% of these women are single, independent and doing their own thing. Trends for men are broadly similar.[79]

On the walkabout, you will notice these women and men in cafés, bars, clubs, on the DART, on buses, in burrito bars, queueing up behind you in Tesco Metro or transfixed by their screens, aniseed vape in one hand, head-to-toe in limited edition Japanese streetwear. One character turns up time and again. You might know him. We will meet his girlfriend in a bit; but for now, let me introduce you to The Sleeve.

THE MORNING AFTER

A tattooed arm bursts forth from the sheets and searches in vain for a glass of water on the bedside table. Slowly a shaved head and beard emerge. The Sleeve, nervous as a fawn, delicately tests the parameters of the hangover.

Another pint too many in Grogan's. Why didn't he just go home after the gig? But how could he? The repeal party was rocking South William Street.

The Sleeve was only supposed to go for the one after but it just sort of escalated, somewhere between Hogan's and Against the Grain, before winding up in … was it The Black Door? It's difficult to be certain if that was last night or the Friday before. There was definitely a kebab involved, at any rate – the Zaytoon wrapper is still on his bedroom floor – devoured with the raging appetite of Cronus after being carefully cradled home in a 3 a.m. MyTaxi like a newborn.

Why, at the age of 33, does Guinness still seem like a good idea after midnight? The mysteries of his own decision-making evading him, The Sleeve groans and rolls over. What happened his vape? He doesn't smoke, but that doesn't stop him from feeling the fuzz of a few rollies bummed off an overly enthusiastic intern. The kid dressed like a modern-day Patrick Bateman. The Sleeve just didn't get it at all. And how come none of them have spots anymore? What happened to the bad skin his generation was gifted with? Was he that self-confident when he first started working? He'd consider asking someone, but can't, as he's never stayed in the same job for more than two years.

His miniature pitbull, licks the pocket-watch-and-playing-cards tattoo on his right forearm and whines. He senses the boss is hanging. The Sleeve wonders if the watch and playing cards aren't getting a bit too commonplace these days. Time was, he was one of the few. Now they're everywhere.

He had wanted a full-size pitbull but his two-bed cottage in Ringsend didn't come with a garden. It seemed perfect when he bought the place with help from Mum and Dad five years ago, but between the dog and the newish girlfriend leaving her stuff everywhere, he's not so sure.

Herself has been showing him a lot of pictures of her mates' humanist boho weddings lately and even asking to meet his parents. In fairness, they're both getting on a bit. His own parents had three kids almost reared by the time they were his age. It feels to him like every weekend is a wedding this year. His Facebook and Instagram timelines are permanently taken over by floral headdresses, Ted Baker suits and chalkboard 'I dos'. The plan was to go to Japan this autumn but the holiday quota has been taken up by his cousin's do in Santorini, a trip to Turkey they booked last year after something herself had heard on a SheerLuxe podcast, and a chain of mental, coked-up stags in Prague, Glasgow and Galway.

The first hour of The Sleeve's weekend is spent scanning through social media. The vote was extraordinary – 78% 'Yes' in Ringsend. This took him by surprise.

The 'fear' subsides as none of the photos on the work WhatsApp group appear to be of him. He ritualistically checks his Tinder (which he still hasn't deleted – shh!) and that one awful message he sent to the popular girl from his old secondary school he matched with last year. Still nothing.

He scans his floordrobe to find an option amongst the pile of clothes and a 'Make Your Own Gin' kit that never made it out of the box since his birthday. A pair of skinny jeans, a vest and camo shirt, sleeves rolled up so you can see the bespoke tattoo drawn up by Mo Coppoletta in London, but creatively directed by himself, of course. A retro Jesus and the Sacred Heart intertwined with doves.

He's running late. She'll be at Herbstreet already. He gives himself a quick up-down in the hall mirror, buttons the shirt over the growing craft-beer paunch, throws on the aviators and sprays on ample Sauvage by Dior for good measure before heading.

It's only a 10-minute walk but he curses the Luas again for evading the Google Ghetto as an orchestra of cranes, saws and piledrivers whizz, burr and clunk around him. Doing nothing for the head, this racket. Don't they know people actually LIVE here? Whatever happened to lazy builders who don't work weekends? He avoids most traffic via the Dodder and passes a bunch of them devouring protein shakes and chicken fillet rolls outside Spar. They actually look pretty fit. Not a Breakfast Roll Man among them.

Waist-wise, things have kind of gone downhill for The Sleeve since burritos and burgers became a legit breakfast choice in Dublin, so he resolves to do something. But not just yet. He has tickets for Kodaline in Malahide Castle. He never misses them live.

Maybe he should take the lads up on the offer of inducting him into gym life. Get his shit together before the Christmas reunions back home. Or he could finally get around to trying kite surfing. That looks cool. He stares at the zipline over Grand Canal. Maybe not.

Nor has he committed to EP yet – for the first time in years. Passing out briefly in the Spoken Word arena last year was a bit scary and overnight camping is starting to seem like a bit of an ordeal. The Salty Dog at four in the morning isn't quite the craic it used to be.

He hasn't forgiven the lads for last year – losing the guitar he had since he was 15. He had every ticket from every gig he'd ever been to taped to it. They used to slag him a lot about that. Actually, they slag him a bit too much about everything in general. But he knows it's only because they're a bit jealous. The lads didn't get on the property ladder before the latest madness. They thought he was crazy not to spend the money from Gran's will on travelling but now he's the jammy fucker. He has an actual job, in design. Gran would be pretty happy with him, really.

But though he's been working for years, there's nothing left at the end of the month, ever. Worse still, a lot of design work is being outsourced to India. He googles PeoplePerHour.com. At these rates, no one can compete. The work is excellent and living costs in Mumbai are a fraction of Dublin's. Technology is liberating his social life but could be decimating his work life. Something has to give.

She claims they could save so much money living together and eventually get a bigger place, but he doesn't really see the point. And isn't more debt what destroyed the country last time? What would he need a bigger place for? Kids? Better not think about it. Fumbally last weekend was a crèche.

Should The Sleeve be getting his skates on? With her? Maybe he should have stretched to that crumbly redbrick on the far side of Porto – closer to Blackpitts, really – but at the time the place seemed kind of dead. And well dodgy.

Herbstreet isn't that packed; the queue is only six-deep. Pulling up a dog bowl and chair, he collapses. Netflix and chill beats this. Actual human beings are a bit too much today. He should probably 'adult' and stock up on ready meals from M&S. How is she supposed to be all domestic goddess in his grotty 1960s kitchenette? He makes a mental note to pick up a dine-in-for-two as a treat for them both.

With still no sign of her, he orders an espresso and scrolls through Irish spa resort deals. It's his parents' anniversary next weekend, but they're not getting on. Mum's threatening to move out, just after they got the house tarted up á la *Room to Improve*. His sister suggested taking her away, so she doesn't dwell on it too much. It's a good idea but he can't help feeling his sister would be a lot better at this sort of thing if she wasn't stuck living in Melbourne with IVF triplets. They've been Skyping weekly since then.

Sunday mornings are for the old man. The Sleeve hates golf. Now that Dad has taken up cycling, The Sleeve dreads the invitation to do Enniskerry with him, but it's kind of inevitable. Maybe the golf wasn't too bad. And you never know, it might end up handy in work if he ever gets promoted to director or MD.

He can't understand it. How can two people spend all that time together only to start splitting up right at the end? Both parents seemed pretty pissed off at how he'd phrased that question, though, so he isn't sure if he'll get an answer anytime soon.

But seriously, is that all there is? What was the point? Christmas will be awkward.

Maybe he could do Japan for New Year after all.

THE FRINGE REALISES TIME'S UP

'For fuck's sake!' Just once, The Fringe would like to have a shower without worrying about strangers' pubes snaking up between her toes. She grabs her towel.

She never expected to be still renting six years on, in a bloody house share. Sure, the gaff is huge, it's handy for work, but the people? Jesus wept! Wasn't it Sartre who said 'Hell is other people'? In fairness to The Fringe, she can spoof with the best of them, even French existentialists. And if it wasn't Sartre, who cares, because it's bloody true when you are sharing a big house in Rathgar past the age of 30.

Where to start? The Spanish couple with their noisy sex and even noisier arguments? The mature student from Carlow with the colour-coded cleaning rota and booby-trapped snack box? Her best mate from school who turned out to be a kleptomaniac? The two session mots when there was only ever supposed to be one? The nerdy Bitcoin guy who never leaves his room? The two graduate accountants who simultaneously lost interest in her when they realised they were never getting the ride? Or the skinny French girl who only ever seems to raise an eyebrow and say, 'This, I don't get – why it is funny?'

Eleven adults, one house, one outcome: mutual loathing.

She isn't even 100% confident about their names but it's well past the expiry date of awkwardly asking again.

Friends grossly misrepresented the fun times that awaited her renting in her twenties. But economics is telling her that, at €720 for a double room (excluding bills) she'd be absolutely insane to give it up. Anyway, there are no other options, so sucking it up has become a coping strategy.

Is it push or pull that has her hanging out with The Sleeve? Better keep that thought for another day.

The one thing about all the sleeping around, Tinder, hook-ups and general carry-on is that, when you've so many options, settling for one can be difficult. The paradox of choice. Her mother's generation wanted more choice because they had none. They expected more choice would make them happy. And maybe it did, up to a point, but now that The Fringe and her friends have all the choice they want, both fellas and the girls, it's harder to choose. Why settle when there's always someone better around the corner? All you have to do is swipe right.

Actually, a lot of things are not what she expected since she first started that €28,000 job at Facebook, with free snacks, and could finally move out of Mum and Dad's. The Fringe's mum is Brazilian. Her dad, hard as it is to believe now, was a bit of a dude travelling around the world in the late 1970s because, as he said, Ireland was a kip. He met Mum when he was teaching English in Santa Catarina in southern Brazil. Eventually, they drifted back to Ireland, before Dad became evangelical about selling water purifiers. The Fringe got her Facebook gig thanks to her fluent Portuguese. Her Master's in Journalism was of no interest to them, but that wasn't surprising – it hadn't been of interest to many journalists either.

Her dad is so proud. He tells all his mates in Kildare his daughter's working for 'the Facebook'. She hasn't the heart to tell him it's just a glorified telesales job. She'll get her journalism dreams back on course in a year or so, and in the meantime there's still her blog, dedicated to vintage brand packaging. It's not a lot to show as a 'vocation' after 30 years but she was reading this article about how everyone needs a 'side hustle' now. The Fringe needs to give it another go. Or maybe photography? Her Instagram photos regularly get a lot of likes if she throws a few dozen hashtags on them. #Instahustle? Who knows?

It's the end of the month. She checks the bank balance on her AIB app. Not good. That €40 is going to have to stretch until Thursday. She'd better not take it out in case she's hit with those ridiculous account fees again like last month. Maybe the six months upfront fees for unlimited classes in YogaHub was a bit rash.

Going home to Newbridge at the weekend to save money isn't working. Ending up with the gang from school, dropping the cheeky half and staying up all night like it's 2008 all over again isn't too clever. And there's no renting for them of course; they all have massive gaffs – new builds on that 10% deposit thing. But their cookie-cutter sameness makes The Fringe shiver. It's not for her.

It's just so inauthentic, you know?

The whole thing makes her appreciate again why she got out as soon as possible. Who would actually choose 'renter beige' and a cream L-shaped leather couch from Harvey Norman for their own home?

When The Fringe 'grows up' everything in her ideal home will be original, each a perfect find telling a unique story about who she is as an individual and all the interesting things she has done. Her shelves will be filled with carefully selected hardbacks from Hodges Figgis (currently all stacked in neat, unread piles on her bedroom floor). She'll grow her own herbs out the back and maybe even keep a few Silkie and Plymouth chickens if there is the space. She'll host dinner parties with proper wine and have long talks after dark with friends and neighbours who will never want to leave.

She has some regular savings but it's becoming laughable to call them mortgage savings at the rate house prices are ratcheting up daily. She managed to set up a pension last week, which none of her mates have done yet. She's not completely hopeless, but horizons are narrowing. She can feel it.

Time to head out and meet yer man.

What about boyfriend jeans, brogues, nondescript white t-shirt from @Arka, thin rose gold chains and a vintage Casio?

Naturally, The Fringe hates the fringe – as she does with all major consumer choices she makes. It's ultimately why she never got a tattoo, even though she has wanted a sleeve of botanicals since before it was cool. She's just too fickle for that level of commitment, that permanence. The risk of screwing up is too high. Now she's seeing fringes everywhere, even on the DART. Like classic designer bags, the fringe is becoming so ... basic.

Growing it out and going pink was an option before Mum got there first. Since her early retirement from nursing last summer, Mum has rediscovered her wanderlust. Initially it was just the Camino, but now she's heading to Abkhazia, Georgia and Armenia. When not around the Caucasus mountains, she's on writer retreats out west, Basque region wine tours or taking selfies on nights out at the theatre or the latest restaurant.

Mum's generation is having a laugh. Kids raised, mortgages paid off and pensions kicking in, they are healthy, fit and rich, and The Fringe suspects there's someone new in her life, but she can't bring herself to start that conversation.

The whole thing is grossly unfair. Her mother stole what was supposed to be *her* life.

She throws the Adidas Originals and yoga mat into a gym bag and WhatsApps The Sleeve to order her a supersalad and green matcha almond latte. She pockets the vape he left the last time he stayed over and heads out the door with a 'Bye' behind her – a habit from home – to nobody in particular.

She said she'd be there soon (a lie) but she's not feeling that guilty. Walking past the Savita memorial, it doesn't seem to her like The Sleeve is that bothered after nearly a year of dating. He doesn't even watch her Insta stories anymore. And he has already made plans for the rest of the weekend without her. The last few weekends were spent helping out on the 'Yes' campaign but now it's over, The Fringe kind of misses the whole thing. Maybe there are other things she should get involved with? She was never interested in politics or any of that before, but the campaign gave her a sense of being part of something bigger, a movement.

Her timeline is stuffed with ads like 'Bucketlist Bombshells' and 'Working Nomads' telling her to ditch her nine-to-five cubicle and be her own boss, all while travelling the world. Maybe there's something in it.

CHAPTER 13

SLIOTAR MOM

So we say goodbye to The Fringe, The Sleeve, Flat White Man, and the not-half-as-handsome-as-Cillian-Murphy Peaky Blinder clones. We drive out past the Berlin-themed coffee shops, burrito joints and graffiti, increasingly encroached upon by consumer brands desperate to get hip with the kids. We begin to notice something physical: beards become less resplendent.

Soon, after 15 or 150 minutes, depending on traffic, we reach a place where beards don't exist at all. Facial hair is frowned on out here. We are now moving from the bearded to the clean-shaven post codes. People wear glasses because they are in fact short-sighted. The houses are getting bigger, the gardens too, and European cars replace Asian ones. Bikes tend to have gears and everyone's on them. Out here, public transport is only considered acceptable if you can see the sea clearly from it.

In a stubborn democracy like ours, where a few hundred votes can determine who gets in, the clean-shaven zone is crucial to the fortunes of every political party. These people vote, all the time, on everything.

Sticking with politics, during both Clinton elections in the 1990s, US political analysts identified a new group that was pivotal to the success of any candidate. In 1992, the suburban 'soccer mom' became that most prized and elusive of all American voters – the uncommitted, non-partisan swing voter.

Soccer moms voted in their hundreds of thousands for Bill Clinton and, by doing so, they guaranteed his double victory.

Soccer moms are the type of young mothers who you see all over the suburbs. Their daily lives are one long school run. In the past few years, soccer moms, tennis moms, rugby moms, swimming moms, piano moms and 'whatever else your children must do in their hyper-organised after-school life' moms have come to dominate the suburbs.

Sliotar Mom is the Irish equivalent.

Out here a strange thing has happened to accents in the past few years. The air sounds American. The more Irish the children's names, the more American the children's accents; the more American the names, the more Irish the accents. So kids called Dexter, Cody, Cole or Jayden call their mothers the old Irish Ma or Mam, but little Setanta, Lir, Luan and Caolfhionn all call their mothers the suburban American Mom. She's Sliotar Mom, not Sliotar Ma.

It's suburban Ireland and one of the most significant cultural forces in the country, the GAA, uses Saturday like the Catholic Church once used Sunday. It's a day of devotion. For Sliotar Mom, weekends are exhausting.

She remembers her own Saturday mornings as a kid, glued to *Anything Goes* while her parents slept off the working week and a few Friday night drinks. Saturday was about guilt-free lounging around, a time to relax, chill out and wind down after the stresses and strains of the week.

Not today.

The weekend in 2019 is a time for achievement, for fulfilling promise and for creating the perfect environment for little Lorcan, Tadhg and Aoibhinn to accomplish their dreams.

In the world of organised playdates, Sliotar Mom has banned screen time of any kind on Saturday mornings and afternoons. Saturdays are all about activity. It's a day for self-improvement. It's the new Mass, with equivalent helpings of guilt for those who do not attend.

Her iPhone 7 alarm goes off at 7.15 a.m. That's a lie-in compared to her weekday 5.45 a.m. wake-up call. She was hoping to sleep in until 7.30 but the husband of 10 years is having a pre-midlife crisis after one of the mates remarked on his 'Dad Bod'. He's out doing his best Forrest Gump already, pounding the concrete up and down the beard-free zone, terrorised by his Fitbit. But of course, being an Irish male, the disorganised fool woke her trying to find his Under Armour leggings. 'It's all about the power of habit' is Dad Bod's rosary.

Only his own wife would dare to call him disorganised. In his mind, he could coordinate the raid on Entebbe singlehandedly. After all, Dad Bod is a global supply chain manager at a large multinational. His business card tells the world that he organises Europe, the Middle East and Africa! His diary is perfectly assembled, all meetings are spaced meticulously and every minute of the day is used to its absolute maximum. In recent months, he has become focused on blasting the Dad Bod. But in your forties, it's harder than you think.

Focus is his word of the year. With focus, he can achieve anything. He is working towards a triathlon in the summer and suggested they should all have a go at Hell and Back Family in a few months, claiming it would be an amazing mental and physical endurance challenge and a bonding exercise. In case you have forgotten, this is an Irish family we are talking about, not the marketing department of an American start-up. But there's no talking to evangelicals, particularly fitness evangelicals. The more weight they lose, the more muscle they restore, the more devout they become.

Dad Bod had an epiphany at the last Pendulum Summit. It was the corporate equivalent of taking ayahuasca at Burning Man. As he sat there in the Convention Centre in golf slacks, his all-cotton pink button-down Oxford shirt a little too tight around the midriff, he saw the light. Immersed in the self-help lexicon of Tony Robbins, surrounded by his fellow corporate warriors, who'd also paid €1,200 for the pleasure of 'reaching higher' and 'unleashing their inner champions', he understood the message. Tony was looking into his soul and emoting him to be the best he can be, reassuring him that no endurance challenge is too demanding. Ordinary Iron Man is for pussies when you can do Iron Man barefoot in the North Pole. Since the Pendulum Summit, Dad Bod has been a man possessed.

Sliotar Mom is not too sure about it all. She has seen the pictures on Instagram and Facebook of her friends scaling 10-foot walls and wading through ice baths and has to admit it looks pretty cool. But maybe a hike up the Sugarloaf would be enough for now.

The major upside of doing Hell and Back Family is that it constitutes an accomplishment and out in the suburbs accomplishments matter. The Radical Centre is a meritocracy. Every move carries a score and life is one big exam. Saturday is an activity-laden points race, the year governed by continuous assessment. In this process, Sliotar Moms police themselves, constantly watched by other hyper-competitive Sliotar Moms. No slip-ups are tolerated.

Sliotar Mom already knows how many points each child needs to get into Law with French in UCD, even though the eldest is only nine. Inside her head is a big CAO form, with points going up and down, 500 for this, 570 for that. With the mental CAO form constantly whirring around in her head, Sliotar Mom has been measuring and comparing since the day Lorcan, Tadhg and Aoibhinn came out and she began monitoring for baby development 'leaps' on her Wonder Weeks app.

Sliotar Mom likes a leap. After all, how are you to get on?

And the Leaving Cert is closer than you think.

She's driving the boys, Lorcan and Tadhg, to GAA training this morning. Nespresso to go. Little Aoibhinn has ballet and then she has a birthday party to get to.

As it's May and communions are upon us, Sliotar Mom is starving. May is the new January, a month for getting in shape. For Sliotar Mom Aideen ('Aido' to her friends), two weeks of tofu is losing its appeal. But, with the help of Pinterest and Roz Purcell, she's stayed committed. Still she's pretty sure she will be flexitarian by June, especially now that so many Proseccos are vegan-friendly.

Lorcan, Tadhg and Aoibhinn aren't persuaded by veganism, which is kind of reassuring. They've told her, with a degree of honesty that can only be mustered by those under the age of 10, that everything she's cooked since she began Veganuary looks like sick.

Dad Bod takes Aoibhinn to ballet. Once he's brought her into the studio and popped on her shoes, like most of the other dads he'll grab a coffee and hang around until she's finished. He doesn't know a lot about ballet, but he's pretty sure from looking through the glass in the door that little Aoibhinn is in the top 5% in the class. After all, she can pull off an impressive looking arabesque.

She's almost as good as those drilled Lithuanian children, who raise the ballet bar for the locals. A haughty Lithuanian mother looks in too, Slavic eyebrows arched. In the giant points race, the Slavs have their ambitious eyes on the next generation's prize. Secretly, Dad Bod admires her self-sacrifice almost as much as her impressively toned arms. She knows she's being watched. She knows what he's thinking. But, being a typical Irish bloke, he has no idea that she knows what he knows.

He will join Aido and the lads for their GAA training later in the morning. Sliotar Mom wonders about his sanity when he blows a gasket on the side-line, but puts it down to stress at work following the corporate restructuring. He counters that a bit of bottle will do the kids no harm, give them some backbone and drive them on to make senior when the time comes. She thinks he's going a bit bonkers; he worries she's going soft. In the great parenting points race, soft is unforgivable. As Dad Bod learnt at the Summit, talent is one thing, but character is another. No child of his will fall at the last from lack of preparation or drive.

The sun is out and the Cuala Buachaillí are there in huge numbers. But things don't start well. While her mind was on protein balls, Pilates and animal welfare initiatives, Sliotar Mom forgot that Lorcan's group are leading the club sustainability initiative against single-use water bottles. She's made a cardinal error by giving him a plastic bottle. The other Sliotar Moms are not impressed and, in truth, amongst this driven tribe, there is no greater source of joy than to see another Sliotar Mom stumble. Everyone else has reusable ones; the gung-ho ones have bottles labelled in the club colours. Cursing them under her breath, she immediately finds out where they bought them. She's not going to let the side down next week. No more schoolboy errors.

Saturday afternoons are for parties. They all happen in some place called Something Zone – Jump Zone, Fit Zone, Party Zone. It's Aoibhinn's birthday in a couple of months so Sliotar Mom is highly attentive. This is an opportunity to get ahead of the pack. She'd love to find somewhere new for Aoibhinn so she can be the first in the class to have her party in 'New Zone'. Giddy Studios worked well last time and it was nice that the kids were working with pottery. Who knows, if the boys don't end up running a large corporation, they could be the next Stephen Pearce. But this year Aoibhinn wants something different, with unicorns.

It's all unicorns and glitter with her at the moment. She's becoming quite the girly girl – as Sliotar Mom's friends, who *didn't* adhere to the gender-free toys for toddlers rule, delight in reminding her. Sliotar Mom makes a mental note to buy *Goodnight Stories for Rebel Girls* as part of the obligatory birthday book pile. Aoibhinn has Sheryl Sandberg written all over her – at least that's what her mother sees when she comes home from school with stars on her copybook.

While Dad Bod is spending some quality time giving extra coaching to Tadhg, Lorcan is also off to a party, this one in the senior school gym hall. It's his little pal Setanta's birthday. They've hired the hall and are having a Dave's Jungle Party. Lorcan is mad excited; he'll be playing with real snakes, spiders, scorpions and iguanas. Sliotar Mom is worried that Setanta's family might be pulling away from the pack. As Gaeilgeoirs, they already have extra points, and it's hard to beat iguanas. They're fun and educational.

For Aoibhinn's party, Sliotar Mom is already ordering the contents of the party bags. It's getting harder each year to uncover uniqueness. She's recently discovered AliExpress, China's answer to all her Pinterestable party prayers, but there's a six-week delivery time, so she's stocking up. She's ordered the unicorn party bags, animal snap bracelets, mini Beanie Boo keyrings, scented pencils and LED bangles. She needs just one or two more things to make the bags memorable. A party bag to rival those at the Oscars.

Once she has the kids fed and her weekly food prep Tupperwared and frozen, Aideen gets ready to go out. Tonight they are off to dinner with Kathleen and JP, who they met through Dubai GAA. It's Asian so she's not too sure about the vegan options, but it's Saturday night so she'll allow herself a little leeway. And anyway, herself and Kathleen have a weakness for 'Lady Petrol', as Dad Bod likes to call rosé.

Alannah, the babysitter, arrives at eight. Her rate is €12 an hour; Aideen bargained her down from the €15 she was looking for. Easy money for watching Netflix and Snapchatting for a few hours. Still, she only lives across the road, so there's no extortionate taxi fare home.

Sunday mornings start promptly at eight. Swimming lessons are at nine and this is the last week of term, so the kids need to be on their game. Today at the end of class their instructors will decide if they progress to the next level or not. Dad Bod, always one for a conspiracy, smells a scam. They keep them on lower levels for longer to get more cash out of the parents.

Because the kids are in different groups, the lessons, combined with showers and dressing in the oppressive heat of the tiny and clamorous changing rooms, take three hours. Bod and Sliotar are hoping this won't aggravate the hangovers neither of them is admitting to having from their night out. Let's just say the Lady Petrol kicked in early.

None of them mentioned the referendum. They don't talk about those things in public as they're from places where abortion is a conversation-stopper. Their hometowns all voted against abortion in 1983, but now that they live in Dublin, it's different. Both were amazed at the strength of the 'Yes' vote in Munster. Even Dad Bod's mother, a national school teacher – regarded as one of de Valera's devoted foot-soldiers – voted 'Yes'. She's changed, mellowed as she has become older. The Ireland she came from is gone. Sliotar Mom and Dad Bod spent close to a decade in the Gulf, from where Ireland seemed like a liberal haven. And in truth, that's what it has become. They've taken a pay cut and a massive tax hike, but they are home, ready to do their part, driving the Radical Centre forward.

She's got a 4.45 a.m. airport start tomorrow. For the Renaissance Nation, the points race never sleeps.

CHAPTER 14

STOVELAND

KILN-DRIED KEVIN

L eaving Sliotar Mom and Dad Bod, the sprawling GAA pitches, the Saturday afternoon Jump Zone parties, corporate mantras and Iron Man training schedules, not to mention a few too many bottles of Lady Petrol, let's jump in a truck for the next part of our walkabout and cruise out towards the more salubrious areas, home to Kiln-Dried Kevin's most valued customers.

Kiln-Dried Kevin has never been busier. He can't keep up with business. So much so that he's delivering on Sundays. He's got three trucks on the road and one more on the way. Despite the hottest summer on record, there've never been more orders placed, as if Irish exceptionalism will extend to a new geological concept called global freezing. His production processing unit, just past Trim, is working non-stop, but his customers are in the swankiest parts of Leinster, Galway and a few as far south as Cork's Victorian suburbs. Ireland is in the middle of an epidemic. Up and down the country, perfectly decent fireplaces are being yanked out and replaced with wood-burning stoves.

You don't need me to tell you that we have a new housing crisis. Prices are going up five times faster than wages, rents are higher than they have ever been, but the leading indicator of where the market is going might not be interest rates or planning permissions, but the sale of wood-burning stoves.

We know that property porn in its filthiest incarnation is back with a vengeance. Open up the pages of any newspaper and you will read the same lustful vocabulary, stimulating our animalistic desires. If you thought that humans learnt from bitter experience, our recurring property obsession would not give you much confidence in the species.

This year's fetish in property porn is stoves. You may have thought that the fixation with photos of wood-burning stoves in estate agents' brochures was coincidental. It's not; it's real. Sellers suggest that a good wood-burning stove can add a decent €20,000 to the price and, more crucially, will accelerate the sale by a matter of weeks, if not months. If you are in the flipping business, buying a rundown terraced house, and doing it up to flog on, then a stove is a must. Like decks 10 years ago, nothing betokens upward social mobility like a stove.

And the ground zero for stove porn is Stoveland. Stoveland is the Upper Redbrick Zone squared – an old established suburb, preferably built around the time of the Land League. These places are hives of reinvention; scaffolding and skips litter Stoveland. Here the Renaissance Nation is at ease. These places voted overwhelmingly for repeal and are in the middle of rampant one-upmanship when it comes to stoves. While it is Trumpian to lavish money on anything mechanical, electrical or fast, it is a sign of true sophistication to fork out on something as environmentally friendly, family-friendly and frankly Danish as a wood-burning stove. If you can combine a wood-burning stove with a gravel drive or, better still, steps up to the door, you are ascending into Stoveland status heaven.

To be a proper member of the Stoveland aristocracy, the house should never, ever have a name, particularly one acquired in the past three generations or less. Nor should the lawn be too clipped, a sure sign of status anxiety. Excessive symmetry is out too; a matching pair of anything is a dead giveaway in Stoveland. That extends to matching bay trees at either side of the entrance. Studied nonchalance is the effect of choice in Stoveland.

Homeliness is central to the self-identity of Stoveland. The image of the warm fire, keeping the family toasty when the Beast from the East strikes, bespeaks comfort, security, radiating heat in your own familial cocoon, protecting you from the dangers outside. A thousand years after the Vikings came raping and pillaging, the Scandinavians are back, but this time as a lifestyle choice. Irish people are finding their inner Sven and Ulrika. Stovelanders have gone all Jutland with candles, cosy blankets, oversized scarves and throws over the couches. The tabernacle of this warm, friendly cavern is the wood-fired stove.

For a few years, Kiln-Dried Kevin's delivery run was a map of upmarket Ireland – Victorian redbrick Donnybrook in Dublin, the Edwardian solidity of Taylor's Hill in Galway, or the grand homes of Montenotte in Cork. But now, as befits the great blurring of the Renaissance Nation, the Radical Centre is spreading and so too are the stoves.

The best way to pick up trends are in the once-again-burgeoning property sections of our newspapers. Wood-burning stoves featured in a total of 25 articles in the *Irish Times* property section in the first five months of 2018 – eight in May alone – and in nearly 300 articles over the past decade. And, in a true sign that the craze has jumped over into popular culture, wood-burning stoves even featured in the construction exam paper in the 2018 Leaving Cert. The Radical Centre has embraced the stove.

In recent years, the *Irish Independent*, *Irish Times* and *Irish Examiner* have each published guides, tips and odes to the efficiency of stoves. Aside from wanting to be as tall, tanned and well-read as Ulrika and Sven, Stovelanders cite economic sense, because those parsimonious Scandinavians figured out that stoves can wring the BTUs out of a variety of fuels, instead of gifting the heavens up to 80% of our hard-earned heat. And, naturally, from the green perspective, wood-burning stoves are carbon-neutral, have very low emissions and the wood ash is good for planting and gardening. What's not to like?

But, in truth, Stovelanders regard themselves as that bit classier than the rest, and hygge is a regular feature of their home lives.

Like the Scandinavians they revere, Stovelanders are a tolerant bunch, have no problem cooking scrambled eggs for stay-over teenage boyfriends and they love Leo, or at least they love what they think he is when he is running with Justin at Farmleigh. They also feel secure in this fiscal-probity/social-promiscuity combo. They are open-minded and easy-going, and dislike Jordan Peterson intensely.

When left alone, Stovelanders immerse themselves in cultivated spending and the prodigious brainpower that propelled them to the pinnacle of the education system can now be applied to researching the tiniest details of their stoves. They love heritage and tradition, so will investigate their Norwegian stove intimately, swotting up on the long history of craftsmanship that the Norwegians can draw on, as they've been coping with the cold for centuries. Their bookshelves are ceiling-to-floor bragging walls underscoring their gargantuan educational achievements, and the vinyl collection – the more obscure the better – pushes the sense of accomplishment.

Stovelanders also display what David Brooks called professional shopping, where it is quite alright to spend enormous sums on professional quality kit when it has nothing to do with your profession. In the Renaissance Nation, nowhere is this more evident than in cycling, the new sport of choice for Stovelanders. Why buy an ordinary bike to head out to Marlay Park for a spin when you can splash out on a retro-carbon replica of the machine that Eddy Merckx rode when he conquered L'Alpe d'Huez to win the 1975 Tour de France, or the same kit that Stephen Roche wore when he won the famed Triple Crown in 1987?

So let's leave Stoveland and head out on Stoveland's favoured mode of transport to see how the rest of the Renaissance Nation is getting on.

CHAPTER 15

WHERE MAMILS ROAM

L eaving Stoveland, we head out past the 1960s estates, built for the guards and nurses of this world and now only available to millionaires, professionals, tech workers and, of course, the hurling aristocracy of south Dublin. Heading out of the old suburbs, we pass the huge empty churches, built in the 1970s for an observant, Mass-going population that no longer come.

As it's the weekend in Ireland, let's take the form of transport much loved of the Renaissance Nation: the carbon ultra-light bike.

Kingfisher's Kitchen, just opposite the town clock in Enniskerry on a Sunday morning any time after eight, is a perfect spot for Mamil-watching. That's Middle-Aged Man In Lycra. Here they are so self-assured, you don't even have to sneak up on them. Secure amongst their own species, the otherwise socially anxious Mamils congregate with carefree abandon.

They luxuriate in the bright sunshine, resplendent in multi-hued mating plumes of bright pinks, greens and blues. Amongst some primates, the more radiantly red the bums, the higher up the social hierarchy. Similarly, the more incandescent the Mamil's clobber, the more splendid the specimen. There's even the occasional risqué, lurid tangerine, lime or even lilac, although it takes a proper Bull Mamil, out to make a name for himself, to carry off such a display.

The Bull Mamil, rarely threatened, is assured of his place in the pecking order. Hierarchy is signalled by the marque of the bike, where expense is a significant indicator of status, but not the only one by a long way. The arriviste Mamil might make that schoolboy error, but the true aficionado knows retro beats contemporary, and it only requires a touch. Small things matter enormously. It could be just a little hint of depth like an Italian Molteni cap, but it says enough. You are in the inner sanctum.

Up here, the rarely seen female of the species, the Swallow (Skinny Woman All Luminous Lycra On Wheels), struts her stuff flamboyantly. The Swallow is an increasingly common, but not yet everyday sight. She is still a little nervous on the hard shoulder. Unlike some of the more solitary Mamils, she rarely travels alone and it's not uncommon now to witness a group of trim Swallows picking at avocado toast, poached egg and rocket salad on the terrace of Kingfisher's.

Once refreshed, the packs of Mamils and Swallows get back on their carbon-framed Ridleys, Specializeds and Canyons, bikes that would set you back more than a new kitchen, and head up the steep Wicklow hills. Cycling is the fastest-growing sport in Ireland and this Sunday's weekend warriors are just one example of the activity of choice for a rapidly growing segment of the Renaissance Nation.

According to the Irish Sports Monitor 2017, cycling is now the fourth most popular sport in the country, with 5.1% of the adult population participating regularly.[80] This puts it behind personal exercise (12.4%), swimming (8.5%) and running (6.2%), but ahead of soccer, GAA and the rest.

The growth in the past five years has been extraordinary. Cycling Ireland had 29,333 members in 2017.[81] This is almost a doubling from 15,331 members in 2012, and up from a measly 2,000 in 1980. There are new cycling clubs opening all the time, all around the country. Today, there are 483 clubs operating and, in 2017 alone, 538 newly trained coaches arrived on this burgeoning scene.[82] In total, 948 events took place in 2017; 490 of these were leisure events and 458 involved competitive racing.[83] All over the south and west coasts, cycling 'sportifs' are extremely popular and, over the summer, you will see thousands of Mamils and Swallows grimacing up some of the most beautiful passes and mountains, hurtling down some of the most scenic routes in the country, and much of this done for charity.

Rarely can a government initiative have had such spectacular results as the Cycle to Work Scheme. The health aspect of the surge in cycling should not be overlooked. Cycling is hard, it gets people fit and, even if the caricature of the Mamil is as much defined by his paunch as his mettle, imagine the size of that paunch without the wheels? The Cycle to Work Scheme nudged along a sport that was already growing rapidly, not just here but all over the world.

One of the most fascinating economic aspects about the popularity of cycling is how the sport has jumped a social class or three. This is all part of the social blurring of the Renaissance Nation.

Tom Daly's wonderful book *The Rás* – a definitive history of Irish cycling – reinforces this idea that cycling was once the sport of working men and the sons of small farmers. The cycling royalty of Ireland, the aristocracy on two wheels, were families from corporation estates. The Kimmages were from Crumlin, the McQuaids from Finglas, Stephen Roche from Rosemount in Dundrum. Sean Kelly left school early to work on his father's farm, becoming an apprentice bricklayer before taking to the road professionally. When Stephen Roche became only the second rider ever to win the Triple Crown of Tour de France, Giro and World Championship in one year, cycling was very much a minority sport largely involving blue-collar men.

However, by the time Tipperary's Sam Bennett won three stages at the Giro d'Italia in 2018, cycling in Ireland had become the professional class at play, at least in its weekend incarnation. I suspect there is a large crossover between the hurling peers of south Dublin GAA and the resplendent Mamils of the Wicklow Way.

Cycling is not for the faint-hearted; it is difficult and demands commitment. Only a person with a certain inner drive gets up on a saddle. That's why it's popular. Remember, the new Ireland is all about pushing yourself on to greater feats, extending yourself to the limit, competing all the way. This is part of the make-up of the successful professional in this hyper-globalised world. It may also be because it is expensive to get kitted out. Only the reasonably comfortable middle-aged, with children almost reared, have the time and money to commit to a top-of-the-range rothar. Or maybe the camaraderie of a congress of Mamils and Swallows, head-to-toe in flamboyant, tight-to-the-point-of-autoerotic clobber, is simply too irresistible.

And cycling doesn't destroy the knees the way five-a-side football does. Dad Bod's five-a-side team is threatening to atrophy as it hits the mid-forties. Joining the rainbow peloton, which the N11 becomes on a weekend morning, seemed like the obvious progression. The last bike he was on was a second-hand Chopper. However, a few months in and it's as if he's joined the Moonies.

They're everywhere, not just in Wicklow, but on Howth Hill, the Naul, Blessington Lakes, Connemara, all over west Cork and beyond. The great outdoors is swarming with Mamils and Swallows by 10 o'clock on a Sunday morning. The hard shoulder has become a rich savannah. Although there are lone rangers, Mamils tend to travel in packs. The Bull Mamil is difficult to spot initially in the sea of colour. But the road is unforgiving and in time he will emerge. Sometimes the pack is stretched as naive riders, usually a pair of bucks, head out, injecting speed and extending the peloton. The car is the enemy for good reason: it's the predator.

THE VELOMINATI

Cycling is the new golf, beloved of the professional class. Years ago, when Ireland almost merged into one large golf course, cyclists were few and far between. These days, as golf clubs shut up shop or desperately drop their membership fees, cycling is booming.

The Mamil driving the cycling revolution is a middle-aged family man with a decent enough income. Flash cars are so Celtic Tiger. Today's mid-life crisis is all about getting fit on the bike.

And it's not just any old class of ride; once you join the Mamil tribe, the gear, not just the bike, is crucial. The innocent starter Mamil gets hooked and in no time he graduates to the holy of holies and enters the world of the Velominati.

But it's not just men's fitness that is at stake. The Mamil is the latest holy grail of marketeers and advertisers all over the world.

Strange as it may seem in a world that appears to be dominated by Sky Sports, transfer windows and soccer, cycling is now the biggest sporting goods market in the world in terms of revenue, according to a survey by multinational market research company NPD Group.[84]

Global sales totalled nearly €36 billion in 2014 (about the same as the losses at Anglo). It is, like the Irish economy, growing rapidly. Some 133 million bicycles (including electric bikes) were sold in 2014, with the average price estimated at €191.[85]

Last year, globally, cycling accounted for a massive 15% of all sporting goods revenue.

As more people start cycling than start any other sport, the market for bike sales in Ireland and the UK is predicted to grow by more than 20% to €1 billion. The cycling market, including accessories, footwear and clothing, is valued at €2.2 billion in Ireland and the UK, twice as much as the €1 billion soccer market.

But what is important for marketeers and advertisers is that the Mamil is a largely middle-class creature. The Bull Mamil is a fully paid-up member of the Radical Centre. To marketing departments, the bright, taut 50-year-old in a yellow replica leader's jersey is the lucrative upmarket version of the bloke in an XXL Man Utd jersey, glued to his widescreen.

Research carried out by Mintel reveals that cyclists who use their bikes at least once a week are more likely to shop at posh supermarkets and have a household income in excess of €65,000 a year.

Halfords Group, which is the biggest Irish and UK bike retailer, posted sales growth at its cycling division of 15% in the second quarter of 2012, faster than any other unit. The lucrative road bike market is the smallest part of its overall bike sales. Halfords has 24 shops in Ireland, from Cork to Letterkenny. But Halfords is the Aldi of bike sellers; the real place to spot a Mamil is in one of the many specialist bike shops that have sprung up to meet demand.

While the Cycle to Work Scheme rekindled cycling interest in the Chopper generation, the commuting cyclist has morphed into the serious weekend sports enthusiast and he has provided a bigger opportunity for retailers. While a commuter may spend up to €1,000 on a bike, helmet and high-visibility jacket, a weekend road-biking Mamil will lay out significantly more.

For the starter Mamil, there isn't much change from €1,500 on the bike. You can expect to fork out €300-odd on clothing, more than €100 on shoes, and another €100 on the helmet, as well as an endless array of accessories. But the Bull Mamil will spend multiples of that.

The neophyte Mamil will quickly discover the rigours of bike etiquette. Rule number one: any bike displayed on top of a car should be worth more than the car itself. Rule number two: kit confusion is not entertained when you decide to worship at the chapel of Mamildom. Shorts have to be black and never baggy or voluminous. Sloppiness may affect the aerodynamic look of the rest of the pack. Shorts and socks have to meet the Goldilocks rule – they must be neither too short, like 1980s tennis players, nor too long, like those beloved of Spanish footballers. Rule number three: all saddles, bars and tyres must match. Rule number four is that the weight ratio of Mamil to bike should be at least 100 to one, 100 kilos of chunky Mamil to one kilo of carbon.

This list is only for starters. Like any sect, strict adherence to the rulebook will reinforce your position as a Mamil of good standing. Things that make no difference at all to the outsider are of enormous significance to the insider. For example, when a helmet is not worn, it should never be carried around, but draped symmetrically around your bars. The Mamil practises perfection in small things; the smaller, the more exacting. When it comes to gear and kit, understanding the smallest piece of machinery on the bike is a key marker of the Bull Mamil. Bike porn is an essential part of the Velominati and the home-made model, customised by you to satisfy your own tastes, is where most Mamils want to worship.

But this takes time and enormous application, vision and above all dedication to the Velominati. The cycling widows out there understand that, when the Mamil gets hooked, he is unlikely to be seen at home over the weekend ever again. Which is why so many Swallows get up on the bikes themselves. This is an infectious syndrome.

For the Bull Mamil, the more homoerotic the look the better. The hardened, fully kitted out Bull Mamil, trussed up in tight rubber cap, goggles, clasps, rubber tubes rammed into pockets, skins and arm warmers, wouldn't be out of place in a Berlin dungeon bathhouse. Sure, wasn't your man in *Fifty Shades of Grey* a Mamil?

Dad Bod looks in the mirror, lathers the smooth cream over his legs, opens the razor, a shining, fresh Mach 3. Moving against the grain, he elegantly begins to shave. With each effortless, sensuous glide of the blade, he is closer to the tabernacle of the Mamils. Each swish of the wrist positions him deeper into the sect. The smoother the legs, the classier the Mamil.

He has ascended to suburban heaven. He is a Bull Mamil, a true disciple of the Velominati.

CHAPTER 16

APPLEGREEN LAND

By tracking the Mamils and Swallows, the multi-coloured hard shoulder peloton guides us deeper into the most vibrant zones of the Renaissance Nation. We move out to the commuter ring, where house prices fall as the commuting distance rises. We find ourselves far away from the Lower and Upper Redbrick Zones and Stoveland, miles beyond the old suburbs with their revitalised GAA clubs, their Sliotar Moms and mini-All-Irelands.

We are in search of the displaced Dubs, priced out of their own territory by the hurling aristocracy and the Stovelanders in the older suburbs, and by Flat White Man and Ballet Blonde in the Lower Redbrick Zone. Stay with us as we track the Mamils and Swallows on their Sunday morning trajectory.

This zone is a place of over-crowded primary schools, new estates and long, long commutes. This is Ireland's fertile crescent. In 2005 the youngest town in the country was Naas. Today, as the country has spread out farther and farther, the youngest town now is Portlaoise, while the fastest-growing suburb in Ireland is Drogheda.

We traverse the country, past Delgany, uphill towards Brittas and then on to Arklow, in towards the sunny southeast, moving farther out from the cities into deep countryside, where the old settlement pattern of the boom reasserts itself with large estates circled around formerly provincial towns.

We see the same type of development in Louth, Kildare, Meath, south Cork and east and west Galway. This is commuter land. Every day 32,208 people leave Kildare to commute to Dublin; 27,795 head out from Meath; and 23,160 flood into the capital from their homes in Wexford and Wicklow.[86] If you drive into Dublin from Newbridge, Navan or Gorey at six in the evening, the miles and miles of oncoming traffic looks as if a panicked city is being evacuated following some tsunami or nuclear strike.

But isn't this Deckland, the place that became infested with decks during the boom? Yes, it was. Critically, the decks, like the credit at the time, masked a secret. They were hiding something. In the same way as the credit proved transient, so too did the decks. The death of Deckland is a sorry tale.

Let's remember that, during the boom, so many houses were built in the wrong place. These were the ghost estates – that odd, slightly creepy description that came to me on a lazy afternoon's drive back from Mayo to Dublin in 2006. I'd no idea the term would catch on like it did. These rows of empty shells outside country towns remained empty and, ultimately, were vandalised. But ghost estates were only the extreme version of what was a more general problem.

As the boom became more frenetic and the borrowings became more short term, the pace of building had to rise so the developers would not be caught with unsold houses when the music stopped. As the pace became more hectic, the quality of the land that builders were prepared to risk building on became less suitable for houses. Homes were built on floodplains in soggy hollows, which farmers were only too willing to sell and the councils were only too happy to rezone so they could trouser as much revenue as possible in the form of builders' fees. In Ireland, one of the wettest countries in Europe, one consequence of all this building on sodden land was certain: over time, these places would flood, or at least not drain properly.

(As an aside, have you ever wondered why so many American trailer parks seem to get hit by twisters? They are built in the wrong place, places where nature hammers down a 'Danger: Keep Out' sign, because they are on a destructive twister path. While not of the same devastating scale, building on land that doesn't drain in a wet country like Ireland is asking for trouble.)

So these back gardens were prone to flooding. But one other thing was happening: it's called burying the evidence. When a new estate is built, there is an enormous amount of concrete, bricks, steel, bits of plastic, sewers and stuff that must be covered, and covered quickly. It would be expensive for a builder to lay a new garden with deep, decent-quality soil. He would also have to pay to get rid of this general detritus. So why not simply bury the stuff? Who's to know? So Breakfast Roll Man, the under-pressure builder, would lay a thin veneer of topsoil over this rubbish at the back of the house. It looks good cosmetically, but, like an iceberg, it hides something much bigger under the depths.

The cheapest way to cover this waste and the sparse topsoil is to install a cheap deck on top of it. With a quick trip to the builders' suppliers, the back garden looks great, allowing the punters to sit outside at night on those balmy evenings for which Leinster is world famous. A bottle of Tesco Finest wine and a few veggie burgers and we are set.

In 2018 Coillte introduced their most durable decking product, made from a highly treated, super-strength hardwood, with a maximum 25-year warranty. After that time, even this super-specific garden decking wood putrefies.

Now consider the second-rate, soft, untreated wood used in Deckland during the boom. Let's think about what nature does to such cheap wood over the years.

Ten years on, this wood is about as durable as wet wallpaper. The decks are rotten and large bits are breaking off and splintering the children on communion days, if they haven't already been concussed by falling off the trampoline, even before the fairy cakes and the selfies with Granny.

Now lads are out the door pulling down decking all over Deckland. The fad has passed. Decking is going the way of crazy paving in the 1980s, never to be seen again.

Most punters out in Deckland were on the trading-up buzz, but that buzz was wrecked by head-melting negative equity. The homes they were hoping to trade up to, closer to Dublin, Cork or Galway, have recently become extortionately expensive. So the former Decklanders are stuck.

And what do Irish people do when they are stuck? They self-improve! That self-improvement starts by pushing the kitchen out into some mini-cathedral structure with vaulted ceilings, leading to the black Indian limestone patio, complete with its high-end Broil Imperial XL barbeque. You never know who will drop by, who you might need to impress.

Not everyone goes for the top-of-the-range barbecue, but one constant amid the decaying decking, extended kitchens and domestic makeovers is the trampoline. Welcome to Trampoline Drive, Trampoline Grove, Trampoline Crescent, Trampoline Downs, Trampoline Heights or, more aptly given the sodden decking, Trampoline Hollow.

There's nothing like a trampoline to scream dynamism, hope and the sleepless nights of demented, Calpol-brandishing parents. Where a back garden in Stoveland is an altar to the Bloom Festival, a verdant ecozone of dahlias, purple millet, foxgloves and hollyhocks, the typical garden here is a smaller area covered by these super-sized Vegas-style launching pads that cover 86% of the available square footage.

This commuter belt stretches in a vast arc from Drogheda as far as Portlaoise, sweeping south to Carlow and east to meet the sea in Gorey. It's a commuting world of 24-hour petrol stations and these industrial-sized trampolines. I'm not sure I remember when we began to think that we were a nation of child gymnasts, but if you want to see the vibrancy of the country, get a drone to fly over these areas. The places with the highest ratio of trampolines to Skoda Octavias is where the babies are. These are the new suburbs, places full of children and knackered, sleep-deprived, 20-hour-a-week commuter parents. It's a vast area of Giraffe crèches, Costa coffee and donuts at the weekend.

We are in the stomping ground of Applegreen Man, the breakfast-on-the-go, muffin-chomping, commuting hero. In fact, he doesn't limit his pre-dawn carb consumption to muffins. You will see him in the Applegreens up and down the country, faced with the Applegreen Conundrum: should he go for the obvious Burger King option and tell no one, or the middle-of-the-road 'Bakewell', the more traditional selection which bullies him with the 'Eat Smart, Think Smart' logo? Or, ultimately, should he go for the 'Freshii' alternative that apparently 'energises the healthy', according to its strapline?

All this choice and the day's hardly started.

THE WEXICAN WALL

This Sunday morning is bright and sunny, as it always is in Gorey. You are in Wexico, migratory home of displaced Dubs forced out by high house prices. Given the enormous invasion of Wexicans who stream, unrestricted, over the Wexican frontier towards Dublin every day for work, it's surprising there haven't been more calls to build a wall.

The true Wexican is a Dub stranded in Wexico. In the same way as Mexico is a huge source of labour for California and Texas, Wexico provides the worker bees that keep the Dublin economy going and growing. It is thought that the Dublin economy couldn't function without Wexicans. Despite cultural differences, even after one generation the cultural chasm is significant.

Indeed, in the same way as Mexico is the number one holiday destination for Americans afraid to venture farther abroad, Wexico is the destination of choice for unadventurous Dubs. This is particularly the case for coastal resorts close to the border in northern Wexico, like Courtown and Kilmuckridge. Southern Wexico, whose capital is Kelly's in Rosslare, is for a different tribe of Dubliner.

Americans tend to travel over the border to get bargains and sample indigenous produce that has not yet made it to Macy's on Fifth Avenue. Dubliners also cross the border to Wexico to avail of Wexican fashion. If you doubt this, visit Gorey's boutique quarter. Here you have Liz Collins Boutique, Skyfall, Shoe Style International, New Vibe, Fifth Avenue, Ruby Rouge, Losam and Contra Clothing – all high-end boutiques, more Wicklow Street than County Wexford. Up the street is upscale jeweller Ashanti Gold, trendy children's outfitters The Cosy Cot and Jahlandi Kids,

Lilly Bloom Interiors and the Gas Lamp Gallery. And when you want coffee or a quick bite, there's Partridges Bistro, selling coffee grinders, or the Gorey Book Café, a bookshop and café in one.

High-end shops, cafés with bookshops, interiors boutiques and expensive shoe shops used to be the preserve of cosmopolitan Grafton Street. Not anymore. It's a whole Brown Thomas quarter by the sea. Is it any surprise that Wexford voted 'Yes' by 68% to 32%, a complete reversal of the 1983 number?

There is no rural Ireland in the old sense of the phrase. What we have is a great moderation of views, coalescing around the live-and-let-live middle.

Applegreen Man swerves to avoid a congress of Mamils and Swallows. The Bull Mamil knows he is no match for the Skoda, not a hundred kilometres into alien territory. Still, he gives Applegreen Man a withering look, the message clear: *an overweight, flaccid species like you wouldn't last a day out on the safari with us hunter-gatherers.* Deep down, Applegreen Man is a bit envious of these wild creatures, whose stamina must surely come from some unnatural desire to survive in inhospitable terrain. In the suburban Darwinian battle for survival of the fittest, the vigorous Mamil has the upper hand over the ailing Wexican, and the Wexican knows it.

As the Mamils head back towards the city, they pass through the old suburbs where the new elite of Ireland live. Don't think just because we became wealthy and share many values in the one nation that the old hierarchies have disappeared.

However, one thing has changed profoundly and it is that the Radical Centre works at a pace and with an ambition unheard of in the short history of this state. We are a 24/7 society where time waits for no one. This is particularly the case for the new arrivals, those hundreds of thousands of people from all over the world who have come to the Renaissance Nation in search of something few of us would have ever expected a few years ago: the Irish Dream of self-transformation, self-improvement and opportunity. When Pope John Paul II came, who would have predicted this? But the growth freak that is the Irish economy is sucking in all sorts from all places.

Here's one of them to close our weekend walkabout.

IMRAN'S DILEMMA

Imran checks his Carlow Cricket Club WhatsApp group for news of last night's game. He is still buzzing from seeing Pakistan in Malahide. Ireland aren't bad, but Pakistan are cricket royalty and his family are Pathani, from the northwest frontier close to Afghanistan, and everyone knows the Pathani are cricket maestros. Imran Khan, the Cristiano Ronaldo of cricket, and now Prime Minister of Pakistan, is Pathani. This morning, the weather hasn't been too bad and picking up at this hour is always the same. It's the usual Monday in Ireland. The client ordered the cab on MyTaxi the night before. Imran knows in advance what state his passenger will be in from the time the cab was booked. It's 4.40 a.m. now and the sun is just coming up. The car was booked just after midnight, so this will either be the silent grumpy type or the still-pissed, chatty type.

Carlow Cricket Club was established in the 1880s but was disbanded for over one hundred years until the Rohingyans re-established it in 2012. Carlow received 13 Rohingyan families from a Rohingyan refugee camp in Bangladesh as part of a UN resettlement programme in 2009. The community has grown steadily since. The cricket club has gone from strength to strength, moving up two divisions. It is comprised of Pakistanis, Indians and Rohingyans. In the same way as Irish and English tend to gravitate towards each other on holidays (rather than, say, Irish and Germans) because we share language, culture and Man United, Muslim Pakistanis and Hindu Indians, despite tensions over there, get on famously over here. In truth, once people leave their own backyard they often leave their prejudices behind.

The captain of the club, Muhammad, is also from Carlow via Pakistan, but he's Punjabi. They met up driving taxis first and then later, at the Blanchardstown mosque, they bonded through the two supernatural powers, Allah and Pakistani spin-bowling. Imran has recently moved in, sleeping on the floor, with relations in Hollystown on the Dublin/Meath border. There are lots of Indians and Pakistanis living around there. He loves it in Ireland and has set himself a €10,000 target to send back home this year. He is going to build a house, close to his parents, but just for holidays. Pakistan is his past; Ireland is his future.

Listening to cricket matches on his headphones keeps him going as he drives through these depressing Irish nights. Sometimes he wonders how this pasty Celtic race survived up here in the darkness and the cold for thousands of years. The winters are interminable. The wind, more than the cold, gets to him. But it's a small price to pay for freedom and the dream of his own business importing clothes from Lahore.

His uncle wants him to marry a distant relation on his mother's side who lives in Manchester. There aren't enough suitable brides in Ireland, the family claims, and she is a doctor. In Pakistan, the social pecking order is everything. Nothing comes close to a doctor. It's a bit like Cork in that way.

Unfortunately for Imran, he has fallen for one of the Rohingyan girls. Hafsa, a sister of one of the players, breaks all the rules. The one insurmountable Pakistani prejudice that remains is a ban on marrying a Rohingyan. In the pecking order back home, the Rohingyans are lower than the Bengalis.

Arguably, more important than ethnicity is skin colour. Hafsa is not fair enough for his family. Skin colour matters in Pakistan – a prejudice that pre-dates the English colonisers by thousands of years. Discrimination remains to this day. Imran is sure that the 2014 Miss America, Nina Davuluri, of Indian descent, would not have been Miss India or Miss Pakistan as she would be considered too dark. Good enough for America, but not back home. This is what Imran loves about Ireland, the freedom.

He sighs as the passenger bundles herself in.

'Terminal 1, please.'

Sliotar Mom hardly takes in the driver. She's comatose.

Our Ireland is a 24-hour economy. After dark, it changes colour, accent, religion and manners. The local Irish retreat and are replaced by the immigrants. Each with their own story, their own dream, their own new life to lead, each one a new member of the Radical Centre.

PART 3
BANANA REPUBLIC

CHAPTER 17

THE PESSIMIST SOUNDTRACK

NOT PERFECT, BUT BETTER

The Radical Centre has delivered many positives for the country but there are several threats. Some are obvious and some are hidden in plain sight. In this section, let's look at those less obvious threats.

When things are going well you can be sure that lots of people will tell you the place is going to hell. It's fair to say that the better the country is doing, the closer to damnation we all are. Why so many find fault with general prosperity, higher incomes, more income equality, better health, better education and significant technological advancements is hard to understand. We've lived through crushing poverty, early death, poor health, mass ignorance and manual labour, none of which was too pleasant.

The Italian Marxist philosopher Antonio Gramsci – no friend of our heroes of the Radical Centre – coined the phrase 'pessimism of the intellect and optimism of the will'. By this he meant that we tend to be pessimistic in our mind, sceptical of big claims and notions, yet optimistic in our will, meaning enthusiastic in our everyday life and efforts. This seems like a sensible way to look at the world. However, there may be another way of interpreting this pessimist-versus-optimist, intellect-versus-will dichotomy. The other interpretation is that intellectuals tend to be pessimistic, while most other people tend to be the optimists who get up every morning and drive things forward. They tend to believe that tomorrow is going to be better than today, which is why they go on.

If we were to wait around for everything to be perfect before we do anything, nothing will get done. Progress is a process of trial and error, the result of tinkering around, seeing if it works, adjusting and then trying again. Progress comes from experimentation. It never starts at perfect and works backwards. It works the other way round, starting at good and getting to better, and then better still.

Could an obsession with the perfect be the reason why so many people – particularly commentators, bloggers, political activists and protestors – appear to be incensed by the progress of the past generation? Do they start at some idealised notion of perfect and work backwards, quick to point out what is not perfect according to their worldview, rather than seeing the headway we have made, which is pretty good?

The heroes of the Radical Centre might not be daring in the traditional sense, in the perfectionist sense. You won't get murals of their struggle painted on ghetto walls, urging the people to rise up against the power. This might be because gradually, little by little, more and more people have taken more and more control of their own lives. That is what progress does. Our progressive heroes don't have the chiselled revolutionary perfection of Che Guevara, but they are pretty good skins.

As we evolved away from communal positions towards personal responsibility, society blossomed, the economy surged and we became much more open to all that is 'other'. The population grew and prosperity flourished.

No, it's not perfect. Walk around Dublin or Cork city or indeed any town in Ireland any afternoon and you will see homeless people, individuals for whom life is a series of crises. For them, the huge upswing in general living standards is something of a phantom; the surge in the prosperity of those in the middle only reinforces their own sense of isolation and desolation.

There are, despite the enormous increases in education throughout society, too many children who still don't get a fair chance. Take a cursory glance at the few postcodes where the majority of Mountjoy prisoners come from; this reveals a great deal about social exclusion.

There are problems, but these are challenges to be overcome, not reasons to reject progress. The dramatic improvements in the quality of life in Ireland have been impressive. They are worth preserving and are worth celebrating. Few other countries have achieved what Ireland has achieved in terms of an increase in the general standard of living since Pope John Paul II's visit in 1979.

That said, one of the major economic failings in Ireland lies around the issue of housing, land ownership and wealth inequality. We'll look at these failings in Part 4. At this stage, take heart, because there are ways to tackle these serious problems.

LITTLE UTOPIAS

To a utopian sloganeer, 'heaven on earth' is a much better mantra than 'a little bit more of the same', which is why 'Make America Great Again' became such a rallying cry. It's utopian and claims the power to eradicate all imperfections in one fell swoop. The message was simple: vote for Donald Trump and everything will be wonderful.

The same applied to the Brexit catchphrase, 'Take Back Control', where the message was: one vote can deliver the perfect future. In the Brexiteers' utopia, the British people would take control of events from those horrible little Europeans.

I witnessed Marine Le Pen roar '*On est chez nous*' at a crowd in the Marseilles Velodrome. 'This is our place.' She was pushing all those buttons, implying that France is for French people and if it wasn't for those nasty foreigners, France would be Nirvana – mind you, they wouldn't win the World Cup.

These instances are examples of the same thing: let the perfect bully the pretty good.

The problem with the pretty good is that it doesn't sell books, or make headlines, or grab our attention. Pretty good, when it is happening, is boring, relentlessly dull – until it stops happening.

As a result, the non-confrontational Radical Centre, the easy-going political and economic rules-based system, which has delivered so much for so many, is under attack from incoming assaults on an hourly basis. The list of crimes supposedly committed by the most inoffensive, egalitarian political and economic system we've ever experienced reads like the charge sheet of a serial societal killer.

Of course, in Ireland there's another local spice that further poisons the discourse. Let us reacquaint ourselves with our old friend, Mr Begrudgery. The offence committed by the Radical Centre is the crime of success, an unforgiveable sin in the eyes of some. In Ireland, you are not so much a *victim of* your own success, but a legitimate target *because of* your success. Why be good when you can be mediocre?

Having the audacity to excel at something demands a response. You are just asking to be taken down a peg or seven. There's always the lad in the corner of the pub ready to sneer and remind everyone about the time when you hadn't the arse in your trousers. And what goes for the individual who is getting ahead goes for the country. Sure what else would we have to talk about?

THE DEGENERATION GAME

Despite all the evidence to the contrary, you will regularly hear on the radio and TV that society is falling apart, the place is going to the dogs. The pessimistic cacophony comes from all sides. Professional nostalgic chin-strokers contend that Ireland has lost its soul. We are being overrun by foreign corporations and foreign immigrants. Our identity is being undermined. International cosmopolitan influences are attacking our very Irish DNA. We might be rich but we are, in truth, poor. Our communities are fracturing. Rural Ireland is on the verge of extinction, threatened by creeping suburbs. Urban Ireland is too, threatened by creeping over-development, gentrification and vulture funds.

The lifeblood of the cult of pessimism is cynicism, nihilism, suspicion, distrust and a general sense that something is just not right. The currency of pessimism is that we are just one catastrophe away from total breakdown. The culprit is us, the modern individual driven by greed, narcissism and self-regard.

The attacks come in from the left and the right, from the old and the young, from the eco-warriors in the countryside and the hipster urbanites in the city. The central message is that we are in a chaotic tailspin towards disaster.

And it's all the fault of progress because progress is catapulting us away from the authentic Ireland. To its detractors, at the heart of the calamity are two of the building blocks of the Radical Centre: choice and individualism.

We, the individuals, are the problem. The optimist-versus-pessimist dichotomy raises its head again. Where the optimist sees effort, drive, ambition and individual self-expression, the pessimist sees vanity, desire, lust, cravenness and obsession with celebrity, which is corroding the soul of the nation and obscuring the true meaning of life.

Old-school religious people blame excessive individualism for rotting the bonds of obligation and service. They recommend a return to the old days of deference and order, as if turning the country into some sort of nostalgic battalion of a new moral army were the solution. But in their keenness to turn back the clock, they are joined by their secular allies in the environmental movement, who also blame individual consumerism for the ecological travesty that has befallen the earth. So you will see the recent fears about plastic in the ocean – very real fears – being used as a moral stick to flog modern lifestyles.

There is a strain of self-flagellation in these new moralists. We must get more out of less, or totally reshape our worldview, putting temperance and self-sacrifice at the centre of our daily lives. Moralists of all hues see a degenerate youth destroyed by crass, excessive hedonism, drug-binging and over-the-top spending. Dundrum Town Centre is Sodom and Gomorrah. Individual self-expression is the problem, so let's abandon it and go back to communal living.

The second culprit propelling us towards degeneration is choice. What could be so dangerous about having a choice, you might think? But pessimists see choice as a scourge. You can have too many restaurants promising the culinary delights of various parts of the world. You can have too many TV channels. You can have too many career choices. You can have too many sexual partners. Pessimists see this as the paradox of choice, whereby with too many things and so many desires to be satisfied, we can never be happy. The fact that survey after survey indicates that Irish people are extremely happy with life is overlooked.

Evidence is overruled by the gloomy background noise which says that not only are we not happy, but more and more of us are depressed, cocooned in our bubble of materialism, which is reducing the very essence of our lives and denuding us of meaning.

As more and more boundaries come down, the pessimists don't see freedom, career enhancement, new dreams and new opportunities. They see dangerous exceptionalism and a lurch away from traditional Irish values. The pessimists imply that only a certain type of deracinated Irish person can thrive in this world without frontiers, an effete cosmopolitan elite who are equally at home in Canada, Cape Town or Kiltimagh. This elite, they say, has lost touch with the homeland and has more in common with overachievers from other countries than with the people they were born beside.

Irish people like this are not, it is argued, the patriotic Irish of 1916 and the War of Independence, but the opportunistic, expedient Irish of *Game of Thrones*. We have become nothing more than a global franchise. The real, authentic Ireland and Irish are wiped clean by synthetic, globalised Ireland.

Pessimists forecast disaster and massive dislocation, arguing that the modern world divides into two sorts of people, as David Goodhart claimed in his interesting book on Brexit: people from somewhere and people from anywhere. The former are people whose identity is granted to them by where they were born; the latter acquired their identities along the way through their personal achievements. Brexit and Trumpism and other nativist movements can be seen as the victory of the people from somewhere over the people from anywhere. It is the triumph of blood-and-soil nationalism over ephemeral globalism.

In truth, the anti-expertise tirade that was the Brexit campaign was nothing more than a rallying cry for nostalgia against modernity, for voodoo over science, for sentiment over economics. It was the ultimate pessimists' alliance.

For the media, especially the daily radio talk shows, this outsized pessimism is rich soil. It keeps talk shows talking. The presenter knows the game. The more shocking and outrageous the claim, the more indignant the angle, the better the ratings. So all sorts of complainers, theorists and quack peddlers come on, filling the air with angst, foreboding and warnings.

Right-wing economists warn of another property crash, which will destroy the middle class again, and too much regulation is to blame. Left-wing economists alert us to another property crash which will destroy the working class, and too little regulation is to blame. Traditional anti-abortion moralists and worried liberal social commentators say we are losing our compassion. Dyed-in-the-wool environmentalists and 32-county nationalists are at one.

NOSTALGIA SQUARED

All around Europe and in the USA, the pessimists have taken charge or are on the cusp of power. The Brexit message, the Trump message, the Le Pen message, the Italian Northern League message, the German AfD message and the message of various other mini-Trumps in Austria, Hungary, Poland and Slovakia, are repackaged nostalgia claiming that the past was a better, purer, safer place. Nostalgia for more community, cleaner air, greener fields, more certain morals, more focused identity, more religion and certitude to protect us from being overrun by outside influences, crass consumerism, and corporate power.

The very dynamos that drive the modern world – individualism, choice, freedom, creativity, ambiguity – are vilified in favour of hard-and-fast rules, collective angst, strictures and prohibitions.

So, you will hear that we are working harder and harder only to feel less secure in our jobs. We are having more children but never see them. We are outsourcing parenting to understaffed crèches and will reap a vicious harvest in a future generation of depraved children. We are building more golf courses than children's playgrounds. We are buying houses, pinning ourselves to our collars, but vulture funds are taking all the profit, while we drown in yet more debt. The corporation is destroying the family. Too much one-off housing is destroying rural Ireland. Not enough one-off housing is destroying rural Ireland. Our spiritual values have been destroyed and all we do is click our lives away in a sea of vacuous online retail therapy. We are losing our emotional ballast in a transient quasi-pornographic life dominated by Tinder. We are becoming atomised. No one talks to anyone anymore. Relationships are negotiations. Friendships are bargains.

We are in the grip of a death wish. But that death wish is also called modernity. Nostalgists characterise modernity as an insatiable lust for choice, freedom, pleasure and democracy, which releases a degenerative decay at its core.

The repeal campaign revealed old-fashioned right-wingers in the Iona Institute who claim we are losing our sense of family, community and God and replacing these solid foundations of our identity with the spurious gratification of consumerism, brands and nail bars. Left-wing anti-water protestors also say we are losing our humane sense of ourselves and our communities as we succumb to the power of corporations, greedy landlords and a faceless state apparatus that favours the interests of the rich and attacks the bonds that gel class-struggle solidarity. The state apparatus claims to be under attack from the extremely rich in the courts, while the extremely rich say they are under attack from the state in the Dáil.

Greedy landlords say they are being undone by stodgy civil servants, while stodgy civil servants say greedy landlords are the problem. Builders say planners are the problem and planners say builders are the problem. Anti-globalisers claim that Ireland is a self-serving tax haven, while pro-globalisers point out that we are a tax-haven that actually raises too much, not too little tax from too few corporations. Large corporations claim they've never paid more tax here. Apple is accused of tax evasion and counter-claims it's the largest single taxpayer in the world. The EU says our government is owed $13 billion by Apple and our government says it doesn't need it. Tax-efficient, Revenue-avoiding accountants claim the Revenue is being unreasonable, yet the Revenue blame the scheming accountants for unpaid taxes. But all the time the tax take miraculously rises.

The foreign corporation states it is providing jobs, thus keeping the Irish family together, while talk-show psychologists claim that foreign corporations are putting far too much stress on Irish workers, undermining families by damaging mental health. Traditionalists argue that commuting is turning grandparents into childminders, while grandparents point out on afternoon TV that less emigration means they are the first generation of Irish grandparents to know their grandchildren.

Web Summiteers say the country is too expensive, while the country says the Web Summit is too expensive. Atheist, bearded trade unionists worry about the industrialised destruction of the food chain by the likes of Aldi and Lidl, but so too do their former enemies, bearded rural Catholic fundamentalists, who worry about the future for small farmers. Pro-choice left wingers worry that we are losing our sovereignty, but so too do anti-choice Christians.

EU-loving social democratic politics professors take to Twitter claiming that American-style consumerism is the enemy, while American-style free-marketeer IBEC members see European-style social democracy as the problem holding back the country. The old see the young as lazy and coarse. The young see the old as lucky and smug. The EU-loving gay cosmopolitan sees the young being corrupted by American branding, but the American-influenced moral fundamentalist sees the EU as a hive of sexual permissiveness and STDs.

The architectural snob sees a lack of planning and the ubiquity of the car as the scourge of Irish life, while the rural realist who actually lives in the countryside sees too much planning and too many architectural snobs as the problem.

As we've seen in so many cases all around the world, when countries least expect it, the perfect can bully the pretty good; the utopian can arm-wrestle the pragmatic; and the pessimist, with his collective ideology, invoking the people or the greater good, can vilify the optimistic, creative individual with his own private, progressive self-improvement project. How else could the civic-minded, inventive and very peaceful bourgeoisie have become the enemy of so many would-be revolutionaries?

This distaste of the middle class lingers. The interesting thing is that, in many cases, it's the middle class, the civic bourgeoisie, who read out the charge sheet against themselves.

NICK CAVE: CLASS ENEMY

On Tuesday, 5 June 2018, Nick Cave, Australian post-punk rocker, held a Q&A in the Abbey Theatre ahead of his gig with the iconic Patti Smith at the Royal Hospital in Kilmainham. Cave is the real deal: razor-thin, slim-fit tailored suit, dyed priest-black hair swept back like a rock'n'roll cross between the 1970s snooker player Ray Reardon and Peter Cushing's Dracula. Cave was generous, raucous and humane, dealing with the personal as well as the professional, dipping into popular culture and creativity, telling yarns, combining little gems from four decades of performing with deeper reflections on life, love and loss. On seeing Cillian Murphy in the audience, Cave bowed to the Peaky Blinder. One artist to another.

It was a freestyle gig, Cave with a mic and a grand piano, unplugged, unrehearsed and on fire. This is actually what punk is all about, the creative artist and engaged audience with nothing in the middle, no mediator, no lens, no script, just pure human exchange. It was a special night. There was something for everyone, Cave being both humble and dominant at once, the revered artist with his adoring fans. The audience held the mic and Cave answered honestly, humorously and, as a father who recently lost his teenage son in the most horribly tragic circumstances, poignantly.

The fans, like himself, are no longer in the prime of youth. If you want to know what that Portobello hipster ukulele player trying to be the most obscure man in the room is going to look like when he gets older, this was it. Lank, dyed jet-black hair, aneurism-inducing skinny jeans, lots of leg, arm and shoulder tattoos – that's the look. The way to define yourself in the Abbey tonight is a faded Birthday Party T-shirt, rocking that heroin chic, Kreuzberg, Bowie Berlin, lost decade, translucent look. Most importantly, you are locating yourself in the early 1980s and therefore signalling to everyone that, as much as you worship at the altar of contemporary Nick, if the truth be known you 'preferred his earlier stuff'.

At one stage, one of Cave's answers struck me. A fan who, like thousands of Irish people, had spent time in Melbourne, asked him about his hometown and his creative relationship with Rowland S. Howard, a mesmeric Australian guitar player, eulogised by many in the know, but unknown to the rest of us. Howard sadly passed away too early, from an excess of booze and drugs, as is the default position for many in the business. Howard and Cave played together in The Birthday Party.

Cave spoke about how he and Howard had met in Melbourne and how Howard had been excited to meet him. Cave had an early reputation for being a flamboyant punk in 1970s Melbourne at a time when Australia's main music exports were the Bee Gees and Rolf Harris. Cave had been the local prince of counter-culture. He remembers meeting Howard in the city before they headed back to Cave's house to listen to music. Cave said – and these are his actual words – that Howard was 'disappointed that it was in a leafy, suburban street, so middle class, so bourgeois'.

At the mention of the words 'middle class' and 'bourgeois' the entire audience in the packed Abbey auditorium guffawed in perfectly timed unison, North Korean-style, as if drilled from infancy to react to these two offensive words. But hang on – what could be more middle class and bourgeois than paying €50 to sit in the Abbey Theatre, the citadel of the Irish middle class, a tax-funded bourgeois arts emporium? What's more bourgeois than politely waiting your turn, civilly and courteously, to ask a question of the great one as he talked about the joys of reading Sebastian Barry? Who do you lot think you are – Dubs supporters at Hill 16? You are Nick Cave fans, for God's sake!

I was struck by the contention that Cave might have been any different. Why would Nick Cave *not* be a member of the middle class or the Australian bourgeoisie? The last major rock band that was *actually* working class was Oasis, described memorably by Noel Gallagher as 'the sound of a council estate singing its heart out'. You can hardly claim the same about Blur, Radiohead or this generation's favourites, The Arctic Monkeys, whose songwriter is the son of two teachers. Rock'n'roll stopped being street a long time ago. Hip-hop is a different story, but we are talking here about Nick Cave at the Abbey on the eve of a gig in that well-known working-class venue, the Irish Museum of Modern Art in Kilmainham. Nick Cave's dad was an English and maths teacher, his mother a librarian. Tupac he is not.

Yet why was Rowland S. Howard so blinkered as to think that the middle class did not produce great art? In fact, art is what you do when you are middle class, when the drudge of day-to-day survival has been somewhat lifted and you have a bit more time to focus on self-expression, self-analysis and self-projection. As Brian Eno states, 'Art is everything you don't have to do.' Look at the Irish greats in music, literature and cinema. Be honest with yourself. Where did they come from? The civic bourgeoisie, I'll bet. I am happy to be corrected, but the vast majority of the artists we fête not only hail from the middle classes but come from the places that cool people love to hate, the middle-class suburbs, like Nick Cave himself and so many others. The much-maligned suburbs are the font of much of society's creativity.

Yet at some stage the heroic, creative, rebellious middle class – Leopold Bloom's people, in fact James Joyce's people - have become a byword for dull conformist pen-pushers. Things are not binary. You can find in the middle class millions of versions of both, a wide spectrum of everything possible. Yet an alliance of perfectionists, academics, intellectuals and journalists has decided that the bourgeoisie are the problem when we are not just the solution, but the font of many solutions.

The Radical Centre is something precious and we don't understand how fragile precious can be. If you don't believe me, just have a look at Trump's tweets and shiver.

CHAPTER 18

THE CONTENTED CLASS

I'M ALRIGHT JACK

We are going to focus on the less obvious threats to the Radical Centre. These threats are not the big ones you read about in the news such as a trade war, Brexit, Trump's tax moves or some major series of events that will ambush us. Some of the most insidious threats that should concern us now are hidden in plain sight.

Those who have done very well out of the past generation's economic and social uplift and now, even though they don't know it, are setting limits on other people's opportunities. They are trying to consolidate their position close to the top. They are the 15%. They are not mega-rich like the easy-to-vilify 1%, but they are the I'm Alright Jack tribe who would now like things to stop moving and the status quo to be preserved. Having experienced significant upward social mobility in their careers, they now want to preserve these benefits for themselves and pass them on to their own families. If you want to know how they sound, sit back and listen to the newspaper review on the *Marian Finucane Show* on a Sunday. (I know I'm on that show regularly; taking the mickey out of your own tribe is half the craic in writing a book like this.)

THE CAVEMAN OF THE BANANA REPUBLIC

Nearly four decades of extraordinary prosperity and calm have led to a type of resistance and form of inertia when it comes to change. Change, or that more fancy word they use now, disruption, is what forged the Renaissance Nation. Little mutinies led to major disruptions. The last 40 years has been a period of massive disruption to old ideas in Ireland, to the way we did business and to the very sense of what it means to be Irish. It was an era of restlessness, dynamism and possibilities. Not all ventures succeeded, not all endeavours yielded positive results, but we did give it a lash. In the process of growing so rapidly and, in some cases, throwing caution to the wind, we did suffer one of the biggest crashes in economic history, which was spectacular in both its size and needlessness. But the Radical Centre is built on energetic self-improvement, involving both societal upsides and financial downsides. The subsequent recovery from the crash was straight out of the Renaissance Nation handbook, gutsy and unexpectedly rapid. It's a resilient beast, this Radical Centre.

Now that a level of affluence close to par with the wealthiest in the world has been reached, we are seeing a certain amount of inertia, more of a 'go-slow' than a 'tools-down'. Restlessness is an energy in itself. Any deceleration can undermine the dynamism that propelled us forward and at the vanguard of this threat are some of the very people who have done best out of the economic surge. This is understandable; why change when you have it all going for you? Why not circle the wagons and hold onto what we have?

THE BANANA REPUBLIC

As the garish-coloured convoys of Mamils and Swallows ride back from Greater Wexico, leaving the Wexicans south of the border, the amateur peloton glides through the older suburbs towards Stoveland, the playground of the professional classes. Gradually you will notice the cars become less diesel and more hybrid. In late May, there is the hushed sense of hothoused teenagers cramming for Higher Level Maths.

These folks voted overwhelmingly for repeal: Dublin Bay North voted 74.7% 'Yes'; Dublin Bay South 78.5% 'Yes'.

In these most salubrious of places, where property prices are amongst the highest in the country, almost four in five voted for repeal. In verdant Castleknock, across the Phoenix Park, where Pope John Paul II once said Mass for over one million, 74% voted for repeal. The old liberal strongholds of Dún Laoghaire and Milltown had similar figures. Moving across from D4 to G4 (aka Galway West), repeal won 66% of the vote. Similar patterns could be seen in middle-class parts of Cork, Galway and Limerick.

Here, repeal forms part of a suite of beliefs along with devotion to Stott Pilates reformers, reclaimed wide-plank flooring and the *Irish Times Weekend Magazine*. It's what the cultivated class believe in – personal health, the environment and restaurant reviews.

The rest of the country is churned up with skips, new roads, newer estates, giant yellow Caterpillar trucks, Polish lads with stop/go signs, endless traffic on roads defiled by Virgin Media broadband cable trenches, jammed Applegreen filling stations and the sounds, sights and smells of a country groaning from decades of breakneck expansion. But these older suburbs are different.

These places look exactly like they did when Alanis Morissette released *Jagged Little Pill*. They are frozen in time. The same roads, the same tree-lined estates and the same bus routes. They are precisely as they were a couple of decades ago. Unlike Greater Wexico, which is almost unrecognisable, nothing in the established suburbs has changed in a long time.

Sutton, Castleknock, Blackrock and Milltown in Dublin, Bishopstown and Douglas in Cork, Salthill and Taylor's Hill in Galway, Castletroy in Limerick or Stranmillis in Belfast are places that favour golf courses over people, static over progress and, more than anything else, they preserve a Stepford Wife-style uniformity, as if still trapped in 1995. They are preserved, the residential equivalent of a creaseless forehead.

The reason is a particularly virulent, professional Irish strain of Nimbyism. Nimbyism – 'Not In My Back Yard' – is the tendency some people have to object to any new development or infrastructure being built in their locality.

We are now in a new Banana Republic, a place preserved in time, where nothing can be built no matter how much sense it makes for the greater good. A Banana occurs when individual objectors get together to form an 'objectionist coalition' to oppose absolutely everything: 'Build Absolutely Nothing Anywhere Near Anything'. Banana Republicans, like any sect, are held together by a creed that invokes all sorts of higher moral authorities such as the environment, obscure endangered species, sensory overload, contamination, congestion and, of course, heritage to prevent anything being built anywhere near them. Build somewhere else, by all means, but not in my manor. I paid for that view, don't you know? Such serial objecting explains why their territory is unchanged.

The religion is enforced by orthodox disciples only too ready to identify heresy, such as new builds, signs for planning permission applications, government plans for an airport Metro, a Luas extension, essential new water infrastructure or potential residential development of any sort.

Within the Banana Republic lie the established suburbs, the ones with the best schools, the best public transport, established shopping centres, public parks and public amenities. They have the country's highest property prices and the highest addiction rate to San Pellegrino and Nespresso machines.

The Banana Republicans are a curious tribe, thin-skinned and open-minded at the same time. They are liberal and tolerant of all comers, until a developer suggests building an apartment block in the half acre of one of their recently sold back gardens, or until the unfair advantages their children have in the education or jobs market are at stake, in which case they turn into a 600-point version of Conor McGregor in the Octagon. At the hint of a threat to their status, these oratorical jousters turn feral and will stop at nothing to destroy progress. They block everything, particularly anything designed to solve the housing crisis that comes within an ass's roar of their new stone patio.

THE CAVEMAN

In this upper professional prairie, The Caveman roams triumphantly. He is the alpha male, the silverback of the Banana Republic. He represents the new governing philosophy of the upper professional zones, called Cave – Citizens Against Virtually Everything.

Cave Dwellers come in all political hues. A left-wing Caveman might object to a mobile phone mast, citing corporate malevolence aimed at poisoning the community, whereas a right-wing Caveman might object to a new development blocking his own right to a view. Cavemen deploy arguments from different ends of the spectrum to hamper the same thing. Posh Caveman sailors will object to an ocean cruiser docking on the basis that it undermines the value of their harbour moorings, while the left-wing agitating Caveman will protest against the same cruise liner on the basis that it will overvalue the same moorings. Neither wants to see disruption. Cavemen might deploy tactics like a GAA club protesting against the MetroLink by invoking their favourite mantra: 'For the sake of the children.'

Father Ted's 'Down with that sort of thing' is their political manifesto. No development, no matter how small, is overlooked. A road, a bus lane, a school wing, a hospital, a new radiography centre, a vaccine – anything that might benefit everyone – is regarded as an existential threat to their cloistered habitat. Naturally, Cavemen love the environment and deploy it to beat up any new initiative. Who can argue with the environment?

And then there's rights. Golf-playing Cavemen oppose residential development on the basis of their property rights, whereas hillwalking Cavemen oppose the same development on the basis of their human rights. But the key word here is rights: my rights, my entitlements.

Cave Dwellers are obviously happy with the status quo. It has been good to them. In their eyes nothing should be, will be, or needs to be changed. They are doing very well, thank you very much. I'm alright, Jack, how are you?

But this is the problem, because if we are not going forward, we are going backwards. If you stop development, you take away an essential ingredient of the Radical Centre – dynamism. If you prevent people living in higher densities in sought-after, well-connected parts of the country, you begin the process of retardation and segregation. You are explicitly saying: you can't come here. This is my place. The Cave Dwellers benefitted from the economic upswing through elevated house prices, good public transport, safe streets, nice parks, lovely views and such like. Now they want to prevent others from sharing this upside, so they block everything. It is an insidious form of privilege preservation.

As befits the professional class, they fight dirty, but make it look clean. Cave Dwellers love a petition. Once they have enough signatures, they can claim to have a community mandate against everything. This community-enforced status quo confers an almost republican zeal on The Caveman because he is not protecting his surroundings for his own narrow interests; he is doing all this selflessly on behalf of others. Is there a higher state of suburban grace than for a man to lay down his time and connections for his neighbours? He can be both bullying and angelic at the same time.

The Caveman is constantly on the lookout for signs of any new infrastructure anywhere near anything, unless, naturally, it's a cycle lane financed through central taxation by poor people who still think bikes are for poor people. The Caveman knows that cycling, far from being the mode of transport of the poor man, is a virtuous stairway to heaven for the man on his way up. Cycling is not for the merely successful, but for that rarefied person, the one who combines material success with self-control. In the old days, the image of a rich man was a fat lad, gorging himself on his wealth and excess. Today this truly virtuous well-off citizen is skinny, gorging himself on self-sacrifice and control.

The Caveman and most of the citizens of the Banana Republic are well educated, well-travelled and well-connected, yet wear their achievements with the incessant humility of only the truly self-assured. They are Camino Christians whose annual pilgrimage is never to some tacky apparition-inspired shrine like Knock or Medjugorje or, God forbid, Lourdes. They prefer all-weather Gore-Tex hiking in Spain's Atlas mountain range, genuflecting to the gods of pintxos, Albariño and crab claws. Theirs is a form of post-religious, mystical, Kabbala Catholicism, combining the holy trinity of deep spirituality, deep reflection and deep pockets, offering them a holistic connection with an earlier spiritual age.

In the hierarchy of global pilgrimages, the Camino is up there with the sacred sites of Machu Picchu, the Great Serpent Mound in Ohio, the

Mayan ruins of Chichen Itza in Yucatan and the Temple of Delphi in Greece. The Camino is the Hajj for people too old for Burning Man and too fond of pinot noir for Mecca. These factor-50 travellers hike the lower slopes, exchanging bragging tales with each other. Amongst the Banana Republicans, travel is about self-improvement. It's not just about going places; where you travel signals what sort of person you are.

Experiences are to be accumulated and retold, reinforcing the message that you're not some package tourist but are amongst 21st-century pilgrims. Of course, a pilgrimage, with its set routes, communal dinners and group discounts, is about as close to an organised package tour as you can get this side of Santa Ponza.

Banana Republicans like their creature comforts and their Irish obsessions. In truth, in their minds they rarely leave Ireland behind for long. In 2018 they got lucky on both counts. With almost predestined foresight, the Camino ended up in Bilbao in May, just in time to see Leinster crush Racing 92 in the Champions Cup rugby final. There must indeed be a God. He wears blue and is a season ticketholder at the Aviva.

THE CAVEWOMAN

The Cavewoman's 'Camino Goldens' WhatsApp group bings. Three of the girls at Pilates are co-pilgrims and prefer 'golden' to 'middle-aged'. They may be the wrong side of the big Five-O, but you wouldn't think it. Downward dog and rowing machines only get you so far; a few small interventions do the rest. Ironically, the one place where The Cavewoman gives large-scale reconstruction carte blanche is on her own face.

Despite, or maybe because of the fillers, she is comfortable 'in her own skin', happy to shop in Brown Thomas and TK Maxx. It allows her to talk to anyone.

The Cavewoman loves life, is good fun, throws a great dinner party and, as this is a high-level socially aspirational zone, obsesses excessively about food, unlike the uber-posh who don't care and whose entire diet tastes of semolina.

The Cavewoman was formerly head of the parents' council at the local primary Gaelscoil, which both Conor and Sorcha attended. She wanted them to experience 'full cultural immersion' before going to one of the older swanky secondary schools. Now that the kids are grown up, she pours her energy into the residents' committee. Just like the parents' council, the sailing and tennis clubs, the Tidy Towns gang, the Royal Horticultural Society and the local chamber of commerce, the residents' committee is more than just a diversion. It's a calling. Ever since she packed in her marketing career to 'spend more time with the kids' (the same week the nanny was hired), these outlets have been as vital to sustaining life as her nightly tipple at wine o'clock.

Newcomers be warned: if you've recently moved into the area, you don't need to look out for her – she'll be looking out for you. That blind has been twitching across the road since the 'For Sale' sign went up. She'll be the first one over to introduce herself by telling you just how long she's been in the community and, almost as an afterthought, to drop off a copy of the residents' committee guidelines. In the same way longevity bestows status amongst the Inuit, longevity in the Banana Republic also conveys status, simply because having been around a long time, The Cavewoman can recall precisely how the place looked before the uppity vulgarians tried to develop it.

Questions regarding your work and family status may seem like polite chit-chat. In reality, it is ammo-gathering for the next committee meeting. Information is currency in the annual fight for the chair. Her parting shot is a homemade quiche as she fills you in about 'herself in number 4', who tried to paint her house a different colour and applied for an extension. It may seem like an invitation into the circle of trust but, in reality, it's a thinly disguised warning not to stick your own toe out of line.

THE RUMBLINGS OF WAR

When the war comes, the patriots of the Banana Republic will be ready.

In ancient societies, coming conflict was usually signalled by a war dance of some sort; so too for the modern Irish Cave Dweller.

The coming conflict will be signalled by a suburban Haka. The opening salvoes of the Banana Republican Haka come not in the form of a war dance, but via a war missive. Rather than standing on the battle site grimacing, chanting and sticking their tongues out at the builder who wants to break ground, they do what all educated people do. They send a letter.

They don't simply 'write' this letter, they 'craft' it – deploying phrases like 'cultural vandalism' and 'the lived heritage' alongside that other objecting Caveman's gem, 'monstrosity' (pronounced nasally with the emphasis on the middle vowel).

You know there's trouble ahead in the Republic when this outraged letter to *The Irish Times* appears, signed by a residents' committee populated by people with capital letters after their names, listed on top of each other in alphabetical order, as befits such unimpeachable democrats. This is mandated objectionism.

Then the patriots sit back and wait. *The Irish Times* letters page does the rest. Outrage spreads in book, wine and golf clubs all over the country. The torch has been lit.

The chilling message to other Banana Republicans is, 'If you tolerate this, your tranquillity will be next.' Pastor Martin Niemöller showed them how it goes if they don't stand up now:

> They came for Stillorgan and we did not speak out because we weren't from Stillorgan.
> They came for Douglas and we did not speak out because we weren't from Douglas.
> They came for Malahide and we did not speak out because we weren't from Malahide.
> They came for Mount Merrion and we did not speak out because we weren't from Mount Merrion.
> Then they came for us – and there was no one left to speak for us.

Banana Republicans all over the country are galvanised and, for those so inclined, there is Twitter, the home of passive-aggressive indignation, made for the Cave Dwellers of the Banana Republic. They document architectural atrocities performed by uncivilised developers, robotic town planners allowing entire panoramas and vistas to be wiped out, cultural heritage destroyed and worse still, the 'wrong sort' moving in. Banana Republicans fear social housing like flat-earthers fear falling off the edge, and as all development needs to come with some social housing, better to have nothing at all.

Needless to say, the Gonzaga An Taisce revolutionaries, who didn't get enough points to do architecture, are up in arms.

Their objective is to stop change and block dynamism – the very dynamism that the Radical Centre needs to reproduce itself to the next generation. The Radical Centre is all about ongoing, gradual revolutions. The rigid status quo, so beloved of the Banana Republicans, is the enemy of progress.

NIMTOO

Once the missive has been sent, the next phase is the passive-aggressive public meeting. The first to feel the heat of the Banana Republicans on their collars are the local politicians. In the Irish proportional representation system, electoral margins are tight, often going down to the wire on the sixth or seventh count. Therefore, not causing offence to anyone or, more crucially, to any local voting bloc becomes a survival tactic.

In fact, you could go further and argue that preserving the status quo is the most important political imperative for any ambitious politician. An aspiring party leader might be able to guide a nation through a historic abortion referendum, swaying and influencing millions of voters on a once-in-a-generation national decision. He may even be able to address the United Nations on climate change and inclusion. Yet he can be felled by a four-storey apartment block in the wrong place obstructing the view of less than 50 well-connected, outraged Banana Republicans. This is why it is easier to win a referendum on changing the constitution than it is to build a new Luas stop. Who said all politics wasn't local?

The reality of our electoral system leads to Nimtoo – Not In My Term Of Office. Nimtoo leads to big decisions being postponed or kicked into the next term, which means they're never addressed.

Such is Irish politics in the 21st century. The Irish Water episode was a brilliant example of this, where all major parties were initially behind the very sensible notion that we should pay for water use, an unremarkable idea that is generally accepted all over the world. By the end of the anti-water-charges campaign, all political parties abandoned the idea.

In the Banana Republic, politicians realise that their job is to follow, not to lead. It's quite ironic that these same politicians are currently commemorating the War of Independence fighters, who risked execution. Their job now is to listen to the infinitesimal concerns of their electorate and focus on these specific grievances, no matter how deleterious this might be to the general population. Nimtoo explains why, despite a huge housing shortage, the population of suburban Dublin within the boundaries of the M50 has hardly changed since 2000. It also explains a lot about the ridiculous price of houses in Irish suburbs.

As a rule of thumb, the natural frontier between the wilds of Greater Wexico and the Banana Republic (Dublin Branch) is the M50. There are, on average, 400,000 unique journeys on the M50 every day. In 2016, this 45.5-kilometre stretch of tarmac carried average daily traffic of 142,496 vehicles, according to Transport Infrastructure Ireland (TII) and the National Transport Authority (NTA).[87] This is up 30% from 109,434 in 2009.

The M50 does for the Banana Republic what the Alps did for the Roman Republic: it acts as a natural barrier, keeping out style enemies and those who might interrupt its peaceful but fragile ecosystem. Between two radial routes, 51 million journeys were recorded in 2016, making the M50 by far Ireland's busiest road.[88] To put this in context, that same year, the same number of vehicles used the George Washington Bridge, connecting New Jersey and New York, with its population of 8.5 million. Dublin, by contrast, has a population of 1.3 million, or almost two million if the surrounding counties are taken into account.[89]

However, that's beyond the line. Within the Banana Republic, inside the M50, 45% of the land is green space – 20% is parkland and 25% is made up of the luscious gardens of the Banana Republicans themselves.[90]

SETTLING PATTERNS

Nimtoo also sheds light on the migratory patterns of immigrants in Ireland. Indeed, a cynic might suggest that the aim of Banana Republicans is to keep those sorts out too, so as not to affect their house prices, their school ratios and their sense of suburban tranquillity.

Remember earlier, we looked at the three main zones in Ireland in terms of our immigrant population? The innermost zone is the inner cities, particularly in Dublin, where the immigrant population is highest. Much farther out, once we cross the M50, in what used to be Deckland before the wood rotted, in places like Navan and Portlaoise, the immigrant population is also significant and rising.

Each of these zones is as far away from the Banana Republic as you can get without being accused of actual segregation.

Stuck between these two zones are the tranquil older suburbs of the Banana Republic, home to the Cave Dwellers. Immigrant families here disappear almost completely. In a country where one in six people are foreigners, the Banana Republic estates are overwhelmingly white Irish, populated by people who can tell you who played Miley in *Glenroe* – the sure litmus test of traditional Irishness.

In Ireland, immigrants settle where they can afford a roof over their heads. Our immigrants are early-morning and late-night commuters.

Cave Dwellers in the Banana Republic have been extraordinarily successful in objecting to any new developments, often with the support of a local TD. This means that, within the M50 – where development should be taking place – there are wide open prairies where wild horses roam. So in Dublin and other Irish cities, the success of the serial objectors has pushed all development farther and farther away, either back into the old city towards the Hipster/Howaya frontline, or miles away towards the greenfield sites of Applegreen Land.

In the Banana Republic, a benighted place where we build absolutely nothing anywhere near anything, the motto is: we have what we hold. These are liberal-voting, immigrant-loving professionals who feign awkward surprise that their Lithuanian cleaning lady has to get three buses to come to work for them.

CHAPTER 19

THE MAKEOVER

FROM BREAKFAST ROLL MAN TO HAPPY PEAR MAN

While there are precious few significant new developments within the borders of the Banana Republic, there is still an enormous amount of highly lucrative building work going on. As you move around, you notice a proliferation of skips. The skip is the most accurate early warning sign that an old friend is back.

Breakfast Roll Man surveys the back garden, measuring tape in one hand, clipboard in the other, shaking his head as he pokes at the crumbling gazebo. He is older, wiser, gluten-free and gaunt; think Ian Brown of the Stone Roses after a brief hunger strike. He has gone down five sizes and swapped high-viz jackets for low-res glasses. The rimless spectacles do the trick, giving him that 40-something, austere, greying-temples, Danish-chair-designer look so beloved of interiors magazines and expensive whiskey ads.

He hasn't seen the inside of a hot food counter in Spar since the marriage referendum. In fact, he has adopted a slightly camp manner, not quite Panti Bliss gay, more ripped Manhattan professional gym-bunny gay. It's good for business. No one spends on interiors like a gay couple. Sinking eight pints a night is long gone; he's clean now, hasn't had a drink in years. Tai Chi helps. The fasting does the rest. And, of course, like every born-again life-transforming evangelist, he's taken up open-sea swimming with ferocity. The colder the water, the more miserable the day, the bigger the implicit life-changing brag.

Breakfast Roll Man has returned, resurrected as Happy Pear Man.

Potatoes swapped for quinoa, sliced pans for sushi rolls, and he's no longer a builder; he's an artisan fabricator. Bankruptcy – courtesy of a last, frantic, heavily leveraged ghost estate knocked up outside Mullingar – led to months of self-reflection, a short-lived, last-blow-out addiction to skunk, exile in Goa, followed by a life-affirming dip in the Ganges. The new French yogi wife might have had a thing or two to do with the transformation. Their young son Rufus is now the intense focus of all Happy Pear Man's energies. When it comes to his son's upbringing, he makes that terrifyingly abusive drum instructor in *Whiplash* look like St Francis.

Happy Pear Man has rebranded himself as a cubist. No more 'slap-them-up' jobs out in Deckland. These days it's all about heritage and reclaiming underused areas. He is a creator of space, an exploiter of light, a crafter of interior dreams.

His website cites Picasso. Over a hundred years ago, Picasso, like James Joyce, decided to break things down and invent a new genre, recreating everything in a two-dimensional form so that figures looked like a series of boxes seen from a variety of angles.

In the Banana Republic, Dermot Bannon is our Picasso and Happy Pear Man his devout disciple. The rule is simple: you can build anything you like at the back of your house, where it is unseen from the road, so long as it's a cube. Ceiling-to-floor glazing and flagstone floors lead out onto a perfectly trimmed lawn, with its own manufactured meadow at the back, beside the black bamboo. This is the look.

Peek over any back wall in the Banana Republic and you are likely to see one of these glass boxes. You will probably be able to see right into the kitchen, now the size of a cantilevered airport hangar, needing a satellite tracking system to navigate from the fridge to the Connemara marble island.

Modernism is the future and the Banana Republicans have taken to it – as they do with most fashions – with enormously enthusiastic uniformity. While the front of these houses may be 1960s three-beds, 1970s pebble-dash bungalow, 1980s mock-Georgian or even genuine Edwardian terraced, the backs are an altar to Dermot, the patron saint of Irish interiors.

THE ARCTIC PANTRIES

In the Banana Republic, most kitchens are one of two styles. Either you go with rustic farmhouse chic, harking back to the wholesome countryside our imagined ancestors once roamed; or else you go all sterile Scandinavian. In contrast to the nostalgia-squared farmhouse chic, which thrives on human connection to the past, Scandinavian operating theatre antiseptic chic works on the basis that humans don't really use the kitchen. No one ever had a sneaky tea and toast on these metallic worktops.

In the same way he understands the need to transform Deckland into a sanctuary for trampolines and Woodies barbeques, Happy Pear Man understands his new clients and their need to express themselves not through their pocket but through something much more sophisticated – their diet. This is why the renovated kitchen is the tabernacle of the Banana Republic, a sacred, revered place where the truly chosen ones congregate.

Consider each walk-in fridge, a homage to multiculturalism, the vegan diet, zoodles and Yotam Ottolenghi. The vertiginous shelves of these arctic pantries are stacked with designer salt, guacamole, sushi, aubergines, kale, lemongrass, coconut water, butternut squash, frozen yoghurt, smoked salmon, pesto and, naturally, ricotta.

Each carefully measured triangular workspace signals a Pythagorean understanding of geometry, which, together with an appreciation of the chemistry of cooking and a comprehension of the Fitbit implications of rustling up a rocket-and-cherry-tomato salad, are a given.

Despite the enormity of these kitchens, there are no utensils on display, and not much evidence of cooking, even though cooking is one of the key battlegrounds distinguishing the merely well-off from the truly sophisticated. Microwaves are clearly an offence. The wine fridge should be well stocked with German Gewürztraminer; no New World wines anywhere, apart from the aboriginal co-operative winery in Queensland where the proceeds go towards redrawing the ancient songlines and dreaming tracks of the indigenous peoples.

There must never, ever be any sign of a washing machine or tumble dryer remotely close to the Aga. The 'no clothes in the kitchen' rule is absolute, more sacred than the sixth commandment. Clothes in the kitchen is so Wexico. Clothes belong in the new utility room, in another little cube off the main cube. Picasso would have approved.

The high-end Banana Republican rarely has a TV, particularly one attached to any wall anywhere. He is a Netflix on his MacBook Pro sort of dude, signalling, amongst other things, that he is his own man, his time is his own and he will not have his viewing habits curated for him by some remote, ratings-obsessed, shiny-floor TV scheduler. The Banana Republican is a sovereign person. If he wants to show off his education, the only sound in the kitchen will emanate from a Roberts Duck Egg Replica 1950s radio, the sort of gadget your granny listened to the lunar landings on.

Technologically, we are back to the 1960s. But this is only for technology where the experience is shared. For personal devices, the more high-tech the better. For the communal technology experience, some very confident Banana households get all ironic and go up a decade, locating themselves in the 1970s. The '1970s-were-the-coolest-decade' philosophy is an affectation exemplified by a fondness for Kraftwerk, peach melba and Parker Knoll furniture. This pretension can only be carried off fashionably if you look like Brian Eno or sound like Alex Turner. In that case, you can get away with pretty much anything.

In the more upscale provinces of the Banana Republic, such as Victorian Dublin 6, TVs in the kitchen are most definitely not seen. Strangely enough, in Dublin 4 they are ubiquitous. Dublin 4 has always been more arriviste than it lets on, always a bit more shameless, aspirational and slightly off the pace. Far too many home cinemas, frankly.

The highly educated modernist kitchen will be able to combine the very new with the very old. There will be a reconditioned Aga, a recycled

Belfast sink and maybe a weathered-looking bench, side-by-side with a top-of-the-range Lavazza home-espresso coffee machine. Everything is reconditioned, unless it's made by Italians. The whole place is Bluetooth-enabled, obviously.

THE BANANA PARADOX

Remember, you can build whatever you like, as long as it doesn't increase the population density of the area. The bigger the kitchen extension, the fewer people live in the house. In the Banana Republic, the ratio of house to human is the highest in the country.

But here's the paradox at the core of the Banana Republic's preservation drive. The more they object to development, the fewer houses are built, the longer the housing crisis continues, the higher property prices go and the less chance they have of their kids moving out. So their adult children will stay at home for as long as possible and, before they know what is going on, their son's girlfriend moves into the family home and they are stuck.

In fact, our Cavewoman, she formerly of the Gaelscoil parents' committee, is quite worried that Conor's new girlfriend, the one with the severe fringe that makes her look like a bewildered Amazonian, might be eyeing up just such a move.

The Caveman surveys his home from the elevated vantage point of his home office in his new double-height box – a man-shed for men who don't like Black-and-Decker tools. Banana Republicans dream of giving up the rat race, the commute and the incessant office politics. They fantasise about being their own boss, working when they want, where they want. So their suburban castle has to be turned into a productive centre. After all, if you've spent hundreds and thousands on home extensions, you want to spend time there too.

Banana Republicans voted for abortion, divorce and gay marriage, understand non-binary sexuality and love the immigrants who add colour to the place. But all that cosmopolitan tolerance goes out the window if you are planning to build anything near them. Don't bother them and they won't bother you.

If you do pick a fight, try something as outrageous and egregious as suggesting that there needs to be higher-density housing in the established suburbs, then you can expect a well-placed anvil to crash on top of your head as residents' committees are galvanised, voluntary groups ignited and nasty political threats issued, all under the organisational watch of that deep, deep insider, Quango Man.

CHAPTER 20

QUANGO MAN

Quango Man is having a great Brexit, like he had a great Y2K, a great foot-and-mouth crisis, a great banking crisis and a great Maastricht Treaty crisis. In any crisis, Quango Man is called upon to form a committee, a working group or a task force. He is so deeply inside, he doesn't know where the exit door is. He's been on the government revolving-door circuit for so long, people have even forgotten which party he was with at the start. Quango Man is part of the system, the go-to man in a crisis, the State's fixer, the apparatchik's apparatchik.

Having presided over the massive excavation of his back garden, Quango Man headed North to buy his wood-burning stove during a Brexit-inspired sterling collapse. He threw in an authentic Rajasthani Kadai for chilly nights on the flagstones. He couldn't resist.

He is in the North a lot these days; two cross-border committees, an Invest NI sinecure and the North–South Cooperation Council all sit in Belfast. Who says Brexit has no upside? For Quango Man, the North is a constitutional Lidl, a bargain basement only an hour up the road. It is far cheaper than anything this side of the border and as his salary is determined by equivalence with his Brussels counterparts and topped up by all these state quangos, plus mileage, it keeps getting cheaper.

Quango Man's favourite pit-stop on the way to Belfast is Wilson's Yard, just past Hillsborough. Wilson's Yard specialises in architectural antiques; it is reclaimed heaven, flogging something from the past to the only people in the present who can afford nostalgia. Everything in the Yard is vintage, recycled and reimagined. Nostalgia is pricey. There are vast ornamental gates, stone follies and cast-iron radiators galore. If that doesn't do it for you, what about reclaimed plank flooring salvaged from a whiskey distillery in Scotland or rare oak from a 19th-century Amish barn? This is high-end stuff.

Brexit's been boomtime for Quango Man. The gift that just keeps giving. As well as his usual gigs, he is over and back to London, or representing Irish business in Brussels, lobbying for the specific concerns of the tech sector. St Patrick's weekend was a blizzard of panels, chats and general windbaggery all over the US as part of something called the Ireland Fund's 'Task Force for Brexit, Ireland and the Globe'. Then he's off to give his view of the world at the great Quango Man jamboree, The MacGill Summer School. It's all great fun and, most importantly, all expenses are paid by someone called the taxpayer.

Deep down, despite the necessity of sounding alarmed and concerned in public, Quango Man is loving Brexit, every minute of it. Every twist and turn means more money. And now that the transition period could go on for a few years, there's at least another few massive paydays for Quango Man.

Brexit has also given the Banana Republicans like him permission to be anti-English while still sounding all European and reasonable. Their inner Provo can be released without sounding sectarian, gratuitous or, even worse, vaguely Celtic Park. Most Quango Men learnt their history from the Christian Brothers – hardly an even-handed narrative.

THE QUANGO THREAT

The Radical Centre was created by the resplendent efforts of the average person, having a go, taking a risk and expressing themselves in that part of the economy where the vast majority of people work, the small business sector. A threat to the Radical Centre comes from the emergence of a parallel class, the Quango Class.

Over the past 30 years, a key dynamic opening up in the economy was the movement of society from a 'permission economy', where people's 'pull' and networks superseded their individual talent, to a 'have a go' society, where individual effort was rewarded. As long as there were avenues open for upward mobility, people took them. Anything that closes off these pathways is a threat to the Radical Centre.

The arbiter of success was, and is, having skin in the game, putting risk on the table so that there is a connection between your individual effort and your reward. If a parallel aristocracy emerges with no skin in the game, we have a threat to the upward mobility of the Radical Centre.

Quangos reproduce themselves. Although the number of quangos in Ireland has fallen from 170 in 2010 to 153 in 2017, the numbers employed haven't really budged.[91] Despite Fine Gael promises in 2011 to cull 145 of them, the Quango Men in the long grass, the trade unions, managers and upper echelons of the civil service resisted the removal of quangos.

What we got instead was reform, which isn't really reform at all. For example, the VECs (Vocational Education Committees) were reduced from 33 to 16 but there were no reductions in staff numbers and the chief executives of the culled VECs were redeployed elsewhere, on the same pay and conditions. When Quango Man digs his heels in, he is limpet-like in holding onto his perks. A 2015 report by Dr Richard Boyle of the Institute of Public Administration concluded that 62 state bodies were terminated, but only 10 of those ceased operation completely; the remaining 52 were merged with other bodies or subsumed back into a larger agency or the parent department. And, almost mockingly, 14 new agencies resulted from such mergers![92]

If you look at the 2011 figures for the average earnings in a selection of quangos, at a time when unemployment was in double digits, the deficit was enormous and essential public services were being cut, you can see that Quango Man is paid very well indeed, which is nice when it's other people's money.[93]

Of course, as our Quango Man is on the top of the pile, his slice is much higher. And we know that average public sector wages in Ireland

(€47,400) are 40% higher than in the private sector, before allowing for differences in pension entitlements and job security.[94]

Davy Stockbrokers – in fairness, not people known for underpaying themselves – warns that the public sector enjoys retirement benefits that need to be taken into consideration. They calculate that a private sector worker would need to save €590,000 to buy an annuity that matched public sector career-average salary pensions of €23,000 per annum.[95]

The implication of this €590,000 savings figure is that the average public worker is not just slightly overpaid, but is actually a member of the 1%. Having savings of over €500,000 is wealth that puts you in the top 1% of the country.

The Quango Class is a threat because it feeds off the system, but it is a class that is good at covering its tracks and even better at looking busy. Think of all the public sector scandals over the years and ask yourself: has anyone at the top ever paid for incompetence, or even taken a pay cut? For now, allow that 1% observation to sink in and imagine how you, the taxpayer, will pay for that in the years ahead. In addition, Quango Man, even when close to retirement and about to receive a huge pension, is still taking up seats on this board and that board. These deep insiders hog positions and thus block progression for others. But rather than focus on the obvious financial perils posed to the public purse of such open-ended pension provisions, I'd like to zone in on something else.

Right now, let us focus on the psychology of Quango Man. Because when things are going so well, when you are the cat with a delicious bowl of cream, why would you embrace change? Everything you would do would be aimed at preserving the status quo, beginning with the system itself.

QUANGO MAN TAKES NOTES

This week the schools are closed and morning rush hour traffic in the suburbs has dwindled.

Quango Man slips the 5-Series into fourth, not a gear he hits regularly when he's bumper-to-bumper in the morning. He heads effortlessly down the M1, chuckling at the strangely upbeat tones of the Dutch weatherman on *Morning Ireland*. Quango Man listens, more intently than normal, to news of the untimely demise of a government quango engulfed by a political scandal. Let this be a lesson to Quango Men all over the country. The world of quangos is a highly lucrative one, and rule number one of the gravy train is invisibility. On boarding the first-class, free-loading quango carriage, understand that extracting cash from the state is a delicate business from start to finish. If successful, there never has to be a finish line; you can move seamlessly from one sinecure to another without leaving a trace.

It's well understood to insiders in the quango world that a 'public interest' position is never really offered to the public. For the quangos to prosper, transparency must be kept to an absolute minimum. Of course, for optics, there has to be a 'notional' procedure where the job is advertised in public. This is only for show. The real decisions are taken before the job is ever advertised. The best way to disguise this process is to engage a well-known executive search company, preferably fronted by an impressive brunette who went to Mount Anville. The Mountie will pretend to scour the market for the best candidate. This will cost, but hey, the taxpayers are paying, so who cares? What purer definition of public/private partnership can you get? In cahoots, private sector head-hunter paid by the public purse – you couldn't make it up.

The executive search company will place an expensive ad in the business section of Friday's paper. The ad, scripted with extensive use of a bespoke business thesaurus, will use all the right words like 'dynamic', 'exceptional', 'goal-orientated', 'leadership' and the like.

Innocents who don't understand the deal may believe that they are in with a chance. Typically, but not always, these hopeful candidates will be nostalgic emigrants looking to come home, who have forgotten how some bits of the old sod work, or maybe more plausibly, who can't quite admit to themselves that the place still works this way. So, they throw their meritocratic hats in the ring. Lambs to the slaughter. Baa, baa.

On the inside, deep in the bowels of the state apparatus, the generic rejection letter has already been written. The head-hunter gets paid, Quango Man gets another sinecure and we carry on.

As long as the productive core of the Radical Centre keeps innovating, trading, buying and selling, employing, being employed, and paying taxes, there is enough money for everyone. Jam time for Quango Man.

UNDER THE RADAR

Quango Man is the stealth bomber of public servants. His job is to do the job that should be done by existing civil servants, without anyone even being aware of the rampant double-jobbing and small-scale extortion. The last thing you need to be is rumbled. Keep your head down, take the cash and never, ever upset the politicians. Never draw attention to yourself. This means never becoming the story.

The priority of any Quango Man is to make the politicians look good. Never force them to justify to anyone why you are there. Quango Man also must walk the treacherous fine line with rival civil servants. Unlike the politicians, these tricky creatures are impervious to elections and riven with jealousy, so they are dangerous. Envy, rather than talent, runs much of the upper service. They are the departmental Robespierres who will happily accuse, try, hang, draw and quarter you before you even know what's going on, only to slink back into the crowd.

Every Quango Man understands that in order to survive, the buzzards in the media need to be avoided like the plague.

If some in the media are buzzards, the puffed-out columnists are the colourful peacocks. Their vanity is their Achilles heel. They want to be on the inside and therefore can be offered information in return for quiescence. They breathe the anxious oxygen of publicity and status. Their anxiety comes from being the cleverest boy in the class, yet unrecognised by everyone bar themselves. Not being recognised early breeds bitterness. Only academics are more bitter and envious of each other's success. But, in truth, the columnists are easy pickings for a devious Quango Man. He would meet them happily for a pint in Doheny's on a Friday. Doesn't he meet these peacocks on chat show panels regularly, where he can talk about everything and anything at all? Chutzpah is not rationed in Quango Land.

For Quango Man, the political hacks are a different species. They pose a real and present threat. They are far too territorial. If the columnist is a preening, self-absorbed peacock, the hacks are the predatory buzzards, angry and suspicious, waiting to swoop. Such a breed lives off access and intrigue, unlike the columnist, who wants to comment, analyse and skate eloquently on the surface, pirouetting in his own brilliance. The hack wants to dig, driven by a manic urge to expose.

Such an adversary presents a minefield for a jocular Quango Man who, after all, lives in the twilight world of nods and winks, commissioned reports and obfuscation. Whatever you say, say nothing. Maybe Seamus Heaney was describing something far closer to home.

He switches over to Radio Nova for an early morning dose of Truck Rock. By the time he is crawling along under the flyover, he's belting out 'Hold the Line' by Toto, air guitar at a 45-degree angle to the steering wheel, imaginary plectrum squeezing out riffs. Pity he can't fit into those pants anymore.

CHAPTER 21

THE INDIVIDUALLY WRAPPED CHILD

The number plates are a dead giveaway. Quango Man can tell, not just from the South Tipperary plates but from the hesitancy, that the woman in front is not a regular commuter. Regulars know if there's a gap it's an imperative, not an invitation. Switching lanes aggressively is all part of the morning commuter game. It's *Fortnite* for people with nine-to-fives.

There's an orchestral quality to the movements of Irish commuters, as if directed by some invisible conductor who calls on them to move, then allows the flow to stream, left or right, then calls on them again to make their intervention. Instinctively they know their notes, their tones and their timings. They know where the entire concerto is heading, when to nudge in, who to let go, how to *just* break the lights and precisely when to move out of the bus lane, feigning innocence like Luis Suarez after taking a bite out of an opponent.

Quango Man, off the motorway now, can see him in the wing mirror. He is almost like a dot on the horizon but he is coming up fast, very fast. He is in a race against himself. You can see his face grimacing as he times himself, powering past other cyclists. He needs to be avoided if you know what's good for your wing mirror. As quick as he saw him in the mirror, the cyclist is gone, hurtling to another personal best. Quango Man contemplates his own Lapierre carbon-framed bike in the morning, but satisfies himself with a recreation run to Enniskerry with the boys at the weekend.

On a daily basis the driving commuter's greatest enemy is the school run. When schools are off, the drive is pleasant. Once the schools restart, the roads clog up and the commute becomes hell.

Sliotar Mom is Quango Man's adversary this morning as she, also a seasoned commuter, nudges, weaves and criss-crosses her Citroën Picasso through the morning madness. Eight stone of human in 240 stone of metal. When did we start naming hunks of metal after modernist painters? More to the point, when did we start getting away with naming hunks of metal after modernist painters? When did we stop noticing the absurdity of it all?

Maybe it was when we started driving kids to school en masse. Clogging up the roads with school runs is a relatively new thing. It's a by-product of the Radical Centre. A generation ago, children were not driven to school. Households didn't have second cars and children were not as hyper-protected as they are now. The individually wrapped child, shielded from every possible danger, morning to night, is a fragile creature imported from suburban America.

The travelling trends are extraordinary. According to the census, in 1981, just after the first papal visit, 20% of primary and 8% of secondary students were driven to school.[96] By 2016, 60% of primary school kids and 42% of secondary students were driven to school. This is a massive societal change and is much more significant than can be explained by deficiencies in public transport or distance from schools – although those may also be factors.

Is all this mollycoddling good for little Lorcan? Sliotar Mom worries that children in the hyper-competitive economy of the future might need to be a bit more exposed. She hears ghastly stories about young adults, living with their parents, not being able to wash their own clothes, unable to feed themselves or look after the house. How will they ever compete? As the kids' heads are stuck in their devices, she considers whether they need more protection, not less, from the vagaries of life. Will they build up resilience to the ups and downs of life if she keeps agonising about every danger, real and imaginary? Her own mother never worried about her. At 18 she was on her own, up in Dublin. And she was certainly never driven to school, trussed up in a car seat with more safety features than the cockpit of a MiG-29 fighter.

She knows that the jobs market is changing rapidly. When candidates come through her office door, she's now looking for attitude rather than qualifications or credentials. Anyone can have credentials; fewer have balls, spark or the innovative brain to have a go. Could her anxieties be the very thing that drags her kids back, despite her thinking it's the one thing that is giving them a leg up?

Listening to Gift Grub take the mickey out of Michael D, Sliotar Mom worries about the logic of excessive parental protection and handholding of her children. Does the new chaotic world of projects rather than careers, and of short-term gigs rather than permanent and pensionable jobs, demand this level of child protection? Or does the hyper-competition that she sees everywhere suggest that children need to learn to stand on their own two feet, to deal with upset and to develop coping mechanisms in a globalised world where economic opportunism may be the key determinant of success?

Sliotar Mom rarely gets a chance to be philosophical, but the commute allows her to think. Looking at other faces in the traffic, she wonders are they, too, cocooned in their thoughts.

THE ROAD AHEAD

According to a recent survey by Red C for the National Youth Council of Ireland, 47% of Irish workers under 29 are on temporary contracts.[97] This is 170,000 people employed in the so-called 'gig economy'.

As more and more people work in this freelancing economy, we are witnessing a massive transfer of risk away from the employer back to the individual. When permanent and pensionable jobs were the norm, a significant amount of economic and financial risk was carried by the employer. Now, with globalisation, the pendulum is swinging back to the worker, who is assuming an increasing amount of the risk.

The days are over when you could get a job for life at the same company, gradually climbing the corporate ladder. Only 10 years ago, the largest companies in Ireland were banks, offering permanent and pensionable careers, status and stability. Those days are over. We are entering a world where sole traders will live on their wits, selling their services in a competitive market where their work is reviewed and rated, as a restaurant would be on TripAdvisor, for all to see. The good ones will thrive, the mediocre will fall away or do something else.

Look again at the clogged suburban roads of Ireland. Think of Sliotar Mom who drives the children to school. Will she still be driving them when they are teenagers in a few years, healthy kids who could easily walk, cycle or get the bus? She is trying to protect her children, to minimise the risk they face, but is this the right thing to do?

What if this urge to protect could stunt the child's capacity to meet failure and unpredictability head on? If the aim of modern life is to minimise or squeeze the last drop of spontaneity and adventure out of life, in an effort to make life more predictable, what happens when something unpredictable happens?

One of the most harrowing aspects of the recession was seeing many contemporaries being laid off and knowing they had no capacity or resources to deal with this shock. All their resources had been committed to trying to eliminate risk from their lives, playing meaningless office politics and climbing up the corporate ladder. But we know deep down that risk is ever present. If we could eliminate it, the insurance industry wouldn't exist. However, for many millions of people, career progress is one large process of laying off risk, trying to minimise chance events. But running away from risk doesn't make risk go away; it makes us more vulnerable when the unexpected happens. And the unexpected always happens.

As the economy becomes more globalised, random events happen with greater frequency because they come from more directions. The most important career characteristic might be resilience in the face of adversity, to be able to dust yourself down and carry on. The ability to face up to economic, commercial or financial adversity will depend very much on resilience, which you learn at a young age.

Such dexterity is what drove the Renaissance Nation. We took off the shackles and embraced risk, morally, emotionally, economically, and the results have been phenomenal. If we mollycoddle kids from a young age, how will they be able to stand on their own two feet? Particularly if we put too much store in the education system, in minimising risk and rewarding only those who express themselves in conventional ways?

Sliotar Mom hears the loud hooting. Bollox. She has allowed the car to roll onto the yellow box between junctions. Putting on her mascara in the mirror is a tricky business. Now she is blocking the oncoming merging traffic. Quango Man is furious, late for his twentieth Brexit speech of the year.

Sliotar Mom is distracted, deep in her own thoughts, worried about the little ones, the future and whether she is doing the right thing. Is sixth class too early to start maths grinds?

CHAPTER 22

THE TESTOCRACY THREAT

THE LONG GOOD FRIDAY

The enemy of dynamism is stasis. If society gets stuck into a rigid way of doing things only because this is what we have always done, it leaves itself open to complacency. In our globalised world, there is little room for complacency. Remember, the Radical Centre is the product of freeing the minds of millions of Irish people. What is the point of freeing our minds of one set of rules, only to genuflect at the altar of another?

In this chapter, I'd like to explore the threat to the Radical Centre from that institution which many believe to be one of our strongest attributes: our education system.

Let's see what is happening on that most Irish of days, Good Friday. In the past few years, many of the sacred cows of Ireland have been slain. Is nothing sacrosanct? The ban on both gay marriage and abortion have gone. We've got a gay, half-Indian, physically fit Taoiseach under the age of 40 who is more interested in bench pressing than pint drinking. And to top it all, the ban on pubs opening on Good Friday is gone.

The lengths to which we went to acquire alcohol on Good Fridays is an entire chapter in itself. Around here in Dún Laoghaire, people used to go to England on the boat, not just for abortions but to get booze on Good Friday. I am not messing.

These strange cultural rites used to be seen as bizarre rituals that distinguished Ireland from other countries. They defined us, even if most of us were moving away from them. These edicts or practices made us stand out from the rest of the world. Most of these unique Irish customs have gone, swept away in the Radical Centre revolution. But there's one that remains stronger than ever: the grind.

Religious observance may be gone, but the Leaving Cert is bigger than ever. Easter signals not the resurrection of the Lord, but the start of the early cramming season. There are only two months to go, so it's time to get your act together. And all over the country that means grinds.

The Leaving Cert is the great Irish rite of passage. Rites of passage to adulthood are a cross-cultural phenomenon. They have existed throughout human history. Christians have confirmation, Jews have Bar Mitzvahs and, in tribal cultures, coming-of-age ceremonies can be elaborate and truly terrifying. For example, the Algonquin tribe of Quebec bring their young men to a secluded area, often caged, where they are given an intoxicating medicine known as wysoccan, an extremely dangerous hallucinogen that is said to be a hundred times more powerful than LSD. The intention of the ritual is to force any memories of being a child out of the boy's mind.

The Leaving Cert does the opposite. Rather than cleanse the teenager's mind, our tribal ritual is designed to cram the teenager's mind with short-term memories and lists of entirely useless facts that they will never use as an adult. In my case, it was mad stuff such as how many of Peig's children died before she left the Blasket Islands. I'm fairly sure I have never been asked that question since. Nor has knowing the lifecycle of a liver-fluke been of much value during my adult life.

Yet the Leaving Cert can hinge on such meaningless intricacies.

It is a bizarre national memory test of triathlon dimensions, cheered on and agonised over by the entire nation, working the place into a midsummer communal frenzy. Terrified teenagers are exalted to wilder and wilder mental feats, memorising sacred texts, repeating mantras and praised the more they memorise.

Future generations of anthropologists, when deciphering the ways and motives of their ancestors, will be flummoxed by this one.

For example, nowhere else in the world are national radio programmes devoted to the final school exam results. You don't see photos of smiling children who do well in school exams beaming out of the newspapers in *Le Monde*, the *New York Times* or the *Daily Telegraph*. But you see them holding up their results on the front pages of the *Irish Independent*.

The whole family is involved. Agitated parents who should be agents of calm become peddlers of angst, responding to an innocent request to go out for dinner in early June with a resigned look and a sigh:

'Sorry, but we've got a Leaving Cert at home.'

To which the only obvious answer is:

'You are not doing the fucking exam!'

The entire country – or, more accurately, the citizens of the Banana Republic who run the place – whips itself into paroxysms of agitation and neurosis about the Leaving Cert, prompting thousands of otherwise normal teenagers to scour the dark web for Ritalin, porn or both. Pushy parents cause much of the anxiety with their constant pressure and have accepted the Leaving Cert's dictum in the same way their grandparents accepted McQuaid's.

As the nation marches trance-like towards June and our young people's meeting with destiny, families report levels of anxiety normally only experienced by people under sustained aerial bombardment, leading to a ridiculous Blitz spirit which advises the nation to 'keep calm and carry on'. It's stiff-upper-lip time.

The children are isolated from their friends and families for hours on end, locked in their rooms, trying to absorb as many facts as possible into their little internet-addled brains. By mid-May, it has reached national hysteria.

Generations before them have been through the same ceremony without questioning it. It's part of the process of being a member of that weird post-Celtic tribe, the Irish. But when we have such uniform acceptance of a ritual, should this very conformity be a cause for concern? Rather than question the entire logic of the ritual, normally intelligent and supportive parents abandon their panicked, demented and emotionally fragile children to the system.

They are warned that 'repeating' is the alternative. Failure is not an option.

THE EXAM WHISPERER

Just as we are reaching the climax in this national madness, just when the poor, academically soaked victims are being shoved up the steps of the giant Mayan sacrifice temple, she arrives – the Exam Whisperer.

Like Robert Redford in *The Horse Whisperer*, who has a special way with horses, the Exam Whisperer has a special way with the Leaving Cert. She understands the exam, the marking scheme, the pattern of questions likely to be asked and how to answer them with a view to extracting the most marks. Enjoying the subject, appreciating the topic, loving the nuance, does not come into the ritual.

Maximising points is the name of the game. Deciphering the encryption is what it's all about and the Exam Whisperer knows the code. Once the code is broken, the student can gain admission into the rarefied class, not of university graduates, but of graduates from the right university.

A few hours a week with the Exam Whisperer and the lost teenager is found. The no-hoper is put on the right track and the Leaving Cert, like a wild mustang on the Montana plains, morphs from being a terrifying proposition to one that can be moulded.

But the Exam Whisperer costs and the more she costs, the bigger the wedge driven between the families that can afford grinds and the ones that cannot. This renders what looks like a fair system grossly unfair. This is a way for the Contented Class to reproduce their privilege – by making the educational playing pitch uneven. Again, no one is going out to orchestrate such an outcome, but it comes from the very success of the Radical Centre and from a system that looks highly meritocratic, but may be evolving into something else.

The Exam Whisperer used to be a high-achieving teacher at one of Ireland's high-achieving secondary schools. But in the get-up-and-go spirit of the Radical Centre, she took a career break to set up on her own. That's the beauty of the Irish public service; it provides an insurance policy for ambitious, talented people who joined the public service when there were no alternatives, when Ireland was a different country.

Now the Exam Whisperer, typical of so many who were once trapped in the permanent and pensionable mindset, has gone out on her own. She is liberated and she hasn't looked back. As the High Priestess of the Leaving Cert cult, she is a revered figure. As the weeks count down to the ritual itself, her value soars. Parents are prepared to pay through the nose for their children's salvation. By late May, the country, egged on by editorial writers, TV producers and the schools themselves, reach moving-statue levels of religious zeal.

FROM THEOCRACY TO TESTOCRACY

Ironically, having freed itself from a theocracy run by clerics who were good at obedience, Ireland is at risk of replacing it with a new system of rule: a Testocracy, run by people who are good at exams. Over the past generation, the country has become divided into exam passers and exam failers.

Let's consider this.

Imagine being ruled by people who are particularly good at table quizzes. And not just people who are good at table quizzes, but people who are happy to spend hours remembering the answers for a massive national table quiz.

Once the outcome of the table quiz becomes a significant arbiter of progress in society, the original fairness of the test becomes compromised. The people who have money and power will try all sorts of tricks to make sure their spawn have the best chance to go to the best universities and, therefore, on to the best jobs, to live in the best areas and pass on their privilege to the next generation. It's human nature.

The Testocrats, people who are good at exams, are the clear winners in this giant quiz system. In Ireland's great Radical Centre economic surge, the Testocrats have emerged as the new aristocracy. Testocrats are not the 1%, who everyone loves to hate, who are easy to vilify and target. They are more like the 15% and they get there by doing the bidding of the top 1%, in law, in finance and at the top of the civil service, allowing them to be privately complicit but publicly virtuous.

Testocrats vote left but live right. They talk cosmopolitan but baulk at the notion of refugees moving in beside them. And whatever about refugees, they won't have Travellers – our own wanderers – within a country mile of them. Being educated masks all sorts of contradictions. At the upper end of the professional Testocracy, they are happy to take money from Denis O'Brien in their business life, but feel free to bitch about him behind his back at dinner parties.

As the Leaving Cert is the bottleneck that restricts access into the Testocracy, it is elevated and worshipped. After all, if you are at the top of the system, it must be defended at all costs. The stranglehold the Testocrat has on the Irish education system is asphyxiating and the grind system reinforces this, giving maximum advantage.

The Testocracy is a form of rule based on a narrow sort of merit or value, where your intrinsic value equals your IQ combined with hard work, with an emphasis on memorising. Passing school exams is an extremely narrow definition of human capability. But when you consider what went before – the old system of land based on a hereditary hierarchy, followed by industrial/mercantile power and seniority based on age – maybe it is not too bad.

The Testocracy, armed with their impressive CAO forms, have taken power in Ireland. They are the serial objectors in the Banana Republic, the coffee aficionados of Portobello and a fair few Swallows on their €5,000 Lapierre carbon-framed bikes heading over the Beara Peninsula at the Sportif. The Testocracy has led to a new form of acceptable prejudice. It is no longer acceptable to have a problem with sexual orientation, race, social background or religion. All this is progress. However, it is implicitly acceptable to hold an unspoken, but unambiguous prejudice against people who find it hard to pass exams and by extension towards those who are not quiz test masters.

Testocrats have assaulted power everywhere. Barak Obama was the ultimate Testocrat, which is why the Irish Testocracy loved him. Trump is everything they hate, particularly as he luxuriates in his love of 'the uneducated', as he said on the campaign. Emmanuel Macron is a Euro Testocrat, which is why the Irish Testocracy love him too, despite the fact that, as we will see in a while, he poses a huge threat to us.

When America elected Obama, he was everything the Testocracy lusted after. He was black but not too black, left wing but not too left wing, fresh but not too militant. He was fêted abroad by all the broadsheets. The vision of America that Obama projected to the world was straight from the playlist of American Testocrats. He was the ointment for a wounded and divided society. When sophisticated Americans held up a mirror to themselves, they saw Obama. And they loved what stared back at them. In the great American culture wars, they had won – or at least that's how it seemed initially.

Testocrats regard themselves as ultimately reasonable people. Nothing too extreme is ever really indulged. Being extreme means you haven't read enough. The angry hectoring left and the bat-shit crazy right are both regarded as slightly infantile and insufficiently considered.

Leo is the ultimate Irish Testocrat. Politically, Leo is to Ireland's Testocracy what Obama was to America's. When Testocrats see our fit, photogenic, well-spoken, intellectual Taoiseach, who also happens to be a doctor, walking arm in arm with Justin Trudeau, speaking French at Montreal's Pride parade, they think that's what their new Ireland looks like.

In the same way Obama was black but not too black, Leo is Indian but not too Indian, gay but not too gay, the type of guy you'd bump into at the sourdough counter in Griffin's Artisanal Bakery in Galway's Shop Street. He is socially left, but economically right – so he will follow the Testocrats' social agenda without threatening their wallets.

If he didn't exist, the Testocracy would have to invent him. He's our Obama. He has the exotic foreign surname, the EU love him and, even when he is bashing the unionists, it never feels like Sinn Féin nationalism. What's not to like?

The Testocrats work in both the public and private sector. They can be on the liberal left or establishment right, but veering to the centre. What unites them is the points race, the entry point to the Testocracy. They are the people who go into hysterics over the Leaving Cert, whipping themselves into a frenzy of familial achievement.

THE ANTI-TESTOCRAT

Affection for the points race is mirrored by a visceral dislike of Conor McGregor. Has there ever been an elite Irish sportsman, in this sports-mad country, who so splits public opinion? The real dividing line in Dublin is not the River Liffey, but Conor McGregor. Where you stand on Conor McGregor reveals a lot about the type of person you are, what class you belong to, what generation you were born into and how you see the future of the country.

McGregor is a threat to the Testocracy because he is from the people who don't pass exams. As a product of the Facebook generation, he understands the urgency of now. His west Dublin, trash-talking swagger embarrasses the Testocracy – particularly when he's abroad.

However, he represents a forgotten tribe. His tribe also gets up early in the morning. They are working people – which the Testocracy regularly confuses with poor people. They don't feature often on radio or TV. They're rarely editorial writers.

In McGregor they see a flawed hero, a man who has achieved extraordinary things, who doesn't hide his ambition and understands that he is in it for the cash. They also understand his fragility.

The McGregor tribe despises the Testocracy because, frankly, Testocrats despise them. In contrast, McGregor's tribe respects the rich. And they truly respect self-made rich men or women. Interestingly, this tribe never vote left, despite starting out poorer than most. They have constantly disappointed liberal Testocrats because they don't vote for the guy who said he was going to give them handouts, as left-leaning Testocrats expect and encourage. This electoral fact is why the Labour Party never does so well in working-class constituencies, largely because the modern Labour Party doesn't understand its supposed constituents.

The McGregor tribe, their fathers and mothers, have spent their working lives taking orders and want to be the guy who gives orders. McGregor gives orders. They want to be like him, rich enough to give everyone the two fingers. They don't respect the Testocrat who has status conferred on him by some club, university, title or exam. They respect the guy who has made it in the free market, who has done it on his own and who has earned his corn in places like the hyper-competitive bearpit that is MMA. That's their Irish Dream and that is the attraction of Conor Mc Gregor.

Both Leo and Conor represent an Irish Dream. Both men are outsiders; both are emblematic of our country and its various tribes. As befits the blurring in modern Ireland, Leo is the northsider who is refined and polished; Conor is the southsider who is rough and feral.

CIRCLE THE WAGONS

A new dividing line between the classes is academic achievement, splitting the world into exam passers, who have the merit, and exam failers, who slip back, the unspoken conclusion being that they have no one to blame but themselves. It might look fair, because we start with natural talent and add in personal effort to generate merit, but there is something more sinister going on.

New studies suggest that the most important indicator of whether or not children do well in exams isn't the schools they attend but the degree of privilege they inherit from their parents. According to *The Irish Times*, 'For schools where both parents of many students were graduates, and where they have been supported throughout their education, getting a college place is no great reflection on the success of their school. Alternatively, we are keenly aware that for schools in disadvantaged communities, securing third-level progression for even a small proportion of students is a reflection of highly motivated teachers, and is a fantastic achievement.'

So the winners reinforce winning ways in their children.

This explains how the system works and the grind school simply reinforces the inequities. The Leaving Cert system only looks fair because all the kids sit the same exam, with only serial numbers to define them. The selling point from the perspective of equity is that no one knows who they are or where they are from. But their preparation is profoundly different, favouring as it does the sons and daughters of the Testocracy. The Exam Whisperers give kids a leg up and they queer the pitch in favour of those who can afford grinds.

The Testocracy is also a ferocious master, demanding greater and greater achievements. A generation ago a job demanded a 'good' Leaving, then it was an undergraduate degree and now it's a Master's. All the time the bar gets higher and higher.

But pushing the bar up might be an implicit tactic of the top 15%. Because, after all, it's expensive to stay in education and who can afford to finance their kids through college for years and years? The already wealthy, of course.

As a result, now that the country has experienced this wonderful surge in growth, opportunity and educational achievement, there is a real danger that all this begins to falter. The consolidating Contented Class, the top 15%, are starting to block the constant social fluidity we have experienced over the past two generations. So, ironically, it is the education system, one of the creators of the Radical Centre surge, that is now being subtly used to put the brakes on and circle the wagons.

And can they circle wagons!

One other threat from the Testocracy is a lack of dissent. At this stage, it is worth remembering that all the 'little mutinies' created the economic surge. These little mutinies were encouraged by the fertility of dissent within the minds of millions of Irish people. Dissent breeds creativity. What happens if the Testocracy turn out to be well educated, but not particularly questioning?

Could it be that their very education may have beaten the enquiring side out of them? Such a contention sounds counter-intuitive because we tend to regard education as being the same as curiosity. But an education system that sets a large memory test as being the arbiter of intelligence doesn't even appear set up to create curious minds. After all, it was the 15%, the Testocracy, who ran the country and drove it off an economic cliff in 2008. These were the cleverest boys in the class, so why didn't they see trouble coming? Could it be because their minds were too closed off to the possibility of being wrong?

In the years ahead, if Ireland is to continue being a world beater, the Radical Centre needs minds that are not full of rigid information, but full of innovative possibilities. Such minds need to be agile, flexible and open to making mistakes in our quest for creativity. And they need to develop coping mechanisms to deal with failure so they can get back up and have another go.

Is the Testocracy, despite all its education, able to deal with uncertainty and knocks? Might the Testocrats who come out top of the class ultimately be the grown-up versions of the mollycoddled children in the back of Sliotar Mom's car?

As well as rule followers, we also need rule breakers, unconventional thinkers in a truly unconventional world.

CHAPTER 23

THE TYRANNY OF CONVENTIONAL WISDOM

T hink about all the changes to the global economy you have experienced in the last few years. Think about how the job-for-life culture, which dominated many professions up to now, is beginning to disappear. Think about how the pension system has moved away from being employer-funded, to one in which you have to look after yourself. Think about all the opportunities that have presented themselves for creative people to innovate and improve their lot.

Underlying all these shifts are large-scale changes to technology, demography and the very way in which we consider the economy and our place in it. People who prosper in the years ahead will be self-reliant tinkerers who face each crisis, adapt and get stronger as a result. In his book *Antifragile*, Nassim Taleb sets out the reality of our world, a world where we cannot eliminate risk and change no matter how hard we might try.

I was thinking about this proposition as I watched the 2018 World Cup. The most beautiful thing about football matches is that things go wrong. The coach's job is to try to bring order to what is essentially a disordered affair. This is why they often look so helpless and agitated on the side-lines, roaring instructions at footballers who are also trying to pick apart the opposition's defence. As the game ebbs and flows, the coach becomes more frustrated. All it needs is one collision with the other team and disorder reigns if they are unable to adapt to the game. All sport is like this; no plan survives the first collision with the enemy. Or, as Mike Tyson put it more succinctly: 'Everyone has a plan until they get a punch in the face.'

The truly great football teams are the ones that can respond to the adversity and figure out a way of winning, not *when* the game plan goes out the window, but *because* the game plan goes out the window.

The economy is similar, because it is nothing more than the accumulation of lots of little human experiences that we all go through every day.

Taleb's central point is that there are essentially three types of humans and, by extension, three types of human system. There are the people (and systems) that wilt in adversity. They are fragile. There are the people (and systems) that survive adversity and cope with change. They are robust. And finally, there are the people (and systems) that thrive on adversity and don't just survive, but embrace change, getting stronger the more change, disorder and randomness they experience around them. They are antifragile.

Bear this in mind as we examine the basis of the Irish Testocracy, the experience all of us go through in school during our formative years.

Is there a danger that being a test passer, a national table quiz winner, might breed a type of conformity when a lack of convention is what we need to prosper in the Renaissance Nation? When the world or the economy is changing, maybe thinking unconventionally is what we need to do. If you allow yourself to think unconventionally, you may see things that others don't.

Conventional thinkers, on the other hand, might not give themselves the freedom to entertain the unexpected. But the unexpected is precisely what happens at tipping points. And maybe, just maybe, the unconventional lateral thinker, who sees the world a bit differently, can see the big picture more clearly.

When the economy is in a state of flux and technology is accelerating the pace of change at an extraordinary rate, the value of being an unconventional thinker, the advantage of being able to think the unthinkable, is unquantifiable.

Are the Testocrats unconventional thinkers? Does the system that the Exam Whisperer has navigated with such robotic application, produce thinkers who are prepared to form their own views and escape the tyranny of the Testocrat peer group?

To answer this question, we must go back to the place where thinking – or at least education – all starts. The Irish classroom, ground zero of the Testocracy.

THE CLASSROOM

Let's go back to school for a few minutes. Do you remember your class when you were 16? Or 13? Or even earlier? Can you remember who you sat beside? Where are they now? Maybe now you appreciate why you skipped the last few school reunions. Alternatively, as you get older you realise that those school bonds are real, shared and affirming because you liked each other.

Now think about the many types of brain that were in your class. Think of all the different types of intelligence on display. What types of intelligence were rewarded by our school system? Did school reward the unconventional brain or punish it?

I'm asking this because, as we get older, we realise that there are many different types of intelligence. But in school we reward or give preference, and thus dignity, to one type. We tend to reward the linear, conventional brain, which can absorb information, store it in a compartment in the head and, in the Leaving Cert, regurgitate it logically on a page in a set time. This is a highly literate brain, capable of performing quite amazing tasks of memory and recollection, within a set time, on the written page. This is undoubtedly a form of intelligence, but arguably it's a conventional intelligence. This type of brain is a bit like a computer, only slower and less accurate.

This aptitude certainly demonstrates astuteness, but it's only one form of many. As Ken Robinson points out, it's the type of intelligence that is great if you want to be a university lecturer. But is that what the system should be, a giant machine mimicking the aspirations of university professors?

Some academics are nice people. I know them and I work with lots of them. In fact, I am one myself now, having recently taken up a position as adjunct professor at Trinity. But the highest form of intelligence? In my experience, many are the opposite of Taleb's gold standard antifragile person, displaying all the features of the truly fragile: insecurity, out-sized pride and intellectual vanity. When they are challenged, their fragility becomes obvious. Academics are very fond of telling people they are wrong and often use their normally quite narrow knowledge base to bully rather than to question and elucidate.

Once you abuse learning like this, you soon end up in dodgy territory. We all know that there are no absolutely right answers, just right questions. People can be both right and wrong at the same time. More of this later. Given that we need to produce antifragile rather than fragile creatures, maybe we are getting it wrong!

Back to the classroom. What about all the other brains in the class? What about the lateral thinkers? The tangential thinkers? What about the daydreamers, those who spent their schooldays looking out the window? What about those unconventional brains? Were their brains rewarded or punished? Were these children, whose beautiful, developing brains worked horizontally, not vertically, offered dignity by the system?

It's fair to say they were not. Their amazing brains were punished and discarded and, maybe more depressingly, they were humiliated and shamed – not because they were not intelligent, but because they possessed a certain type of intelligence that school didn't recognise.

My class was full of these types of brain. People who were demeaned in the great scholastic drive to create a nation of people who look like university professors, but might have great difficulty keeping a corner shop open for a few hours. Consider the impact of being mortified in school on a weekly basis. Many of these people who have gone on to have amazingly interesting lives after school will tell you unprompted that they hated school.

Maybe it wasn't so much that they hated school, as school hated them.

Today, there are many incredibly intelligent people walking around Ireland who left school feeling very stupid. This is unforgiveable. But the corollary may also be true; there are plenty of quite stupid people walking around Ireland who left school feeling very clever.

This is truly terrifying and dangerous.

Terrifying because of the effect that elevating a narrow-gauge Testocrat form of intelligence can have on a small society. Dangerous because of where this leads.

Small societies rely on networks and biases. Networks work; if you are in any doubt, reflect on the history of the Freemasons, or even the Jesuits. In a small country, networks work dangerously well. Rather than expanding the base, which is what an open network like Facebook can facilitate by making all sorts of random connections, closed networks like educational, collegiate and professional networks can have the opposite effect. Such networks can narrow the pool rather than expand it. Whether they are a bunch of Jihadis or a suburban book club, networks tend to reinforce their own biases.

CONFIRMATION BIAS

Think about the children whose conventional brains were rewarded and fêted from day one in the Irish education system. For years, the teachers told them that they were brilliant. They were top of the class in the top stream in the top schools, doing honours everything. Every day, this impression of being part of an elite was reinforced. These are the chosen ones. Their mammies, of course, told them they were the best.

The system is their system, devised by people like them, the university professorship, at a time when work was industrialised and intelligence was very much linked to memory. A world before Google.

It is also a system that believes in the single right answer. As noted above, as we get older, we realise that there are many right answers, but in the school classroom there is only ever one single right answer. How many times have teachers – through no fault of their own – dismissed the inquisitive student by telling them, 'Don't be worrying about that, it won't be coming up in the exam'?

Unfortunately, the teachers too are trapped in the system. I come from a family of teachers, so I have huge sympathy for them. They see the problems, but their job is to grind the kids through the system, particularly the points system, because Testocracy reigns. Parents, who now sneer at their own parents and grandparents for their religious faith, put their entire store of faith in a coming-of-age ritual whose worth is dubious, to say the least, and is nothing more than a university bottleneck through which many beautifully creative teenage brains are squashed every year.

Rather than focus on the ones who were disgraced in front of their peers in class, our Testocracy focuses on the winners. Is it any surprise that these students, the winners, who do very well in school, then go on to college and do very well again, begin to believe that they have all the answers? I'd feel that way too if I was being told I was great and eulogised all the time.

Then these people get jobs in the big institutions, the corporate world, the civil service and above all, the Irish professions. The relative worth of their conventional, literal and narrow-gauged brains is constantly reinforced. The behavioural economist Dan Ariely points out in *Predictably Irrational* that all humans suffer from a dilemma, an inbuilt bias which nudges us first to surround ourselves with people who think like us and, ultimately, to employ people who think like us.

This phenomenon is called confirmation bias in behavioural economics. As Ariely points out, we humans in general like people who confirm our own biases, who hold similar views to us, who make us feel good about ourselves and secure in our positions. It's human nature. It's nobody's fault. That's just the way we are.

But in a small society like Ireland, it is not hard to see why, gradually, as the conventional tribe of exam passers climb up the corporate and bureaucratic ladder, we get groupthink at the very top. In no time, all the key decision makers end up thinking the same way, which is when things begin to get dangerous.

When the supposed smartest people in the room coalesce together at the very top and look at the world and its possibilities in the same way, they can make massive errors.

Speaking of errors, there is another small problem with groupthink at the top. The people in this group derive their status, both professional and personal, in always being right. All their lives, they were the ones with the right answers. They were the ones at the top of the class with their hands up. If you have always been right, it's very difficult, almost impossible, to admit that you might be wrong, not least because your sense of yourself is wrapped up with always being right. But you are only truly learning when you are wrong. You are not learning when you are right, because you know the stuff. So being wrong is the way to true knowledge.

But if admitting you might be wrong is an affront to you, there is a possibility that you will cling on to thinking you are right, even when events are telling you that you are wrong.

It's not difficult to see why groupthink at the top, allied with this pathological fear of being wrong, can be rather alarming in a small society. Think about the great Irish economic, housing, banking and credit bust in 2008. Why did so few warn of the housing bubble building from 2000 to 2008? What were the conventional brains, the people who ran the place, doing? Why did they not see it coming? It was because they all employed their mates at the top, people who thought the same. No one was brave enough to break away from the tyranny of the peer group. So rather than listening to the few who said, 'Hang on, this thing is built on sand,' the smartest people in the room tried to humiliate, degrade and undermine the doubters. This is what they had learnt in school when the sceptical kids whose brains worked differently asked questions: they needed to be humbled rather than entertained. The same thing happened here as the Testocracy marched the country off a financial cliff, repeating the 'soft landing' mantra.

The conventional brain does not like to change its mind. As the great Canadian economist J.K. Galbraith observed wickedly: 'When faced with the choice between changing his mind and finding the proof not to do so, the conventional man always gets busy looking for the proof.'

In the years ahead, when faced with randomness, risk and serendipity, will the Testocracy change its mind or get busy looking for the proof?

This is a huge and unexplored threat to the Radical Centre. We have, over time, replaced our ideology, the conservative censorious theocracy that governed Ireland from 1920 to about 1990. This form of fundamentalism squeezed the cultural, artistic and economic life out of the place. The little mutinies gradually emerged victorious, liberating millions. We need to make sure that that fundamentalism isn't replaced by another form of zealotry, a Testocrat fundamentalism, whose creed is the Leaving Cert, whose high priests are citizens of the Banana Republic armed with Master's degrees, ready to snuff out dissent, discord and thus creativity, just because it doesn't suit their accepted suite of beliefs.

THE EXAM WHISPERER GOES OVER THE PAPER

The Exam Whisperer looks down at the class. The final grind before the big day. They look petrified. There is so much to cover and so little time to cover it. The trick now is to go over as many past papers as possible. Don't bother with anything that might not come up. Let's focus on the four big questions. Learn your four essays off by heart. Remember the marking scheme. The examiner doesn't care about your opinion. List the facts. Don't elaborate. Make sure you give each question the same amount of time. Show your workings so the examiner sees your methods. Remember, regurgitate the notes.

It's all about the Five R's now. Repeat, Rehearse, Reiterate, Recite and Restate.

Take a deep breath, open the paper, scan the questions, mark the ones you recognise and … ready, steady, go! Write like fuck!

CHAPTER 24

TOO MUCH OF A GOOD THING?

It may strike you as odd for me to pick out the Testocrats and the Banana Republicans as being a threat to the prosperity of the nation, particularly as they hold so much of the prosperity of the nation. Surely you might think that the biggest threat to the Renaissance Nation is an upsurge in the type of nativism that we see in Trump's America, Brexit Britain, Le Pen's France, amongst the Catalan nationalists or indeed the Italian Northern League, driven by the outsiders, the excluded and the marginalised who vote radical to recover a stake in society that they have lost.

This story, in which discontentment with globalisation, stagnant living standards and social exclusion drive populism, is the one we all accept. This is the story that fits nicely into our worldview. It sounds plausible. The only problem is that it's not true. Have you ever considered that possibly the opposite is the case and it wasn't trauma that led to Brexit or Trump, but the lack of trauma? The always excellent Janan Ganesh of the *Financial Times* suggests that the driving force of populism isn't so much hardship but the lack of hardship. His argument – and also that of US economist Tyler Cowen, one of the finest economists writing anywhere in the world these days – is that complacency, not exclusion, drives radicalism. When you look at the numbers this is a more plausible story than the one about the great uprising of the unwashed against the establishment.

The majority of people who voted for Trump were not just the white underclass, but the white middle and upper middle classes too. Polls from the Republican primaries revealed that only a third of Trump supporters had household incomes at or below the national median of about $50,000. Another third of Trump Republicans made $50,000 to $100,000, and the final third made $100,000 or more. In fact, in the presidential election, Clinton defeated Trump handily among Americans making less than $50,000 a year. And while Trump won white voters at every level of class and income, they weren't just angry white men. The majority of white women voted for the misogynist Trump over the white female feminist, Hillary Clinton.

The same goes for Brexit. The people who voted 'Leave' were not only the council estates of Sunderland, but also much of the affluent South East, home to the broad middle class of England. In addition, the leaders of both nativist movements – Trump himself and the Eton-educated cabal of Johnson and Gove – are not refugees from the lower orders intent on overturning the establishment. They are in both cases the pinnacle of the plutocratic establishment itself.

So there is something else going on.

Could it be that a generation of stability, economic growth and relative luxury has made the middle ground of the US and the UK so complacent that they are prepared to take massive political risks, simply because they have forgotten where taking a risk can lead you? They dabbled with radicalism not because they were poor but because they were bored? Perhaps the fainter the memories of bad times, the more willing the middle ground is to take a big political leap into the unknown. Countries where the memories of hard times are vivid and real tend not to oscillate wildly and gravitate towards the centre, understanding that politics is not theatre; it is real and can lead to real outcomes. On an individual level, if your memories of life are of hardship and sacrifice, the decisions you make are serious. If your most challenging recent decisions in life were a decent holiday, gluten-free pasta, a second car or a kitchen extension, you are more likely to see the drama, but not the seriousness in politics. Such weakness for drama or free-wheeling adventure is what leads the bored, complacent voter to opt for the celebrity romp of Donald Trump or Boris Johnson.

When we look at the numbers, we can see that extremism is an almost adolescent reaction from people who have had it too good, rather than too bad. In Ireland, the threat to the Radical Centre from the Testocracy, Quango Man and the Banana Republicans is something that we should not overlook. At this stage, the main threat to the Radical Centre is not a giant leap in the dark but more likely a stubborn dragging of heels from the Testocrats and Banana Republicans who are slowing down the regeneration needed to drive the Renaissance Nation. Any sanction on building and development to protect their own patch slows down the very physical acts of moving. For Ireland to continue to maintain our rates of economic achievement, we must remain a restless nation, moving houses, changing jobs, migrating in and out of the country. As Tyler Cowen observes, 'the purpose of moving is self-transformation', and so anything that seeks to limit these opportunities, limits individual, and thus national, self-transformation. Earlier in the book we looked at how virtues like hope and belief in the future are the essential background noise for the 'have a go' nation. Anything that stops that, stops the self-recharging battery of commercial self-expression.

THE TAXI DRIVER VERSUS THE UNIVERSITY LECTURER

The Testocracy is that, of course, the educated cohort regard themselves as tolerant, and will readily tell you so. Traditionally, when we think of the typical intolerant, we think of a taxi driver mouthing off about this and that. In contrast, the quinoa-eating, Voltaire-reading, Arcade Fire-listening, hyper-educated Testocrat is the paragon of liberal diversity and freedom of expression. But when we dig a bit deeper, we find something very interesting.

The key aspect that drove the Renaissance Nation was the victory of the free-thinking individual over the censorious Cleristocracy. The Cleristocracy bullied and suppressed the individual, until finally the individual couldn't take any more, prompting the millions of little mutinies. The Cleristocracy was all about telling people what to do, how to think and how to act. Once they were confronted and defeated, the great energy of hundreds of thousands of enquiring minds sparked the Renaissance Nation, seen most evidently in the growth rates and all the attendant social achievements. Once we stopped telling people what to think, the country was transformed.

Now, here is the dilemma.

Survey data shows us that Testocrats, the exam-passing aristocracy that run large parts of the country, are highly intolerant, not tolerant. In fact, taxi drivers are more tolerant, free-thinking and more likely to encourage others to think what they want than university lecturers. The latest survey evidence shows those with Master's degrees are much more likely to want to tell people what to do and how to behave than the typically lampooned taxi driver. The Testocracy runs the risk of being the new Cleristocracy in censoring the nation.

In a recent survey,[98] people were asked whether they agreed or disagreed with the statement that 'People should be free to do as they wish. This creates a better society.' Before we dip into the results, take a second and honestly ask yourself: where do you stand?

The odds are that you're likely to rank amongst the broad swathe of Irish citizens who adopt the statist view – the 57% of us who disagree with the statement, rather than the 43% minority of free spirits whose conviction is that people should be free to do as they wish. Of course, I am assuming you're of a certain vintage. There's an old quip that if you're not a liberal in your twenties, you have no heart; if you're not a conservative in your forties, you have no head. This is borne out in the survey, with a whopping 73% of millennials (aged 18–24) being more free spirited in their outlook. This compares to the minority of around 40% amongst all other age brackets.

Of course, age is not the only dividing line on this issue. Indeed, based on party affiliation, Fine Gaelers emerged as the most statist with 70% adopting the view that people should not be totally free. At the other end of the spectrum, Sinn Féin was the only party with which a majority of free spirits identified, and even then, the margin was a slim 52% free spirit to 48% statist. Of note, however, is that this poll was conducted before Leo

Varadkar, who himself identifies with the live and let live position, took over the helm and, perhaps, broadened his party's support.

More interesting still is that the most educated amongst us, those who excelled at the upper-echelons of the Irish education system, tend to be far, far more statist than those with little formal education. A mere 34% of those with a university degree believe people should be free to live their lives as they wish, compared to 48% amongst those whose education ceased following the Leaving Cert. Meanwhile, those who dropped out of secondary school (55%) and those with only a primary school education (59%) are by far and away the most live-and-let-live people in the country.

We see the knock-on effects of this when we look at which career paths have the most statist and free-spirited individuals. As I mentioned earlier, it is the lecturers and solicitors amongst us who are most statist, with 100% of both surveyed feeling that restrictions must be placed upon the freedom of others. They are not alone, of course, with others who tell people what to do or what to think for a living, such as teachers (83%), social workers (82%), nurses (78%) and bankers (77%) adopting the statist view. By contrast, it is the understanding and tolerant taxi drivers, who actually have skin in the game, earning their keep day in and day out in the private sector, who are the most libertarian. Joining them in their belief that people should be free to live as they see fit are the reliable secretaries (100%), the humble bus drivers (80%) and the unassuming electricians (82%).

A word of warning: we see an element of triumphalism among some of the repeal campaigners after the 'Yes' vote. I understand the urge, believe me I do. However, what carried the day were the silent revolutionaries. This is the Radical Centre and it lives side by side with the 723,632 anti-choice voters. There may have been twice as many 'Yes' voters, 1,429,981 in all, but there is no future in vilifying the 'No' vote.

Such almost evangelical certainty and haughty sneering at the other side of the culture war threatens the Radical Centre because it is the broadest of broad churches, capable of housing the maximum of responsible individuals under its architraves. If the Testocrats become an over-educated but intolerant caste, we risk groupthink, and we all know where that got us in the past.

A final thought on the threats to the Radical Centre from the Testocracy. As society progresses and technology delivers more and more artificial intelligence to us, it is quite likely that the types of brain valued by the exam-passing class are the ones that will be most easily cloned by robots. The national pub quiz winners have great memories, but they are much slower than robots. The robot can easily replicate IQ, but it can't replicate emotional intelligence. Those people with emotional intelligence will be extremely valuable. They are typically the people who are not the best at passing exams but are very good at people skills.

If robots take over from the exam passers, do you think the exam passers who are used to the nice fruits at the top of the tree are going to give up without a fight? Such a shift in the tectonic plates of the country could be very damaging, because the exam passers were always told that they were on top because of merit, that in some sense they were better than the others, that it's their achievements that have them on top. It could be hard for them to adjust downwards.

The disruption might not be so welcome this time.

In order to make the Renaissance Nation ready for the future, we have to make a few small changes to make sure that inertia and stasis don't replace the restless drive that propelled the Pope's Children forward.

PART 4
THE NEW REPUBLIC

CHAPTER 25

THE ROAD AHEAD

In the previous few chapters, we have been examining the silent, seemingly innocuous threats to the Radical Centre and the Renaissance Nation, which can be found right in front of our noses.

These threats are insidious because they are slow burners, rooted in complacency and driven by a desire on the part of those who have done very well to preserve their wealth and status. These are the sorts of threats that sneak up on you slowly, and gradually elbow out the people who want to energise the economy. The Quangomen and the Testocrats in the Banana Republic might not even realise what they are doing, or at least they can't see the big picture. Through no fault of their own, they don't tie it all together. They don't understand that when you add up all the little protests against development, all the modest strictures to more people moving into already wealthy areas with great public services, good transport connections and lovely open spaces, you denigrate the very dynamism and restlessness that fuelled the Renaissance Nation in the first place. When you object to intensive development and when you pay for grinds for your kids, you are making the playing field unequal.

At the heart of macroeconomics is something called the paradox of aggregation. This can be understood through the idea that what is good for the individual is not always good for the collective. So when a small group of individuals, acting in their own self-interest, succeed in blocking a big infrastructure project like a metro line, they deliver something good for themselves as individual protestors, but they undermine and damage the interests of a much greater number of people, known as the entire collective or the greater community.

Because of this, it is very easy for the entire country to be hijacked by the vested interests of these individuals, thus slowing down the entire process. And if like-minded Testocrats are at the top making decisions, rather than the more diverse talent pool that reflects the broad population, we will make mistakes. Inertia is the enemy of progress because inertia is essentially about avoiding risk.

The catalyst to national economic energy is taking a risk, backing yourself and having a go. This is the essence of commercial self-expression and individual self-transformation. One of the jobs of the state is to encourage this endeavour and to dignify such individual effort so that taken together, it becomes an irresistible collective force that propels the nation forward.

So it's not hard to see how the Radical Centre could be threatened by the Contented Class, who want to preserve the status quo. The more we preserve the status quo and try to insulate ourselves from change, like the individually wrapped child, the more we will become fragile and less capable of dealing with the immediate threats we face in a rapidly changing world.

In this final section, I am going to look at the broader economic challenges the Renaissance Nation faces. I'd like to take you on a small journey into the future – not too far, just a few years from now. I would like to examine a number of things we could do in Ireland to make the Renaissance Nation more robust, to spread the wealth around, to fix the accommodation conundrum and to re-energise the place.

THE CHALLENGES

The first of our challenges is technology and globalisation. Since 2008, Ireland has become much more exposed to global trends – and globalisation has been good to Ireland. Think of everything we associate with it: free trade, global communications, multinational companies investing all over the world, the internet, Spotify, Facebook, cheap travel, Ryanair, dairy-free milk, Tinder, democracy, tolerance, free speech, marriage equality, Sky Sports, hip replacements and, of course, the free flow of people in and out of the country. You may say that we Irish suit the global village. We've been globalised through emigration for years; when the great world opened, we were happy to hold the door and then jump into the party.

Accompanying globalisation is technology. The economy has been changed so profoundly by technology that the economy that crashed in 2008 is a totally different beast to the economy you are living and working in right now. Although technology is a great enabler, it also increases the price of failure. If you have a weakness, technology will find it. In the old days we could make mistakes and be secure in the knowledge that these mistakes could be rectified because there would be time to deal with the failure. Today, technology is making the economy accelerate so quickly that the costs of mistakes are amplified and are levied immediately. We will discuss the impact of technology on the jobs market and the housing market in Chapters 26 and 27.

Speaking of houses, another economic challenge we face is feudalism. Yes, you read it right. By feudalism I mean when the interests of a landed aristocracy are squeezing the life out of a generation through high rents and unaffordable housing. We see this most clearly in the Dublin housing market, but I will explain how it infects so much more and, in economic terms, how it is making the underlying growth engine weaker, while appearing to make it stronger.

If this feudalism is not addressed, it could lead to a political and social youthquake, because the young are being penalised and the old rewarded. As I get older I can see this more clearly. They say that you know you're getting old when you think the cops look very young; a true sign of ageing is when most of the cabinet is younger than you. However, because of the way Ireland's feudal land system transfers wealth from the young to the old, in truth the old are the power-brokers; they have the cash. The young, who can't afford rents or mortgages, feel increasingly left behind. This means they have to stay at home longer than previous generations did.

This is not just an economic dilemma, it also creates a societal dilemma that shifts family dynamics, and it means that growing up in Ireland is not what it used to be. If you can't move out, you don't grow up. This is a simple statement of fact. As mentioned when we met The Sleeve and The Fringe earlier, growing up involves certain milestones, such as moving out from your parents' place, maybe moving in with your partner or sharing with friends. It involves having a job that pays decently, allowing you to save a bit and plan for your future, perhaps with one eye on starting a family if you meet the right person. And for most, these milestones involve settling down and getting your own place. All this was achievable for my generation by our late twenties. It wasn't easy, but it wasn't impossible. This is what becoming an adult means, more or less. It is not open to many of our young people now and these milestones have been pushed out by a decade or more.

If growing up is retarded because of the housing and land market, then this must be fixed. This means confronting some vested interests in society. Otherwise the young will reject the Radical Centre that their parents worked so hard and so long to achieve. The young might not have their own home, but they have a vote.

A GEORGIAN FUTURE?

The vested interest is the land lobby, which retains a feudal-style grip on Irish wealth. This group is at odds with the central idea underpinning the Radical Centre, which is that economic growth comes from innovation, and innovation comes from the liberation of the creative processes of the human imagination. It is the human imagination that creates something out of nothing.

Another conundrum is that our public reverence for land prevents us from taxing that land and the wealth associated with it. This over-burdens taxes on wages and ordinary goods, which (a) reduces take-home pay and (b) increases the cost of living. Thus, despite being prosperous, individuals don't have enough money left at the end of the week to save for a home. The fact that the price of that home is far too high is because the returns to the economy are going disproportionately to landowners, which is, unless it is farmed, a useless, uninventive asset. Easy money leads to a drone class of landowners, skimming off too much of the economy's surplus and passing it on to their children.

Land ownership and land interests got lucky in the sense that the energy released by the culture war, which drove the Renaissance Nation and led to the Radical Centre, was so volcanic that it allowed the country to power ahead without fixing the land issue. The property crash, related of course to the intersection of the interests of Irish property, Irish banks that used land as collateral and the political system gouging tax revenue from property, should have led to a total rethink of the role of land in the Irish psyche. But it didn't. The interests of Irish property, which have ransomed the average citizen for years with ridiculous houses prices and vertical rents, dug in deep, double-downed and emerged from a property crash with an even stronger stranglehold on the commanding heights of the economy. NAMA transferred vast swathes of Irish property to foreign funds, creating a new breed of absentee landlord, a loaded term in Irish history.

Looking to the future, artificially expensive property prices here shouldn't be allowed to last. For example, since 2015, although wages have risen by about 3%, house prices have gone up by almost 35% and rents by almost 42%.[99] This is neither sustainable nor desirable.

Unless we prise away the ownership of the land from the hands of the very few, the youth of Ireland will understandably become restless and the country will become uncompetitive, because all costs will rise in tandem. There is also a significant wealth element to this, which is not consistent with democratic liberal values. Although income inequality has improved in Ireland, and all incomes have risen, wealth inequality has not changed. Ireland is not out of step with the rest of Europe, but wealth inequality, in both absolute and relative terms, is too large. The top 10% own over 50% of the wealth, and over 85% of this wealth is tied up in land. Such a feudal underpinning is not what a modern society should look like or, indeed, rest on. As we know, human creativity drives innovation, which drives commerce. Land has no creative value other than being propped up by a feudal infrastructure of taxes, lobbyist pressures, restrictive legislation and planning impasses. We tax labour heavily relative to land. The tax from land is a tiny fraction of the total.

There is a way to address this implausible state of affairs through gradual liberal tinkering rather than anything too revolutionary. We could go down the extreme route because, as land can't up and leave the country, it's a sitting duck. But that's not the way we do things. We don't need to default to the radical left or radical right framework.

There is a Radical Centrist way of doing this, based on the ideas of the most popular book in America in the 1880s and 1890s. We will look at this in more detail in Chapter 31.

MAKING CAPITAL DANCE

One other economic challenge is how we position ourselves with respect to the multinationals in the years ahead. We could inject an innovative new departure in how the Renaissance Nation treats foreign capital. With the threats to the global economy and our multinationals coming in hard and fast, from various nativist movements of the right, to the 'tax all capital' urges from the left, to the unified corporation tax drive by Macron in the EU, to Trump's 'bring-'em-all-back-home' corporate strategy, it is important that the Renaissance Nation remains one step ahead of the game, offering options rather than just accepting other agendas. There is an opportunity for us to use our sovereignty to completely change the relationship between the nation state and the corporate state by speaking directly to the shareholders of these companies.

The Radical Centre might explore the idea of treating the multinationals like an oil find, taking stock in the companies rather than just taking tax. As Norway does with its oil revenues, we could allow this stock to build up over time into the national wealth fund. Such wealth ought to be used not as a pension fund, but as a start-up fund for the Renaissance Nation, with the state using each citizen's stake in this multinational wealth fund as individual collateral for the next generation to have a go, to express themselves commercially. We should look to it as providing start-up funding for the young, rather than as a winding-down fund for the old, which is what a pension fund actually is.

The logical way of building on the huge commercial and social achievements of the past forty years would be to press on with turning the country into an entrepreneurial vessel, generating the resources to pay for social policies to improve the lot of more and more people. The independent creative worker/owner represents the direction the world is going. Significantly, this development is not driven by politics but by technological changes and the reality of the new economy.

Technology is rapidly disrupting old business models and the world is now increasingly set up to reward the independent commercial player rather than the salaried employee of the twentieth century. As the Radical Centre is founded on the independent entrepreneur or intrapreneur who takes responsibility, we are in a good position to profit from the new technology, the new ways of doing business, the new, skin-in-the-game environment that is shaping our lives. So in the next chapter let's look at the intersection between economics and technology.

Although such transformational change sounds daunting, there's nothing to be afraid of. The Renaissance Nation can and will adapt because its heroes are freethinking individuals who have risen to the challenges of the last forty years better than almost anyone else in the western world. While many of our neighbours have become mired in political extremism, running up ideological culs-de-sac and wanting to turn the clock back, we have been forging ahead, dispensing with dogma, embracing individual freedom and opening the door to all comers. Why not back ourselves again?

At the end of our journey, in the final chapter, we'll look at maybe the biggest challenge of all: the wild card of Northern Ireland. One hundred years after the border was drawn to preserve a Protestant majority in the North, that majority has grown increasingly slender and, therefore, it is only a matter of time before the border comes into play again. Even if Brexit hadn't happened, the demographics are moving so quickly towards nationalism and away from unionism that the border and a United Ireland would likely have been back on the table, sooner or later. Brexit has accelerated the entire process. (A disclosure here: my wife is from that Northern tribe, so my children are the Good Friday Agreement incarnate.)

We will head up to the North, chat to my in-laws, their friends and a few new mates. You might find yourself in a chipper opposite the Seamus Heaney centre, devouring a spice bag served by a Chinese man with a Belfast accent in a Bellaghy Wolfe Tones GAA jersey, or discussing the Bible with the moderator of the Presbyterian Assembly in Ballygilbert Presbyterian Church outside Bangor. Either way, we will try to assess a likely way forward, twenty years after the Belfast Agreement and almost 100 years after partition, against the background of a demographic clock that ticks rhythmically towards a United Ireland.

But for now let's stay down south. Remember what I was saying about growing up not being the same in Ireland as it was when I was in my twenties and early thirties? Let's dig a bit deeper by meeting the people who came of age in the crash. You have met some before like The Sleeve, The Fringe and Flat White Man, but now let's examine the economic challenges that generation faces and why these challenges need to be sorted out if the Renaissance Nation is to progress from here.

CHAPTER 26

THE CRASH KIDS

THE GREAT SELFIE DIVIDE

For most of our journey we have been covering the lifetime of the Pope's Children, beginning in 1979, exploring the peak of Catholicism in the 1980s with the referendums on abortion and divorce, explaining how the economy slumped when we were conservative and regressive and then started to take off when we became more enlightened. In the last 30 years, the economy has grown twice as fast as our neighbours'. Starting in 1990, the performance has generated resources for us to address many, but not all social problems. As we became more tolerant, we became richer.

In this chapter, let's look specifically at the past 10 years. There is a subplot in this part of our story, which will define the next decade or two, and it is audacious in its novelty and breath-taking in its potential opportunity.

We know that Ireland has emerged as one of the most globalised nations on earth in terms of trade, investment, immigration and emigration. We are small, with an extremely high level of immigration and a mobile workforce, many of our domestic companies are exporters and our multinational sector means that we are highly affected by decisions taken far away. We have turned all these factors into positive forces, serving us well.

In contrast, many of our neighbours have recoiled from this globalised world, and indeed anti-globalisation is the rallying cry for many of the new political movements from the nostalgic right to the protectionist left. Popular parties promise to isolate their societies from the rigours of global competition and return to an imagined past, where life was better, purer – but of course this is entirely fabricated. The Renaissance Nation, on the other hand, has embraced the modern world with positive and self-reinforcing results.

However, economics has a habit of affecting different generations in different ways. These distinct generational experiences can have a profound impact on the various generations' worldviews. And when it comes to technological change, every society experiences generational divides as one generation is exposed to change and embraces it as 'normal' while another generation tries to insulate itself against it, fearing change as disruptive or even incomprehensible. So my dad couldn't use a remote control, which was described as 'a cod', as were electric lawnmowers, three-in-one stereos and SodaStreams. I'm the same with my kids and Snapchat!

Such generational distinctiveness always strikes me, whether I'm teaching at Trinity or working with brilliant 20-somethings making documentaries. While I'm not a total luddite, technology is the real divide between my generation, born in the late 1960s and who came of working age in the very early Celtic Tiger period, and those who were in school and college when the economy crashed in 2008. Let's call this generation the Crash Kids. They are referred to as elsewhere as millennials, but because of Ireland's exceptional social and economic history over the past 40 years, quite different to any other country in Europe, and because of the depth of the economic crash here, their life experiences as Irish young adults have been unique. Some of the characters we met earlier, like The Sleeve, The Fringe, Ballet Blonde and Flat White Man, are Crash Kids.

The main divide between us, apart from wrinkles, crunchy knees and not having the urge to photograph my next dinner, is technological. It's time to explore this generation gap and how it will affect the Renaissance Nation in the years ahead. But before we look forward, let's look back.

A few years ago, I was asked to write a little account of my memories of Trinity College in the 1980s. It was flattering to be asked, but I was a shy enough student and always somewhat intimidated by the undergraduate debater types so I really didn't have much to say about college life, bar the fact that I enjoyed it, made some great mates, had a laugh. Academically, I was okay, not top of the class, not bottom either, and I spent an inordinate amount of time in the snug in Kehoes with a few other eejits who have become lifelong friends.

When I submitted the article, the publisher asked for a few photographs of me in college. Amazing as it must sound for younger readers, I couldn't find any. There are hardly any photos of me during my four-year stint in university. I asked my mother, who is normally a treasure trove for such things. She had none. I asked a few of the eejits; they had none either, not of any of us. I am from an invisible generation. We simply didn't take photos of each other during our formative years. Few of us had cameras. This must be impossible for anyone under 30 to understand. I lived in a world largely without cameras.

I have about four photos of myself from the 1970s in primary school, a little gap-toothed freckly redser making his communion with a splendid red rosette in a tiny Guineys suit. I also have plenty of photos of myself with my children from my mid-30s on. But from the age of 12 to my wedding day, I don't really exist. This is cool with me. I have a camera in my head; it's called my memory of those days, vivid pictures in my brain, of great times, wonderful people and significant moments. I am simply from the generation that didn't feel the need to document everything, didn't find it necessary to strike endless poses and, most importantly, I never took a selfie until I was far too old for it.

It wasn't because we were not vain – we were – we just didn't have the technology to look at ourselves constantly, nor did we have Facebook, Instagram or Twitter to share photos. Without the technology, there was no demand for photos, so none were taken.

This chapter will be about how technology is driving and changing the economy in ways we never thought imaginable.

2008 WAS THE BEGINNING, NOT THE END

After writing that piece about Trinity, I began to look at the world differently. I divided it into the world before selfies and the world after selfies. I am from a pre-selfie world, living in a selfie globe.

Us pre-selfie people have a different attitude to things, our careers have been different and our relationships have been quite unlike those of the selfie generation. Different too are the stories we tell ourselves and the factors we deem important. Our narrative is distinct to our generation.

You can see this distinction when you look at how we viewed the events of the last decade.

For my generation, 2008 was traumatic. It marked the end of the boom. For us, the year 2008 is defined by the property market collapse, the banks running out of money and the government being forced to choose between a bank guarantee and a bank run. The year 2008 is about unemployment rising rapidly. It's about builders in ghost estates all over the country downing tools. It was the year thousands emigrated, the year the government began to go bust, the year the tax take slumped. It marked the moment when the deficit started to rise and the Irish bond market, which measured the interest rates on Irish government borrowings, started to show the first signs of panic.

The period between 2008 and the arrival of the IMF in October 2010 is painted as marking the end of an era. The political air was heavy with fatalism and economic despondency. There was a sense that the country which had shone so brightly for a few years had come crashing down to earth. We had reached the end of the line.

In fact, 2008 marked the beginning of something much bigger, something that would profoundly change this country.

For the Crash Kids, 2008 is year zero. Just as the old economy was crashing down around our ears, a new economy was starting to make its presence felt. In a few short years, this new economy would have a massive impact on the lives of millions of Irish people. This generation, the Crash Kids, are the 500,000 people who were of secondary school or university age during the crash, whose memory of the boom is very sketchy.

However, because my generation were adults in the boom and went through the crash as grown-ups, our house prices collapsed, we lost our jobs, emigrated, lost our houses and became understandably angry. The Irish story we told ourselves was one of recrimination, anger and incompetence verging on the criminal. And maybe because most of the media and opinion influencers were from my generation or older, our story of failure dominated the newswires.

But what about the generation that came of age during the crash, the Crash Kids? What was influencing their story and how will that story impact on their lives and, ultimately, everyone's lives?

The countervailing narrative reads a bit differently. As everything in the world of the pre-selfies was shattering, in the world of the post-selfie generation, the Crash Kids, it was going off in a totally different direction, opening up fresh opportunities, new ways of communicating, learning, buying and selling. In fact, a whole new way of life emerged after 2008. In 2008, technological innovations that changed the way we live were being launched, almost on a weekly basis. New technology was not just being made available to almost everyone, but it was being introduced at a pace never before seen in human history.

The pace of things is important because, while the old economy became involved in the glacial trench warfare of recrimination, the new economy sped ahead, transforming everything in its wake.

For example, in March 2008, the share price of Anglo Irish Bank collapsed. That's the old story. Anglo was the canary in the coalmine. Once it went, so too did the rest of the banking system. The end of the banks was something that had been building for years.

But something else also happened in March 2008 which was to have an enormous impact. On 1 March 2008, just as shareholders were selling Anglo, Apple launched the iPhone in Ireland.[100] That month, AOL also bought Bebo, the most popular social network in Ireland at the time.[101] A few days later, Apple released the first software kit for the iPhone and 100,000 copies of it were downloaded in the first four days.[102]

The following month, in April 2008, as the Leinster House media obsessed about Bertie Ahern's long goodbye, the rest of the world was accelerating ahead and focusing on something totally different. The iPhone 3G was launched. The implication of this sort of connectivity was not fully appreciated at the time. Worldwide, one million 3G-enabled devices were sold in the first weekend.[103] That should have told us that something was afoot.

In 2008, the smartphone brought the internet into people's pockets, making the internet much more valuable because it was now available all the time. As Thomas Friedman points out, 'the internet in turn made the smartphone much more valuable because you could plug into the world from your phone'.

But it was not just the union of these two technologies that made 2008 special in Ireland. Even as the banks collapsed, Irish people were beginning to connect across the world and all the time.

In July 2008, the Apple App Store was opened. Ten million apps were downloaded in the first week.[104] A couple of weeks later, in August, while the older generation were terrified by the Irish banks scrambling to pretend they had cash, Brian Chesky and his Airbnb co-founders were selling Obama-themed cereal at the DNC convention to gain publicity for their fledgling site,[105] around the same time as the Anglo fellas were 'pulling figures out of their arses'. Out of work and with only $1,000 in the bank, they had been looking to raise money to pay the rent on their flat, which was $1,150. So the three friends advertised for guests and served them breakfast. The 'air' bit comes from the fact that they originally planned to offer airbeds to their guests. It took off. Punters came to stay and loved the idea that they could hang out with two local young lads for a few dollars and have the craic.

Airbnb would later revolutionise tourism all over the world, Ireland included. It is the largest, fastest-growing hospitality network in human history, an online global home-sharing site with an inventory of four million rooms.[106] Airbnb adds 300,000 new users and 60,000 rooms to its network each week. In contrast, Marriott-Starwood, the world's largest hotel chain, has 1.2 million hotel rooms.[107]

In September 2008, when the banks in Ireland told the government they would be bust the following morning, the first Android OS device was launched,[108] and Intel, based out in Leixlip, introduced nano-silicon material into its microchips for the first time.[109] This allowed computer power to expand exponentially. While the rest of the economy was contracting, the labs in Leixlip were operating at full tilt as the global demand for extra computing power went bonkers with all these new devices powering up.

Within a year, we had the iPhone (the device), the 3G connectivity (the pathway) and the new much more powerful chips (the power), allowing far more computing power to flow into the device in your pocket, transforming the world in the process.

In October 2008, Facebook, a company that was then only four years old, set up its European headquarters in Dublin.[110] At the time, very few people appreciated what this company would end up doing to the world of advertising, of news and ultimately of politics. Three days later, as ghost estates were being deserted and our traditional financial markets were collapsing in Ireland, over in Japan an obscure research paper was published by someone called Satoshi Nakamoto, entitled 'Bitcoin: A Peer-to-Peer Electronic Cash System'.[111] Crypto-currencies were born as our old currency, the euro, came under increased speculative attack.

Meanwhile, a couple of Swedish music-loving geeks, fed up with paying so much for CDs, thought there might be another way of doing things. In October 2008, they launched a music streaming company called Spotify.[112] In a few years, the music industry, which had been a cash cow for decades, would be changed beyond recognition, with enormous (mostly negative) ramifications for artists while a boom for festivals. To give you a sense of how streaming would change the music industry and how quickly, by 2018, Drake's new album *Scorpion* hit one billion streams in its first week.[113] In 2008, streaming was still a thing of the future. The Crash Kids' world was changing at a pace that few appreciated.

A month or so later, in January 2009, Barak Obama was sworn in as President of the USA, and Waterford Crystal, Ireland's premier manufacturing brand, went into receivership.[114] It was the end of another era for traditional Irish manufacturing. TV screens were dominated by the nationalisation of Anglo Irish Bank. But on people's phone screens, something else was happening. Facebook, which would go on to employ more people in Ireland than Waterford Crystal ever did, introduced its 'like' button, mandating users to get involved.[115] The human, the most social of social animals, would never have so many opportunities to be so social with so many people from so many places.

As all this was happening, a small telecom service called WhatsApp was launched.[116] Where would you be today without your WhatsApp groups?

In June of that year, Michael Jackson died and Twitter, founded only a few years previously, crashed, with a record 100,000 tweets per hour being sent.[117] Facebook turned cash-flow positive for the first time ever.[118] That doesn't mean that Facebook was making a profit – that would take another few years – but it meant that for the first time it began to understand how to charge advertisers for marketing. It would become very good at this.

Of course, the financing model of Facebook was also revolutionary. Here was a company valued at billions that had never made a profit.[119] In time, the riches generated by these companies would do many things, including driving up rents and house prices in Dublin. But back then, few saw this huge commercial bonanza.

But one guy did.

In November 2009, tucked away in the Arts Block in Trinity, a few hundred hoodies, many of them out of work, congregated for a geek-fest called the Web Summit. Its founder, a 23-year-old graduate named Paddy Cosgrave, thought he might be onto something. In time, the Web Summit would become one of the biggest tourist events in the country. Back then, it passed off with nothing more than a few pints in town to celebrate not losing its shirt on the first outing. Today it is a commercial monster.

There was lots of life in the economy, but not where people imagined it to be. You just had to look for it.

The day Ireland was apoplectic about Thierry Henry's handball, Twitter was closely tracking its recently introduced retweet button[120] – another tiny innovation that would drive global connectivity and engagement, propelling up the value of this company, again without a cent of profit.

In December 2009, scientists unlocked the genetic code for the most common cancers, ushering in a revolution in cancer care.[121] However,

Ireland, parochial because of the trauma of the crash, was transfixed with a particularly choice exchange in the Dáil which ended with the immortal line: 'Fuck you, Deputy Stagg, fuck you.'

The old system was imploding.

THE WORLD IN OUR POCKET

But the Radical Centre is not that brittle. Bruised? Yes. Down? Yes. But not out. A period of massive dislocation such as a crash and national bankruptcy would in the past have ushered in a radical party like Syriza in Greece. But in Ireland, instead of going for new faces, we did the opposite, voting in Enda Kenny, the oldest serving parliamentarian in the House, as Taoiseach. The Radical Centre took one look at the extremes and scurried back to the middle ground. These were not years for setting a new social agenda and breaking old taboos; they were the survival years for many, but they were also years of opportunity for others.

In our pockets, on our screens, within our networks, a new economy was emerging rapidly, transforming Ireland and the world.

The innovations unveiled in 2008–09 collectively constituted one of the greatest technological leaps forward the world has ever seen. The ability to connect, collaborate and create new ideas throughout every aspect of life and work had an enormous and ground-breaking effect on society. Everything was digitising and this data was being stored more efficiently than ever before. The whole world could be accessed on a small device, and more and more networks meant that we could work, rest and play with the whole world.

Ireland found itself at the centre of this world, both as a consumer and as a business location. Intel made the chips in Leixlip, Facebook placed the ads in Dublin and Apple booked the profits in Cork.

While to the outside world, Ireland appeared to be in an economic tailspin, deep down the lives of many people, particularly the younger generation, were looking up. Their world was not closing in but opening up. Something was stirring and Flat White Man could feel it.

Now, 10 years later, the smartphone is largely the reason that there are over 4 billion people online, with a total of 1.9 billion individual websites on the net.[122] Today – just one day – as you read this book, 175 billion emails will be sent, as will 505 million tweets. There will be over four billion individual Google searches and over 4.5 billion videos will be watched on YouTube. 52 million photos will be uploaded to Instagram and 86 million posts will be sent on Tumblr. Three million new smartphones will be sold. There are now 2.2 billion Facebook users[123] – meaning there are nearly more Facebook users than there are Christians in the world.[124] One club took 2,000 years and numerous wars to assemble that number; Facebook is less than 15 years old. There are 355 million Twitter users, tweeting away all the time. Today, over 200 million Skype calls will be made and over 500,000 laptops will be bought.

The world has shrunk dramatically. We are connected, networked and interdependent in a way that has never happened before. Technology is not just transforming the world; it is reshaping the world into different forms, different tribes, different ways of buying, selling, learning, talking and even thinking.

How you work, how you play and how you make a living are all changing so quickly that it's difficult to gain altitude from this maelstrom to see things clearly.

However, one thing is clear, the economy in which Happy Pear Man is working in 2018 is a very different one to the economy in which Breakfast Roll Man was operating in 2008.

CHAPTER 27

TIME IS MONEY

DISRUPTION STARTS AT HOME

Imran drops Sliotar Mom to the airport. By the time they get to the tunnel she's woken up, checking emails, sending messages. Imran too was consulting Google Maps. They were both in the new economy, fully participant before dawn.

This new economy is full of opportunity but also carries risks. New technology is breaking down barriers and, therefore, breaking down some of the securities that people could count on in the past. This means self-reliance is likely to become the most significant attribute in our personal arsenal.

Consider Imran, our Carlow cricketing friend, to give us a microscopic view of what is happening. He arrived in Ireland from Pakistan not too long ago, when he couldn't tell his Clonmel from his Clondalkin, yet within weeks he was making a living as a taxi driver.

He gets the car, a hybrid Prius, and applies for his taxi-plate. In the old days he couldn't get a plate because the taxi unions refused to allow the state to issue any new plates. In fact, in the old days he wouldn't have been granted a visa to come into the country at all. Now the state allows as many plates as the market can bear and allows immigrants to come and work. Imran then downloads the MyTaxi app and he is in business. He gets contacted directly by the client and is paid remotely, as the money goes from the client's bank account to his. There is no cash, no awkward rooting for change in impenetrable denim pockets or the depths of handbags. He doesn't need to know where he is going because Google Maps navigates for him. Therefore, through a combination of technology, a less protectionist attitude to licences and freedom of movement, he is away and can start to earn his living.

Those who remember queueing for hours for a cab in Cork or Dublin will attest to the fact that this system is much better. There are loads of cabs and the customer certainly wins. All this before Uber arrives here. As the service has improved, the number of people taking cabs has soared, allowing more drivers to make a living from taxi driving, even though there are many more cabs on the road. There are many more winners.

But there are losers too. Older taxi drivers whose knowledge of the cities was their advantage have seen the value of their intimate knowledge of obscure alleys and side streets destroyed. And those who paid through the nose for licences – in effect, burgled by other drivers – have seen their wealth diminish. But it was never really wealth; it was simply trading on a barrier to entry which had the effect of providing a bigger income than was warranted for the skill of driving a car.

This is what is meant by disruption and it happens over and over again, creating new winners and new losers.

The relationship between us and technology, particularly our devices, tells its own story.

Irish people are addicted, full-on screen fanatics. Six out of 10 of us admit to using our mobile devices once every 30 minutes and a quarter of all Irish people check our devices every five minutes. Half of us spend at least three hours a day on our screens and one in five are on their devices more than six hours a day.[125]

Four in 10 of us have been influenced by an ad we've seen on our screens. In business, social media is enormously important, with close to 70% of Irish companies having a presence on Facebook, Twitter or YouTube.[126] In pure business terms, the online market is five times bigger than it was in 2008. A total of €497 million was spent on online advertising in 2017.

It's important to remind ourselves how new all of this is. As we saw in the previous chapter, Facebook was founded in 2004 – that's two years after Roy walked out in Saipan, which seems like only yesterday. Back in 2009 when Flat White Man came out of college, there were only 400,000 Facebook users in Ireland.[127] That figure quadrupled in the following 18 months. And now 2.2 million Irish people have a Facebook account, with close to half in rural areas. On average, Irish users spend close to six hours on Facebook per week. Women between the ages of 25 and 34 are the biggest users. In total 65% of Irish adults over the age of 15 have a Facebook page, with 70% using it daily.[128]

Instagram, beloved of gym bunnies showing us their bench presses or wannabe masterchefs displaying their guacamole, was only founded in 2010, the year the IMF rocked up in Ireland. Now it has 800 million daily users worldwide of whom 71% are women. Worldwide, an extraordinary 40 billion photos have been shared to date, with 95 million more uploaded every day. In Ireland, 720,000 people use Instagram and half of them use it every day. Maybe it's just the age profile, but Instagram has a sort of lonely hearts feeling to it with 260,000 singletons on it – like a more romantic version of Tinder.[129]

FROM TINDER TO TWITTER

Twitter, founded in 2006, is the home of political junkies, journalists and those who display inexplicable bitterness early on in life. Crash Kids have replaced 't' with 'd', so Twitter has become Twidder in the same way as the name Katie has become K-dee.

There are 835,000 of us on Twidder. Unlike Instagram, more blokes use it than women; and six out of 10 people use it for news.[130] It's a place where Ireland's weirdest political gremlins stalk. One unexpected consequence of Twidder is that it has made watching TV immeasurably funnier. It's like having your own version of Gogglebox beside you. For those of us who host TV programmes or make documentaries, reactions can be far too immediate, far too honest and far too accurate! You always needed a thick skin for that game, now you have to hide in a darkened room as soon as transmission starts.

In terms of global news, on the day 'you-know-who' won the US presidency, Twitter proved to be the largest source of breaking news, with 40 million tweets sent that day alone.[131] The combination of the smartphone, mobile coverage and greater computing power has allowed the Tweeter-in-Chief to disrupt the traditional media. He has made Twitter his broadcast channel, from which he can speak to the general public without the interference of fact checkers and the like. Why would you bother? In this sense, Twitter is Uberising the news business and Trump is the prime example of this disruption.

Trump is also a wonderful example of the economics of distraction.

THE ECONOMICS OF DISTRACTION

This notion of disruption brings us to the economic impact and, maybe more specifically, the generationally skewed impact of the new post-crash economy. Let's start with the proposition that Flat White Man and his generation feel left behind. Could it be because they are cannibalising themselves and their economic value by spending so much time online?

Online addiction will have huge ramifications for their ability to pay the rent in the years ahead and may be one reason why so many are still living with their mammies.

Starting with the old adage that 'time is money', if you are giving lots of your time to your smartphone, who is making the money? Certainly not you. We hear in survey after survey that the younger generation are finding it increasingly difficult to make a living. Yet they are the most educated Irish generation ever. So why aren't they making any money?

Could it be that while they are distracted on the phone, their money is going elsewhere? The number of users and the amount of time they spend online provides scale to the network. Scale is what gives the network its advertising reach. And advertising reach is what gives the network its value. The value of your time is captured in the valuation of the company. The company is either owned by shareholders or by private equity creatures. So your time, which is your money, is being captured by a few very wealthy investors.

This is obviously worrisome enough, but there is another time-related aspect that might give us cause to be concerned for the Crash Kids.

THE ATTENTION ECONOMY

When we are bombarded by constant distractions, we can't focus, and without focus and hard work, applied to one thing over and over, nothing of value is ever produced. Do you think Leonardo da Vinci would have painted the *Mona Lisa* if he had constantly been checking Instagram?

On 1 January 2018, sick of all the noise and interruption from frivolous things on my smartphone, I binned this incessantly needy partner in order to write this book. The result was a revelation. My days seemed longer and old-fashioned books more appealing. I was far less distracted, more patient and less irritable.

An unexpected aspect of being free of the smartphone is that other people's small talk becomes more interesting. Because you don't know what's going on in the world on a minute-by-minute basis, you can be surprised by the news and chat with people you bump into. When a taxi driver excitedly asks, 'Did you hear what yer man said today on Twitter?' you are all ears because you have no idea what Donald Trump tweeted a minute ago about Canadians, Koreans or the American Dream. You don't know because the little thing in your pocket isn't beeping relentlessly to update you on the latest presidential outrage.

Quickly, you realise that you don't care what Trump tweeted this morning, that you're not fazed by the latest twist in the Brexit saga, that your life is not enhanced by knowing that Taylor Swift's Croke Park tickets sold out or that Manchester City spent £100 million on some French teenage soccer sensation. Your mind is cleared of lots of clutter.

Daily life without constant emails, Twitter feeds, Facebook updates and Instagram photos is a blessed relief. It feels like you are back in control of your own time and not constantly being tugged by some inanimate force at all times of day and night.

I'm not on a total detox: I check emails, Twitter and Facebook on my laptop once or twice a day, usually in the evening, but not being available to everyone all the time is beginning to feel like freedom.

Giving up the smartphone is not for everyone, and there are obviously degrees of addiction. Maybe it's an age thing, but for someone who has few photos of himself from 1982 to 2002 and led most of his adult life without being compulsively interrupted by an algorithm, it has been surprisingly easy for me to step back in time. For the Crash Kids, the generation described as 'digital natives', it may be more difficult.

Now here is the rub. Like others, I gave up the smartphone in order to work smarter. I realised that the smartphone was costing me money because it was costing me time and time in which I could have been earning. My device was making me not smart but stupid, less focused, less productive, and less creative.

As I work for myself, that expression 'time is money' is relentlessly true. If I am giving my time to my smartphone, where's the money going? Very soon you realise that your valuable time is making money for some lad in Silicon Valley whose networks are made more valuable by my time. I'm doing all the giving and he and his shareholders are doing all the taking.

The more people work in the 'gig economy', the more acute the smartphone dilemma becomes.

Once we appreciate that everything that is creatively interesting or good is difficult and rarely comes easily, then we understand the need for focus, hard work and application. Focus tends to come from clearing our minds of distractions and applying our brains, uninterrupted, to discovering something new, fixing something or making connections we never saw before.

Ideally, of course, we should think about how to use our time wisely, delineating unforgivingly between the frivolous and the necessary.

This brings me to the more general issue of the 'attention economy' itself and its unpleasant brother, the 'distracted economy'.

Historically, the economy has operated in great wealth-creating cycles or ages. The first great economic age was the agricultural age, when land was the source of wealth. This bred feudalism, the landed gentry and peasantry.

Next came the industrial age, when the main source of wealth was industrial capital, breeding the great worker-versus-capitalist divisions of the nineteenth and twentieth centuries.

Then came the 'knowledge economy' of the late twentieth century, where ownership of knowledge or know-how (and locking it in via significant scientific investment and patent protection) generated vast wealth.

Now we are in what is termed the 'sharing economy', where knowledge is disseminated and the network – not the stored knowledge – becomes crucial. Once you have the network, you can sell to it and bypass traditional market structure.

A key element of the sharing economy is the 'attention economy'. Without grabbing our attention, the sharing economy can't work. In the attention economy, all products compete for our attention, not unlike the way great pop songs did in the past. But it's not just products; politics too is becoming an attention event, where an online episode generates the interest that keeps that politician in the news. In many ways Donald Trump is the first American 'Attention President'. And before you think that this is an exclusively Republican trick, Oprah could easily be the first Democrat 'Attention President'.

The point is that the attention phenomenon is seeping into all walks of life, we are all vulnerable and its main transmission mechanism is the smartphone. By having our smartphone on all the time, we give this attention economy permission to operate.

The flipside of the 'attention economy' is the 'distracted economy'. Once we allow our attention to be grabbed, we allow our creativity to be distracted. And once we are distracted, we can't focus or deliver excellent work in an economy that demands quality – whether we are working inside a competitive company or on our own in the market.

If you are online all the time, when exactly do you devote the time to becoming good at something, to becoming special and therefore in demand? Thomas Edison wasn't lying when he said that genius was 1% inspiration and 99% perspiration. Hard work is where all good things come from. Indeed, it's not just hard work, but lots of time devoted to something. Malcolm Gladwell maintains that, to become properly good at something, the human must devote 10,000 hours to it. When you see a footballer bend a ball over the wall into the top corner, this is skill, but it's also the fruit of enormous dedication to the craft.

The 10,000 hours is another way of describing 'trial and error'. Trial and error takes a lot of time. We might tinker away for years before we get that eureka moment. It takes time to come up with even the most obvious innovations. All this takes focus, application and time.

As Cal Newport pointed out in a *New York Times* article,[132] the market rewards rare and valuable things and 'social media is neither rare nor valuable'. In fact, it can be a low-grade, low-value use of your time and no amount of social media networking is going to make it high value. Being good at something requires that you apply yourself with almost obsessive focus. It is hard and it is complicated and it means pushing through an intellectual, emotional or physical pain barrier. That's almost impossible to do if you are constantly interrupted.

In addition, when you become good at something, then work comes to you; you don't have to chase it. Think about the restaurants in a city that come highly recommended on TripAdvisor. They are not recommended because their staff are spending hours on Facebook telling people how good they are. These restaurants are recommended because they spend hours trying to be the best place to eat brunch in town and then they let other people, satisfied customers, tell the world how good they are.

Application and narrow, obsessive focus come first. This demands time and exclusive, uninterrupted effort. The market then finds you, you don't have to go out bragging to anyone. Technology will then amplify the demand for your services at hardly any cost.

But given that doing good work requires focus and discipline, anything that undermines that focus and discipline must be harmful to your ability to make a living. In this sense, social media is not just merely wasteful but is actually harmful because it diminishes that skill – application – that is necessary to create the interesting and valuable work, that allows a person to get paid because other people will pay you for it. In Newport's words, 'It diverts your time and attention away from producing work that matters and toward convincing the world that you matter.'

And while it is seductive to think that people think that you matter, only the very few, the influencers, will get paid for working on their best online version of themselves.

The harsh truth of this new economics of distraction is that most people might undermine their ability to make a living by obsessing about their online status. Thus, what you think is making you bigger may be making you smaller.

UBERISING THE MIDDLEMAN

If this is what the distraction economy and the explosion in connectivity could be doing on an individual level, what is this doing on a more macroeconomic level?

Flat White Man appreciates that there's something unsettling about finding himself at home in bed, under the duvet, Pringles in one hand, remote in the other, binge watching *The Crown*. How did he end up here? He's nearly on the second series and it's still Wednesday. Shit, he's got work in the morning. Still, he takes some comfort in the fact that a significant chunk of the Radical Centre is also addicted. Most of us are at it, at all hours of the night, gorging away on Netflix, checking emails, setting up WhatsApp groups, scrolling down, looking up or buying something on Amazon.

What is this doing to the economy, wages and job security?

A few decades ago, the Austrian economist Joseph Schumpeter came up with the term 'creative destruction' to explain the natural process whereby recessions and human ingenuity create innovations and these innovations produce 'disruptive technologies'. At a macro level, today's disruptive technologies, like Uber, Amazon, WhatsApp, Airbnb, Google Maps or Netflix, destroy old industries, drive down prices and change the ground rules, just as Schumpeter suggested. They undermine the old business model, which has existed since the Bible: the fixed margin model. This was based on businesses maintaining fixed profit margins. In most western societies, these businesses were, in the main, middlemen nestled somewhere between producers and consumers. As middlemen, businesses took a fixed margin and that's how they made their money. If costs rose, they raised their prices to preserve their margin and livelihood. But this has all been disrupted in the past five years.

In 2014, Amazon founder Jeff Bezos famously declared: 'Your margin is my opportunity.' Amazon has mercilessly targeted industry after industry to cut the margins of the existing companies in order to offer a lower-cost alternative to consumers. 'Your margin is my opportunity' is actually an extremely nuanced view of how technology and the internet is shaking up old industries.

Taxis, retailers, telecom companies and all sorts of leisure companies can no longer add margin to their price to make up for increased costs because consumers can see this online and shop around. Think about Airbnb and hotels. Every business with a decent margin is liable to be disrupted.

The middleman is being squeezed everywhere. But the immediate problem is that the middleman is us! In mature western economies, based largely on services, most white-collar graduates are intermediaries of some sort. Disruption that squeezes these service providers squeezes everyone and, worse still, because it attacks the profit of old industries, it makes employers wary about committing to full-time employment contracts. Precarious employment is becoming more the norm for Flat White Man and his generation.

This poses a particular problem for younger workers because it undermines their ability to get a toehold in the labour market. Without a toehold, they can't get experience and many employers want to see two years' experience before they consider taking on a person full time. But how can they get this sort of experience if employers are reticent to take them on in the first place?

New technology makes for the uberisation of the global workforce.

In the past, the Irish labour force was limited to the workers who lived in Ireland. If you wanted a job done, you had to fish in the finite pool of local talent. Now, if you want to get a job done – particularly a job in IT or design – you have the whole world at your fingertips. Globalisation and the ease with which people can check work on screens means that contractors in Ireland can pitch their services all over the world. But equally, workers in other countries can pitch their services to companies based in Ireland.

Websites like peopleperhour.com or freelancer.com allow companies that need a job done to get competing quotes from freelance professionals all over the world. These sites work like TripAdvisor, where work is rated and ranked and all prices are transparent. As a result, large parts of the Irish labour market have been or are going to be uberised. The process is relentless and it means that small Irish companies are going straight to professionals outside the country, who do not face the same cost pressures as Irish workers and thus charge less.

It works the other way too, because the new economy provides amazing opportunities for creative Irish people. The most successful of these have been the Collison brothers and their Silicon Valley-based payments company Stripe, which is disrupting banking. Another example is hassle.com – essentially an Uber for cleaners – which was bought out by German company helping.com.

A favourite of mine is Izzy Wheels. Two sisters from Galway started selling wheel covers for wheelchair users, created through collaborations with famous Irish and international designers and graffiti artists. A percentage of their sales goes to charities and 80% of their sales come from the US, driven by social media exposure. One of their videos has 11 million views and it was the first Irish firm to feature as the main story on Instagram's homepage.

Parkpnp is an app that provides a marketplace for people to list, advertise and then generate income from their unused or underutilised parking spaces, allowing drivers to find guaranteed parking through their PC or smartphone. Oathello is an app that allows you to book and pay for a junior solicitor in your area to come to you and sign those crucial forms, bringing speed, efficiency and convenience to a sometimes tortuous legal process. qCrypt is a piece of software that provides security for documents that is verifiably secure for life, could safely store personal documents like wills and is secure enough for governments to use for national security level documents because the creator, a Dublin teenager, has added 'post quantum security'.

The story of the past 40 years has been one of individual liberation and commercial self-expression. The device in our pockets just makes all that easier, cheaper, quicker and more profitable.

The threat to the Radical Centre comes if the younger workers abandon creativity, feel left behind, hoisted on their own technological petard, distracted to death in the distracted economy. That is why reforming the education system and its winners, the exam-passing Testocrats, is imperative. The Radical Centre rests on the foundation of upward social mobility, being part of a great project in which, if you do the right thing and show a bit of gumption, you will be better off than your parents. Upward social mobility is about having skin in the game and a great stake in society.

The main impediment to acquiring your stake right now isn't technology but something equally global. The real and present dangers lie in wait at the intersection where global capital flows meet Irish feudalism in the local property market, which pushes accommodation beyond the reach of the Crash Kids, stunting their ability to reach the milestones that define becoming an adult. Armed with this observation, let's talk about Irish houses, global credit and expanding wealth gaps in the Renaissance Nation.

CHAPTER 28

GENTLEMEN PREFER BONDS

THE ABSENTEE LANDLORD

Hoping to beat the morning traffic, Kiln-Dried Kevin fills his van at sunrise for his next delivery to the professional classes in Stoveland. Halfway across the world, on Newport Beach, the same sun is setting, a great fireball over the Pacific. An intense young man sits at his screen in a Californian hipster café, surrounded by other young men with luxuriant beards, designer tattoos and piercings, scrolling through single-geared bicycle websites. Beside them, perched over their coconut waters, sit bronzed, unfeasibly skinny, yet remarkably muscular women, who haven't eaten anything bar protein balls since St Patrick's Day.

Californian faces are different to Irish ones. It must be something to do with perfection. Everything is in the right place, in the right proportions. You'll never find a 'sticky-out' ear in Newport Beach, and certainly no bent noses. Faces here are remarkably symmetrical. Teeth are an expensive work-in-progress and lips are plumped. Come to think of it, it's a bit like The Gables in Foxrock.

Even 'Gimme Shelter' sounds better in this south LA café than in rainy Ireland; 'LA Woman' on the M50 doesn't quite match the Lizard King on the Pacific Coast Highway.

The intense young man, the algorithm prince, is a balance-sheet wizard, the type of maths wonk who has been elevated to deity status in financial markets. He works for one of the largest investment funds in the world, based in Newport Beach. In his spare time, he trades Bitcoin, Ethereum and Monero. It's fair to say he's not great with people, so it's rather unusual that he has ended up being a landlord in Ireland in that most 'people' of businesses, accommodation.

Spreadsheet Warrior has a huge position in the Irish property market; his firm bought a large chunk of it from NAMA. Spreadsheet Warrior's job is to make the numbers work. He was in Ireland once for the Web Summit. Seemed like a nice enough place, but it could've been anywhere in Britain for all he cared. Spreadsheet Warrior is all about his sell signals. The firm has been in Ireland longer than anticipated, but the numbers are still fantastic. He looks at his Irish housing investments – 800 apartments – as one large bond which offers him a strong rental income, and capital gains have been massive because apartment prices keep heading skywards.

To Spreadsheet Warrior, on paper Ireland is Treasure Island, a place that delivers unimaginable returns for the people who had the money to buy the place when the Irish went bust. Does he hang on for the rest of the ride or get out now? Normally he follows the 3–3–30 rule: three years in the market, only risk 3% of your fund in any one country, wait till your investment makes 30% profit, and then sell. The Warrior's favourite piece of financial advice comes from J.P. Morgan: 'No one ever lost money by selling too early.' As Jagger sneers 'It's just a kiss away' through the speakers, Spreadsheet Warrior wonders if he should hit the 'send' button. Is it time to trade?

Seven thousand miles and 10 time zones away, his Irish tenants, those people whose high rents generate the yield that makes Spreadsheet's models chime, have no idea where all the money goes. They just know they don't have much left at the end of the month.

In 2010, institutional investors like Spreadsheet Warrior owned zero homes; they now own a large chunk in Ireland alone. This is absentee landlordism for the Tinder age.

And this is one major difference between this property boom and the last one. In the last one, Irish banks borrowed money from all over the world to lend more to Irish people, who then bought and sold bits of Ireland to each other at wildly inflated prices. When the foreign investors panicked, they demanded their money back. The banks didn't have it because they'd lent it out to the rest of the country. When banks have no money, they go bust. This is what happened. Then, in order to stay afloat after the government bailed them out, they had to repossess the assets and sell them to whoever had the money at the time. This was done through NAMA. The people who had the money to buy Irish assets and take a punt on the country, were the big foreign funds.

So the old boom was a boom where the Irish played all the parts with borrowed money. This boom is different because most of the main players are not Irish, they are these foreign funds, alongside some already very wealthy Irish players. Recently, the Irish property boom has largely been a non-Irish affair. This is how you get a local property boom without local credit.

But where did Spreadsheet Warrior get all his cash?

AGAIN, 2008 WAS THE BEGINNING, NOT THE END

Let's go back to 2008 again, where things get very interesting. In the same way that it opened up the world through technology, profoundly changing the economy for the Crash Kids, 2008 also changed the way the international credit system worked.

In 2008, the US Federal Reserve, fearing a 1930s-type depression, began to buy assets from the banks and, in return, gave the banks money for free. Yes, for free. The aim of free money is to drive up asset prices. The Fed wanted to reflate the asset side of the broken American balance sheet. The idea then was that the American recovery would be stimulated by rising asset prices, making people more confident, coaxing them to spend and thus the boats would all rise.

The financial mechanism that facilitated this was called quantitative easing, which was nothing more than driving interest rates to negative and urging the banks to lend. The central banks, for the first time ever, swapped banks' bad assets for good money, forcing the banks to lend this new good money into the battered economy, which they did. They lent to the less risky but already wealthy, who began to buy cheap assets from formerly rich, now poor, asset owners. The new global credit cycle started in the US, but it would change the global economy for the next decade. Back then, no one expected it to last more than a few months. But it did.

In the end the American economy did respond, but who do you think gains the most when the recovery is based on pushing up asset prices? The people who own those assets, obviously. And who owns assets, rich people or poor people? Rich people, of course. That's why they are rich. They own stuff. And the more their stuff increased in value, the more they could use it as collateral to buy other stuff in countries that were in trouble, where stuff was selling at very deep discounts.

In this way, the same forces that were financing much of the new economy, the global private equity funds, would come to buy up most of Dublin's commercial real estate. They became known as the vulture funds.

Spreadsheet Warrior was in fact given the money for free in the sense that the fund he works for was lent free money by the bank because it was already rich and therefore not risky. The best way to get rich in the last ten years was to be already rich. This is how Spreadsheet Warrior in Newport Beach, California came to own a large chunk of Ireland, which he had bought at a very cheap price. Once we appreciate this, we can begin to understand this new Irish property boom and how its dynamics are very different to the last one.

SERENGETI CYCLES

Taking a bit of altitude, we see that the global credit cycle is almost tidal, ebbing and flowing with the global economy. When it is abundant, it flows to Ireland; when it is not, it doesn't. When the global central banks turn on the tap, it flows. When they decide to turn off the same tap, credit disappears.

One way to visualise how the credit cycle affects the economy is to think about water in the great plains of Africa. Credit is the life-giving water of the economy. Imagine the wonderful image of the rains flooding into the savannah of the Serengeti. Once a year, between March and May, the arid, sun-parched plain undergoes an extraordinary transformation as the rains bring life and abundance. Flowers and vegetation bloom, animals and insects return to the lush pasture to graze, mate and generally do their thing.

Then, as the seasons change, the waters recede, first from the remote regions of the plain and then progressively until the last verdant area is a small knot around an almost dried-up riverbed. Where once there was abundance and plenty, there is now only dust and barrenness. The burnt earth can't sustain any life.

The credit cycle displays similar characteristics. Credit in an economy works like fresh water in the natural world. It brings life and hope, as well as a little bit of exuberance, which can go over the top at times. Once a society confers dignity on economic and commercial effort, credit is put to good use. Credit, like water in the wild, is essential for society to thrive and function. When credit recedes, so too does economic vibrancy.

Like water in the Serengeti, credit follows a pattern. When credit is plentiful and investors aren't too worried about risk, money flows into every nook and cranny of the system. Credit rating agencies are prepared to give the thumbs-up to almost any country or company and what follows is nothing less than a deluge of free – or at least cheap – money. Other people's cash is available everywhere. So, in the case of the Irish borrowing binge, ghost estates, with no economic or demographic logic, get financed. People are offered car loans, holiday loans and interest-free mortgages. Bank coffers overflow.

But unlike the animals in the Serengeti, who are conditioned to understand the limitations of the natural water cycle, we humans have less appreciation of the credit cycle. We think this time it's different and we get involved in this effervescent game. With success comes a healthy disregard for the chances of failure – until it happens. This is what happened in 2008, when everything stopped.

But then, fearing global depression, the central banks turned the taps on again, full throttle, and money flowed back into the parched system. Except this time, between 2008 and 2018, it went to very different people. This is the story of the second credit binge, which you didn't play a part in but which drove prices and rents ever higher. And now that rents and prices are high, the average citizen of the Radical Centre is paying again.

THE MONEYED TRIBE VERSUS THE MORTGAGED TRIBE

The Irish property market is a tiny bit of the now global property market. Its path will be largely determined by the global credit cycle. The global credit cycle is more important than the much-discussed business cycle. It is driving house prices and rents here. It also drives a wedge between two financial tribes operating within the broad Radical Centre.

These two tribes can be termed the mortgaged tribe and the moneyed tribe. Let's examine these tribes because, once we appreciate them, we can understand how wealth is divided in the Renaissance Nation and why so many of the Crash Kids can't afford to grow up.

Economics is often counterintuitive, and that holds when it comes to making money. The best time to make serious money is not when the economy is booming, but when the economy is collapsing. The bigger the crash, the greater the opportunity.

But who makes this money?

Here is where the distinction between the mortgaged tribe and the moneyed tribe comes into play. The mortgaged tribe are the people who have to borrow to buy assets. The moneyed tribe are the people who have the cash and don't need to incur debt. So you might look at two people with similar houses, cars, clothes and lifestyles. One is mortgaged, and therefore always vulnerable, while the other is moneyed and therefore always comfortable. Debt makes you fragile to unexpected events and the more debt you have, the more fragile the edifice.

When a mortgaged edifice collapses, it is the moneyed tribe, the people who always had the shekels, who pick up the bargains.

In a recession, asset prices fall significantly and only the moneyed tribe has the means to buy. Therefore, the already rich, who didn't lose everything in the crash, pick up all the bargains. The mortgaged tribe – those people who have to borrow to acquire assets – are excluded from the upswing in prices and real wealth creation.

In terms of wealth, the crash provided a huge opportunity for the moneyed tribe. The already rich took the opportunity to pick up assets at bargain basement prices from the newly poor.

Now, as asset prices have recovered strongly and house prices in particular are roaring ahead, the extent of this transfer of wealth from the mortgaged tribe to the moneyed tribe is becoming apparent. One of the great tragedies is that, in the next few years, it could be that moneyed tribe – like our friend the Spreadsheet Warrior – who will sell these assets back to a new mortgaged tribe, trousering the huge capital gain, and waiting for the next crash to do it all again. Such is the iron law of the credit cycle.

THE LIST

Understanding the harsh logic of the credit cycle explains how wealth can become concentrated at the top or close to the top even when everyone's incomes are rising, as is the case now.

A neat way to see this is to compare the annual *Sunday Independent* Rich List's gains against those of the rest of the country every year. The Rich List is the plutocracy squared, the 1% of the 1%, and is perfect territory for the *Sindo* with its strange, but very successful, combination of star-fucking, models' cleavages, populism and Ballymaloe relish – which is precisely why it is the biggest selling paper in the country.

Usually it is the same names every year. Occasionally an intruder elbows in, like Conor McGregor. In fact, McGregor's entry into the Rich List in 2018 was perfectly mirrored when he drove his jet ski into one of Ireland's oldest yacht clubs in Dún Laoghaire. There's nothing a yacht club hates more than new money and nothing screams new money on water like jet skis.

In the past year, the wealth of the top 300 on the Irish Rich List increased by more than €12 billion. To put that amount of money in context, it's around half of the rise in Ireland's entire GDP.

We should not begrudge anyone who is doing their best and making money, because envy is not only one of the seven deadly sins, it is arguably the ugliest. Unfortunately, we Irish do envy beautifully. It's one of our weaknesses. In a country where you are never forgiven for your success, standing out is not a good idea. This is why Ireland's wealthy tend to be discreet. The key to being truly comfortable with your money is to behave as if you don't have any at all.

However, the growing wealth gap is a serious issue, here and globally, because it leaves so many people behind. It also means that the tax system has to work much harder to keep the whole show afloat. Growing wealth disparities lead to the strange situation where, although incomes are increasing, people don't feel better off because they are falling back in the wealth game. This angst is evident in the Irish housing market right now.

The difference between income and wealth is significant. Sometimes the two are conflated. Income is the stream of money you get every month or year. It is your paycheque. The mortgaged tribe usually gets that from work and they use it to pay their mortgage.

Wealth is different. It is the accumulation of assets, which originally may have begun with good incomes but that were translated into stores of wealth over time. Such assets include houses, property, shares or ownership of a company, a business or even a patent that generates recurring incomes. This is what the moneyed tribe has and the stream of income stemming from an asset is what the moneyed tribe use to pay their bills, often instead of working. It's the stuff that pays you even when you are asleep. In fact, to be a fully fledged member of the moneyed tribe, it is better that there is little or no evidence of work at all.

Those on significant incomes are not necessarily wealthy and the truly wealthy do not necessarily have significant incomes. But the wealthy have assets that they can sell if necessary and, if they play their cards right, they can sell back to the mortgaged tribe those assets which they bought cheaply from them in the first place – at a higher price, of course.

The credit cycle's ebbs and flows are like a giant financial pendulum that swings between the mortgaged and the moneyed tribe. There is a good bit of mobility between tribes, but sometimes that mobility slows down and then the disparity becomes a problem. The issue for Ireland is that Irish property is now part of a global game, where the upside is going to the already wealthy. This exacerbates wealth inequality and the essential social solidarity necessary to underpin a project like the Radical Centre.

Spreadsheet Warrior's tanned Californian finger hovers a little longer over the 'send' button, but then he relaxes, closes his laptop and takes another sip of his kale mojito. He smiles to himself. It's too soon. There's time yet to make a killing.

CHAPTER 29

THE WEALTH DIVIDE

WHAT SORT OF SOCIETY DO WE WANT?

We've seen how property amplifies the wealth divide in the Renaissance Nation, but now let's have some good news. The good news is that, instinctively, we are good people. The vast majority of us feel that having a fairer society is a good thing. When polled in 2018, 85% of Irish people said we want our government to do more about wealth inequality.[133]

We also understand there's a huge amount of luck in whether you end up at the bottom or the top and appreciate the 'accident of birth' notion. Deep down, we also understand that citizenship requires a certain amount of equality for the country to function.

When asked about equality, Irish people take the philosophical approach, contemplating what sort of society we would like to live in if we didn't know who we would become. We acknowledge our own privilege and then answer as if we could just as easily be at the bottom looking up as at the top looking down.

This is all good, don't you think?

Just when you might have despaired, we Irish come out with evidence that we are a decent bunch. Intuitively, we understand that having a stake in the society makes people more likely to behave civilly to each other.

Inequality is psychologically damaging for those on the wrong side of the tracks because the issue is not absolute wealth, but the contrast between what I have and what you have. If I look around and see people doing much better than me, I begin to feel like I am falling backwards. At that stage, I begin to lose hope in the promise of society. The best way to feel that you have a place in society is the sense that you have a stake in society.

Having something – having assets – gives you hope. It is your little bit to build on. So owning a home or having an education fund for your kids gives you something to aim for, because it gives you a claim on, and an interest in, society. Such a reassurance changes the way people view themselves and the way they view the future.

A few years ago, psychologists in the US carried out an experiment involving one hundred poor families. Some of the parents were given a small savings fund on the day their child was born, which was to be set aside for their children's university fees.

The kids were then assessed for cognitive reasoning every two years and, by the fourth year, the children whose parents had the small education fund were performing better in all tests than those who hadn't received the fund. The implication of this is that the parents with this small stake in the future were changing their own behaviour towards their children's education in expectation of a better future education, so they were reading to them, paying more attention to their homework, and so on.

This is extraordinary, because it reveals what having a stake in society, having something to aim for, does to people. It gives them a focus, something to believe in.

If people have something small – a savings fund, a bit of wealth, a sense that they matter and that their future is in their hands – they change their behaviour for the better. Obviously the opposite is the case if they feel they have no hope.

For the future of the Renaissance Nation, and in order to preserve the political ballast of the Radical Centre and to allow the Crash Kids to grow up, land-driven wealth disparities should be addressed. This is small stuff and can be done.

THE EVIDENCE

A few years ago, I worked on a documentary about wealth inequality in Ireland.[134]

Beginning with the idea that people instinctively want a fairer society, we surveyed a thousand people. We asked them: in an ideal world, if you were to share out the wealth of the country, what would you like to see? What would you regard as being fair or equal?

The results were more or less what you would expect. Respondents answered that they'd like to see the richest 20% owning 31% of the wealth, and at the other end people would like to see the poorest 20% having a bit less, at 17% of the total wealth of the country. People thought that would be fair, and fairer than it is at the moment. It would also allow the rich the opportunity to get a little richer and have an incentive to hold onto what they have, but equally it reveals that, while we know there will always be poor people in the country, these people shouldn't be too poor. We recognise the role of luck, circumstance and environment in the outcome.

Then we asked: how do you think the wealth of the country is actually shared out? Unsurprisingly, they thought it was more unequal than they considered to be fair. The respondents thought the wealthiest 20% in Ireland probably owned a huge 60% of the country's wealth, while the poorest 20% have just a meagre 11%. That's how unfair people think Ireland is today – and remember, 85% of us think that the status quo was not fair or as fair as we would like it to be.

So that's what we want, but what have we got?

People believed the wealth gap in Ireland is bad but, unfortunately, it's far worse than they think.

Two major studies, one by TASC and one by Credit Suisse, reveal how wealth is divided in Ireland, and it doesn't make for pretty reading.[135, 136] However, we are not out of whack with the rest of Europe. Wealth inequality is the issue of our time and of course the credit cycle we spoke about earlier is amplifying this gap. Not only are the very wealthy getting richer but the divide between those at the very top and those at the bottom has also increased.

The reality is that the richest 20% in Ireland own 73% of the country's wealth. The poorest 20% don't own the 11% people feared they did: they own much, much less. The bottom 20% of Irish society – that's over 1.5 million people – owns a measly 0.2% of Ireland's wealth.

If we look at the share of the wealth owned by the top 10%, top 5% and top 1% in Ireland, we see something quite troubling. According to a survey carried out by the CSO the top 10% own 53.8% of the wealth of this country; the top 5% own 38% of the wealth; and the top 1% own 15%.

This is the reality of wealth distribution in Ireland.

According to Credit Suisse, the concentration at the top is even stronger. Its estimates suggest that the top 10% own 58.5% of the wealth; the top 5% own 46.4%; and the top 1% own 27.3%. Even taking into account the disparity between the two reports, the concentration of wealth at the very top in both studies is extraordinary for any democratic society.

Indeed, because the CSO data is from a survey which asked people to declare their wealth, there is a very strong possibility that those at the very top decided to understate their wealth, so the very rich might have played down their assets. But both studies reveal that the top 10% own over half the wealth of the country.

Once wealth inequality of this level becomes accepted, it's not only the people at the bottom, but also those in the middle, who feel that they might slip back and could begin to lose hope. We lose hope at our peril. The Radical Centre's triumph is founded on the idea that we can all move upwards. On the basis of income, this is true, and it has been a significant feature of the past few decades. However, if there is a ceiling on this upward mobility, because too few own too much, the Radical Centre will shift to the radical left or the radical right.

So what is making a small number of people so fabulously wealthy?

BACK TO THE LAND

When you break down where this wealth derives from, we are back to the land. We know now that Ireland's wealth is unevenly held, but what constitutes wealth in Ireland? The moneyed tribe owns land and they don't sell it very often. They buy during 'once in a generation' opportunities when the market crashes and then disappear and live off the rent. Not for them the excessive churning of the mortgage tribe, who panic regularly because they are leveraged. Financial panic is similar to 'status panic', which the mortgage tribe experiences all the time. In the same way, they buy and sell frantically up and down the cycle, unaware that the credit cycle will look after them if they don't panic and chill out.

In most countries, wealth is a mixture of companies, shares, bonds, savings and property, but not in Ireland. In Ireland, around 87 cents in every euro of all the wealth of the richest people in the country is held in land, property and houses.[137] There it is, in black and white.

Radical Centre Ireland still displays, despite all the huge strides we have made, something akin to an ancient feudalism whereby owing land is still the best way of remaining rich. Therefore, landowners' interests are extremely powerful.

A feudal economy in a digital world might not be the cleverest foundation for the years ahead. These days, wealth is created within the heads of millions of us, not in the ground we walk on. Furthermore, to sustain the Radical Centre, we need as many of our people as possible to be involved in the innovation nation, no matter how minor that innovation may be. Land is a cost as well as an asset. If the return to landowners is rising, the costs to the rest of us are rising too. For the least populated country in western Europe, having the most expensive land makes no sense and makes us weak.

It's important to rectify the problem and the most obvious place to start is with the tax system. In the next chapter, let's explore whether the Irish tax system is part of the problem or part of the solution.

CHAPTER 30

THE HISSING GOOSE

Y ou can tell a lot about a country and the power of various vested interests from the way a country deploys taxes. In this chapter, let's tease out the interaction between the tax system, the cost of things and the price of land. Let's also explore how land makes everything more expensive and exacerbates wealth disparities.

Before we start finger-pointing, it's important to understand people's personal circumstances and the dilemmas they face. When you are buying a house, you want prices to go down, so that you can afford it; but once you have bought, you want prices to rise so that you can begin to accumulate wealth. One person's asset is another person's cost. As land values go up, they make people who own their own homes feel better off. But while rising property prices might make the homeowner feel a bit better off, property value increases make a few very wealthy people very rich indeed.

This is the insidious nature of housing and property in Ireland.

Because we all need a roof over our heads – including businesses – if property prices and rents are rising, the economy's cost base goes up and therefore our wages have to go up. This squeezes profits and as profits are the referee in the great game of commercial self-expression, rising land wealth actually diminishes creative commercial effort in other fields. It is not self-generating wealth but self-defeating wealth. And it takes money out of people's pockets, money that could be used to seed other initiatives. With that in mind, let's examine how expensive land makes the majority poorer, not richer.

We tend to realise just how expensive Ireland is when we land in a foreign country. After a short time in a neighbouring country, Irish people are often shocked at how much cheaper it is than at home. But we rarely stop to reflect that land itself is a major cause of this.

Let's begin to join the dots between expensive land and the price of everything else in Ireland. One of the main threats to the Radical Centre is the fact that the place is so expensive, freezing out many, particularly younger people because they have no money left at the end of the month. The Fringe, whom we met earlier, is over 30 and still shares two bathrooms with 10 others. Without a hope of getting her own place, what is her stake in Ireland? She might easily be persuaded that we should abandon the Radical Centre and lurch to the radical left or right. The tax system is the first place to look for clues as to why the Fringe, and most of her generation, are being priced out of the housing market.

THE ART OF TAXATION

Over the years, I have never met anyone who willingly pays more tax than they must. This is why we have tax audits, tax collectors and tax officials. Yet one characteristic of the Radical Centre is tax compliance. Over the years as we have become more tolerant, better citizens, Irish people have also become much less likely to evade tax. Avoiding tax legally is an industry which spawns legions of tax accountants, consultants and tax planners. At least half of the Velominati are involved in the tax avoidance racket in some shape or form.

This is, of course, nothing new. States have been collecting tax and people have been avoiding tax from time immemorial. Taxation is an art, best summed up by Jean Baptiste Colbert, the extraordinarily talented finance minister of Louis XIV, who radically overhauled the French economy in the late seventeenth century. In a statement resonating with brilliance and bureaucratic cynicism, Colbert wrote: 'The art of taxation consists in so plucking the goose as to obtain the largest number of feathers with the least possible amount of hissing.'

Tragically for all concerned, those revenues were subsequently squandered by both Louis and his free-spending descendants, whose heads rolled in the French Revolution. However, they did leave some nice buildings in Paris around the Tuileries for tourists to take photos. It's swings and roundabouts really.

Colbert's ability to raise taxes emboldened the French royalty to build more and more of these monuments to their own vanity, fuelling the discontent that led to the Revolution. Wealth inequality can lead to rather radical eventualities, if we are not too careful.

In taxation terms, the goose that hisses the most gets taxed least. In any society, those who hiss most tend to be either those at the top, who are extremely powerful and have most to lose, or those at the very bottom who have nothing to give. Who hisses least? Those in the middle, our heroes, the Radical Centre.

At plucking time, the wealthy goose hisses loudly and gets a free pass. No taxes are levied on his assets. Over time, this ridiculous scenario ends up being regarded as normal. Normalising the abnormal is an important issue and one to bear in mind. According to the Colbert view, the state will levy taxes where it knows the goose will hiss least. Keep the Hissing Goose in mind while we compare prices between Ireland and Germany. Then we can tie it all together and identify the role of expensive land in pushing Irish costs way out of whack with our neighbours.

BERLIN

Let's take a short trip to Germany. Germany is one of the richest, and most successful, economies in Europe. Our average wage is roughly the same as Germany's. The Germans, on average, are paid a bit more than us. Therefore, we'd expect things to be a bit pricier in Germany. Things should cost more or less the same in countries that have more or less the same levels of income and wages, because the main local costs in any country are wages, taxes, rents and the cost of land.

But alas, once again, Ireland is an outlier.

Take transport. Everyone has to get around. If we examine transport alone, a picture emerges of a massive heist perpetrated on the Irish public. Transport costs in general are 38% higher in Ireland than in Germany and public transport is half the price in Germany.[138] The key input cost in transport is fuel. Germany and Ireland face the same petrol prices. Both are oil importers. Average wages in Germany and Ireland are quite similar. Wages are the main local cost for transport. So what explains the 38% difference in transport and nearly 50% in public transport?

When we dig a bit more, we note similar enormous price disparities.[139] For example, prescription medicine is 87% more expensive in Ireland. Going out is also much more expensive here. An Italian dinner for two is 28% pricier here than the equivalent in Germany. A litre of milk is 38% more here than in Germany. This is a strange one. Milk costs €1.20 in Ireland and €0.87 in Germany. But how can this be when Ireland is a huge exporter of milk? Milk exported from Ireland becomes miraculously cheaper when it leaves here.

But it gets weirder.

Coca Cola was, not too long ago, Ireland's biggest agricultural exporter (and currently Ireland's most popular brand). Yet a two-litre bottle of Coke costs €2.24 here and €1.73 in Germany.[140] This is more difficult to understand because the product is exactly the same and cannot be fully explained by differences in tax rates. A two-litre bottle of Coke should cost the same in all countries. It's internationally standardised, internationally traded and internationally acceptable in all countries.

Ireland bottles the stuff, Germany takes the stuff and theory tells us that Coca Cola should cost the same in both countries plus a premium in Germany for transport costs. It should therefore be cheaper in Ireland than in Germany. But it's the other way round.

Let's look elsewhere for more anomalies.

Let's look at housing because you can give up Coke, but everyone has to live somewhere. Housing costs are much higher in Ireland than in Germany. Before we look at the details, it's worth remembering that Germany is the most populous country in Europe, while Ireland is amongst the least.

Therefore, logic would argue that housing costs should be lower in Ireland but guess what? In general, housing is 48% more expensive here than in Germany.[141] This average figure masks lots of variations. For example, rent on a small, furnished apartment in a reasonably upmarket area of Dublin like Clonskeagh is 60% more per month than it is in a similar area such as Charlottenburg in Berlin. The disparity is off the scale.

LOOKING FOR CLUES

To understand why Ireland is so expensive, follow the money. With one eye on our old friend the hissing goose, let's look at our tax system to reveal who pays what, because the tax system truly reveals the priorities of the state.

It costs close to €50 billion a year to run this country. The government takes in almost all of this with taxes and borrows a bit to make the books balance.

Our government took in just over €50.7 billion in taxes in 2017.[142] The breakdown of this figure reveals its preferences. But before we become party political and start roaring for an election to change things immediately, understand that the way we tax things is the culmination of years of policy; it is not something new but something that has evolved.

Here's the breakdown. Roughly €20 billion of all revenue was raised from income tax or taxes on wages. These are taxes on effort and hard work. But these types of taxes also reduce people's take-home pay, adding to the pinch for the squeezed middle. A further €13 billion was taken in VAT. VAT is a tax on buying and selling almost everything (except for food and children's clothes). It's a tax on economic activity. VAT is a tax on commerce and the wheels that make the system go round. Obviously, a tax that pushes up prices on most things reduces the buying power of people's salaries, which are already compromised by income tax. Nearly €6 billion was raised in excise duty – basically petrol, fags and booze, the 'old reliables'. Excise duty also pushes up prices directly and again eats into take-home pay.

This implies that almost €40 billion of the €50.7 billion is taken from the income of the average Joe, the hero of the Radical Centre, who we should be trying to protect. All of which is ultimately taken, in one way or another, from what you could call income, the money sloshing around the economy.

But what about wealth? Remember the massive wealth disparity? How do we tax money that is stored in houses, property, shares and savings? The short answer is: we don't. We only raise €500 million of our total taxes from property, despite the fact that it is the single biggest asset in the country.

While Irish income is looted wholesale by the state to pay for the upkeep of the place, Irish wealth is barely touched by the taxman. Why is the state happy to put a tax on income but not on wealth?

As you'll have figured out, I am no closet Che Guevara waiting to roast the rich. However, the people in the middle will find it difficult to feel financially secure while their incomes are being taxed so much and other people's wealth remains untouched, particularly if large chunks of their income, even after tax, are being spent disproportionately on driving up the assets and wealth of the very people who pay no tax on those assets.

Furthermore, because property wealth is not taxed sufficiently, people continue to look at housing as an asset rather than as accommodation. As a result, people invest in housing and once they have bought they want house prices to rise, driving a social wedge between owners and renters. This division is one of the greatest economic threats to the Radical Centre. Very high levels of wealth inequality will provide the radical left or the radical right with the ammunition they need to undermine the Radical Centre, even though the achievements of the Radical Centre are self-evident. This is Ireland's biggest remaining weak spot.

INCOME VERSUS WEALTH

This choice between taxing income and taxing wealth contributes significantly to the twin problems of the squeezed middle. Even on decent salaries, the combination of income tax and indirect taxes lowers take-home pay and increases retail prices. This means that precious little money is left at the end of the month. This prevents large sections of the population from saving for a deposit to address the other problem: affordable accommodation.

Such an outcome is a threat to the cohesion of the Radical Centre.

Now the outlier here is property tax. Surely if you wanted to bring down the price of property, which is the single biggest cost for most workers, you would tax property and income from property, lowering its attractiveness as an investment, and thus drag down prices?

It would seem logical and in the national interest to tax property wealth more than income, to make working hard worthwhile.

But land in Ireland is barely taxed at all, despite the fact that land – with the exception of agricultural land that is being actively used – is the least productive of all assets.

Our brains create innovation, capital increases productivity, while the economy is increasingly moving to being a service economy. Three-quarters of Irish people work in the service industry.[143] Innovation and creativity don't depend on land or property. They depend on human ingenuity.

Despite this, we raise only around 1% of our tax from houses and property.

CHAPTER 31

THE FALLOUT

lat White Man sometimes wonders why the hell he came back from Brussels at all. Waiting in this queue with the smarmy estate agent, giving out his card and advising the hopefuls to have all their ducks in a row – meaning, have a small fortune ready to disappear from your account to his.

But what other choice does he have? The business is going brilliantly. TripAdvisor loves him and he's free doing his own thing and making more than he would ever make on the continent. Ballet Blonde has already moved in in her head. But with the average house in Dublin costing nearly 5.5 times the average salary, things are getting out of hand.[144]

Flat White Man has a few quid from his parents, not rich people, but retiring civil servants out in Stoveland, unwittingly members of the 15%. They've dug deep, as they did for his sister Aisling. So he is a bit ahead of the rest and Ballet Blonde's parents are also stumping up, thank God. After all, as a self-employed person with his bizarre but amazingly successful 'Leopold Bloom Dublin Coffee Tour' business, he isn't the sort a suit in the bank would be throwing money at.

His mates aren't so lucky.

As a result of the extortionate price of accommodation, houses like Quango Man's are full of adult children who can't afford to grow up. Today in the Renaissance Nation, 280,000 adults between the ages of 21 and 39 are still living with their parents.[145] This figure is rising. It is not healthy because, if people can't afford to grow up, they won't. We also know that more and more of the Pope's Children, and their younger siblings the Crash Kids, are remaining single much, much later. As mentioned earlier, the number of single women in their thirties here has increased more than threefold since 1980 and doubled in the case of men.[146]

Therefore, it's likely that they want apartments within the city limits, not three-bed semis out in Applegreen Land. They probably want to live alone in the city, the way their peers on the continent do. However, we are not building apartments largely because of Bananaism. Every time an apartment block is proposed, with decent heights in the city centre or in the verdant zone inside the M50 where the transport links are, our friends the Cave Dwellers gather to protest and oppose. Politicians with slender majorities run a mile.

Within the city, between the canals – Rejjie Snow's old stomping ground – height restrictions, imposed mainly by lobbyists citing heritage who usually don't live in the area, are preventing the type of high-rise or even medium-rise development commonplace elsewhere. In terms of urban development, Ireland has effectively banned the single most important urban transport innovation of the past two centuries: the lift.

Our aversion to the lift, or elevator as our American cousins call it, a result of Bananaism, means that we have derelict sites in our cities, long commutes from Greater Wexico every morning, and mass evacuation every evening. The Danish capital Copenhagen, hardly a high-rise dystopian conurbation, manages to fit 600,000 people living in an area the same size as that part of Dublin that lies between the canals; central Dublin only manages one-fifth of this, again because of planning restrictions.

Let's take the comparison a bit further. Portlaoise, one of the youngest towns in the country and one of the most ethnically diverse, is what could be called an ethnoburb – a multi-ethnic distant suburb. Every day thousands commute the 90 kilometres from Portlaoise to Dublin. Toyko, the largest city in the world, is also 90 kilometres wide. In the same space, the Japanese have built a conurbation of 35 million people, while we have built, on the same footprint, a handful of towns, full of commuters and 10 Applegreen filling stations.

JOINING THE DOTS

As we have seen, the main reason that Ireland's costs are so out of whack is because the cost of accommodation is way out of line. This leads to upward pressure on the entire cost base and the only way workers can afford a place to live, either to buy or rent, is by seeking higher wages. This in turn puts upward pressure on the cost base of other goods, particularly in labour-intensive industries, and this has the effect of pushing up most service prices.

It also leads to a direct transfer of wealth from young workers to old landlords, amplifying wealth inequality and enriching not so much the 1% as the 15%, the citizens of the Banana Republic who are keen to preserve their privileges. There are many ways of moving to arrest this without waiting for the political pendulum to swing against the Radical Centre towards the radical left or right. However, as we saw, when we live in a Testocracy, run by Testocrats, the possibility of doing nothing and following conventions at the top is extremely likely.

But the Radical Centre was not created by doing nothing. It was created by millions of Irish people gradually saying 'Enough!' It was forged by the little mutinies going off in the heads of millions of us, demanding change, demanding an end to the dead hand of the Church and the state, and granting people the dignity to get up and have a go. So how do we solve this?

GEORGIAN DUBLIN, CORK, LIMERICK AND GALWAY

Henry George wrote the most successful economics book ever. *Progress and Poverty*, published in 1879, sold millions and was quoted extensively by people as varied as Tolstoy, Churchill and George Bernard Shaw. In the 1880s, its sales in America were second only to the Bible.

The core argument of this book, the central Georgian message, is that land is a resource that can be either used or hoarded. If it is used and developed, everyone benefits; if it is hoarded, it becomes a speculative asset that benefits and enriches the individual owner. Therefore, George argues that policy should reward the active use of land and penalise land hoarding.

George also observed that land should be taxed heavily because the value of land is created not by the owners, but by its location. The location is made valuable by other people, through factors like shops, public infrastructure, factories, public parks, transport and other people's money and creativity. Therefore, a tax, called a site value tax, should be levied on it to make sure that this asset, which is quite useless and whose value is enhanced by other investment around it, should be used and not hoarded.

When you know that an idea brings together economists from the right and the left, and one which Milton Friedman called 'the least bad tax', it's worth exploring.

Think about the game of Monopoly, Irish-style. All the different streets have various costs and the idea is to hoard as much property as possible to make as much money as possible. Did you ever ask yourself what makes some areas expensive and others cheap? The reason Dublin 4 is expensive in Monopoly is that that's where the rich people live, but they live there because it's close to town, houses are big, schools are good, infrastructure is excellent, St Vincent's Hospital is just down the road, the RDS is over there and UCD is up the other end. The road out to Wicklow is decent and the DART runs through it. It's filled with decent restaurants and five-star hotels. Even the Aviva is within walking distance.

In other words, sites are expensive because of other factors, largely public factors, financed by taxpayers. Land-owners enjoy unearned income, generated by great transport links and proximity to customers and businesses. Therefore, the site value of the land is not generated by the landowner, but by society in general.

George argued that increases in the value of sites should be taxed and taxed heavily – so much so that countries could eventually replace income tax with land taxes or at least reduce income tax significantly. It is a truly compelling and egalitarian idea and, unlike other taxes, it wouldn't lead to capital flight or to people working less.

In Ireland, such a move would liberate enormous tracts of land for development, eliminate dereliction, reduce the cost of property and free millions of income tax payers from the heavy burden of excessive income tax.

Take, for instance, Phibsboro, where we left Ballet Blonde, Flat White Man and Skin Fade. Let's focus for a moment on the impact of the new Luas line on the area. House values, commercial land values and rents have increased substantially with the help of public investment in the new Luas system. Who paid for this? You did. Who benefits from this? Do you? The lucky local landowner certainly does. What did he or she do for this windfall? Nothing.

So, this is a transfer of wealth from the general population, through taxation and public investment, to the individual in the form of rocketing land prices.

If this unearned windfall were taxed with a site-value tax or a location fee, the impact would be dramatic and the logic would be fair. It would also be much fairer than property tax, as it wouldn't penalise people for renovations they may make. Think of all those aspiring Dermot Bannons; do you want to tax them for living out their renovation fantasies?

A location fee would undermine the stranglehold the property lobby has on Irish economics, help reduce land speculation and hoarding, and penalise the dereliction that has blighted our cities as property owners hoard land, waiting for prices to rise. All areas of the capital city and its suburbs would be covered by a location fee, because land values would be driven up by other people, not the landowner. This is why you never see giant shopping centres like Dundrum built in the middle of the countryside without transport links or population centres.

The value of Dundrum Shopping Centre's site is the people and businesses located nearby, the M50 access, the buses and the Luas. Why should the owner of the land get all the upside when you – the citizen taxpayer – create the value?

Taxing sites so that the gain from public investment and infrastructure is not skewed towards the land-hoarding individual is fair. But most critically, given the dire need to accelerate building in Ireland right now, if you tax sites, you penalise hoarding and dereliction. If, for example, tax on undeveloped sites was set at 80% annually, the incentive to build on them quickly would be enormous, as to sit on the vacant lots would cost the landowner hugely.

The beauty of this is that it puts the incentive on the land hoarder to act. No one compels them to do anything, but economics sets out very clearly the penalties for doing nothing. In no time, Ireland's property crisis would be over, or at least moving in the right direction very quickly, allowing the Pope's Children to get on with their lives without paying the most expensive land prices in what is still one of the least populated countries in western Europe.

The main problem with property in Ireland is supply and the psychology of the land owner. We have lots of land, but it is not being used. Land is being hoarded. Why would you sell or develop now if you think prices are rising? Why not wait until next year or the year after and pocket an extra 15 or 20%? Consequently, policy should aim to encourage active land management as opposed to passive hoarding, don't you think?

In short, a land tax is the way forward. It's also a change that we must make to free our society from land interests without doing anything too radical; gentle persuasion rather than confiscation is the future for the Radical Centre.

Changing taxes is what countries do. Every year, income and indirect taxes are increased or decreased arbitrarily. Why not land taxes? For our Renaissance Nation to keep expanding, nothing can be sacred, no resource off-limits.

Change is the only constant and a site value tax would be a huge step in the right direction.

Now let's leave the land and look at trade. Let's expore rewriting the rules of engagement between the sovereign nation state and mobile international capital.

CHAPTER 32

GLOBAL IRISH

L et's go for a drink, or at least go to the pub. Pick almost any country in the world which has become open to globalisation, where the middle class has grown and where the economy is expanding, and what do you find? An Irish pub!

When Pope John Paul II came to Ireland in 1979, there were hardly any Irish pubs outside Ireland with the exception of the States. Today there are over 6,300 members of the Irish Pubs Global Federation. In fact, the Irish pub is one of the fastest growing food and booze franchises in the world.

As the Renaissance Nation took off, its brand, our brand, exploded onto the international scene in the guise of the Irish pub. The Irish pub has allowed Ireland to project our brand far beyond our small island. While I wouldn't go as far as Tom Friedman and suggest that 'no two countries with an Irish pub ever went to war', what I can say is that as a leading indicator for globalisation, the Irish pub is one of the best. This global take-off in Irish pubs mirrors the take-off in our economy since 1990. In short, as a measure of how globalised a country we are, the mushrooming of Irish pubs isn't a bad place to start.

This Irish pub theory of globalisation came to me many years ago when I found myself in Kiev's Irish pub, Kitty O'Shea's, facing a bit of a dilemma. I was working for a French bank and was charged with explaining what was going on in Russia and Ukraine.

Having met the IMF, World Bank and EU delegations, along with consultants and other bottom-feeders, it struck me that these rarefied bureaucrats hadn't a rashers what was going on in the place. They were typical economists: removed, distant and naive. You wouldn't give them a post office account to open back home.

One of the barmen in Kitty's was a different hawk – a typical Irishman with a roguish sense of humour. We got talking about Irish pubs in Eastern and Central Europe. He knew the market, the demographics, who had money in Kiev and the ratio of expats to locals. He explained how to get import licences and how to weed out crooked 'drifter' Irish barmen.

He knew how to defer tax payments, how to spot a good site and a decent landlord. He knew where to source furniture locally, how to deal with local tradesmen, who to pay first, and how to 'incentivise' officials.

He outlined his marketing strategy and which local movers and shakers to target as regulars. He advised about avoiding the mafia. He emphasised the importance of the brand and the significance of local aspirations. This barman was a mine of information.

He offered advice on pricing strategies. He had figured out how to borrow in euros, hedge his local currency risk and stay on good terms with the bank – quite an achievement. That evening, he outlined the basics of running a cash business in a foreign country.

After a few pints, it struck me that the opening of an Irish pub in a developing city could tell you more about what was going on in the economy than a glossy economic report. The opening of an Irish pub tells you who is investing where, why and at what price more accurately than statistics about inflation, budget deficits or trade deficits. With that in mind, the Irish Pub Index was born. Over the years, I put together this index with the help of the marketing department of Guinness and it turns out to be a helpful indicator of economic development. It also reveals how powerful the Irish brand is and how we are constantly messaging millions of people every day, people who have never set foot in the country. It might be unorthodox but the Irish pub and what we could term global Ireland, the free-wheeling, commercially savvy, tolerant, internationally plugged in, trading nation that we have become over the past 30-odd years, are synonymous.

Traditionally when hard power such as military or political heft was the currency of a country's might, a country was truly powerful if it could project its power far beyond its own boundaries. These days hard power has been supplanted, or at least added to, by what is called soft power. Soft power is the power of the brand, the power of the imagination or the creative power whereby a country can influence the world to see the globe on our terms, without having to resort to violence or coercion. The power of the national brand expressed through the Irish pub helps enormously in projecting a positive, friendly, hospitable image of Ireland all around the world.

Check out this map – the shaded areas show Irish pub presence around the world. In 1990, before the economy took off, there were hardly any Irish pubs outside the country, except in places like Boston which had large Irish communities. Now look at the globe. The British used to say the sun never set on the Empire; now we can look around the globe and say the sun never sets on the Irish pub empire. Anytime, anyplace, anywhere the image of Ireland is being reinforced. And we never had to fire a shot, they just had to drink one!

Irish Pub Presence

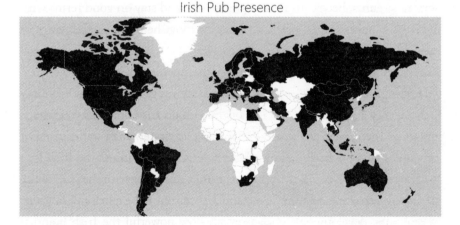

The reason I'm showing you the Irish pub map of the world is because I want to talk about globalisation, modernity and the road ahead for the Renaissance Nation, with regard to our future relationship with global capital, global investment and global corporations. Ireland is and must remain a destination for foreign capital where both Ireland and the multinational can mutually benefit. We would never have succeeded if we'd had to rely on our own market – it is far too small. We must constantly overcome the tyranny of geography and demography. There is a way to achieve this but, as befits the Radical Centre, it demands thinking about things from a different angle.

A TRADING STATE

With the re-emergence of flag waving and nativism in global politics, it's easy to forget that countries and national economies can defy simple geopolitical definitions or groupings. Globalisation has allowed countries, particularly small countries, to escape the tyranny of geography. The Renaissance Nation has embraced this opportunity wholeheartedly. As a result, even though the political rhetoric claims that Ireland is at the 'heart of Europe', the truth is that Ireland isn't really a European economy at all but an Atlantic economy with a brand that is projected all over the globe, profoundly influenced by history, geography, language and culture.

Compared with any other EU country, Ireland is more exposed to Brexit, more open to American investment and more porous to Anglo/American commercial norms and innovations. In addition, our mercantile structure is held together by a shared English-language common-law system.

Over the past two decades, while we have become diplomatically and constitutionally closer to the EU, we have become economically and commercially closer to the American world. Close to 80% of our total exports now come from US multinationals based here, and this figure is growing.[147]

We've done well out of this economic promiscuity, servicing both sides with equal enthusiasm. American capital flowed in, as did European immigrants seeking better prospects. Indeed, the presence of multinationals here, with their Irish and foreign workforces, is one of the most conspicuous successes of the tolerant, business-friendly value system that underpins the Radical Centre.

Increasingly, Ireland looks less like a nation state, or even a region of Europe, and more like a trading hub off the continent's west coast, akin to a medieval Hanseatic city state, an early twentieth-century Shanghai or a nineteenth-century St Petersburg. The 'trading state' has been a feature of economic history, from ancient Alexandria to Dubrovnik.

The growth of services rather than manufacturing, the fall in transport costs, and the emergence of e-commerce have ensured that Ireland is not on anyone's periphery but at the centre of the globalised trading world.

However, playing this trading state game takes skill and vision. Economic history tells us that others, usually bigger players, become jealous of the small trading state's autonomy and move to strip it of its advantages, particularly if capital is moving consistently towards the smaller competitor. Remember, money is like water; it always follows the path of least resistance.

To maintain this position as a home for international capital and a destination for international talent, our trading state must be deft and subtle, negotiating between the great powers rather than siding with one explicitly.

The Renaissance Nation should aim to maintain a footloose commercial status in the face of the relentless march of harmonisation, the enemy of uniqueness.

THE MACRON FACTOR

Over the years, I've often visualised Ireland as a jockey riding two horses: the continental EU horse and the Atlantic Anglo-American horse. When both horses are riding together, the jockey's position is tenable. For years, both horses ran together as the EU and the Anglo-American world were on the same track economically, socially and politically. But three forces – Brexit, US President Donald Trump and French President Emmanuel Macron – have changed the nature of the race.

The Brexit arguments have been well rehearsed elsewhere. In terms of individual countries, the UK is our single biggest trading partner. No other European country is as important to us.

Trump is a threat to our capital base because he wants to reduce US corporation taxes to coax American capital back home.

But while Trump wants to drop taxes, Macron wants to increase them. The greatest threat to Ireland's trading state status might not be the in-your-face, nativist flag wavers in Washington and London, but the behind-the-scenes, integrationist harmonisers in Brussels and, more importantly, in Paris.

Although our annual trade with France is only worth €9 billion – which means we do more commerce in nine weeks with Britain than we do over a whole year with France – Macron may have a bigger impact on Ireland than Brexit.[148]

Because of the dominance of the UK and the English language in the Irish media, we receive a lot of UK-centric and, therefore, Brexit-obsessed news. In the next chapter, we will explore its impact on the North. However, in continental media, Brexit and Northern Ireland rarely holds the front page. For most Europeans, Brexit simply makes detached what was always semi-detached. In contrast, the EU's own backyard has long been framed by the Franco-German relationship. This too is changing.

In Germany there is a sense that this will be Chancellor Angela Merkel's last hurrah. Across the Rhine, Macron realises this and sees an opportunity to remould Europe. Macron is the man of the moment and he realises he needs to construct a new rallying call to combat populism.

In the first round of the French elections, populism revealed itself on the extreme right and extreme left. In Germany, it materialised in the form of the Alternative für Deutschland (AfD) on the right. In Italy, populists are in government. Meanwhile, the nationalist revolt in Catalonia has further undermined European harmony, which was once taken for granted, particularly in Brussels.

Farther east, reactionaries and nationalists with values that run contrary to core EU positions on migration and racial tolerance are in power across a vast territorial arc, from Stettin in Poland to Bratislava in Slovakia and on to Budapest in Hungary. In the old imperial capital of Vienna, an anti-immigrant electoral surge has propelled the extreme right to power.

Macron sees these difficulties within the EU as the signal for regeneration of the European project, a siren call made more acute by the anti-EU developments of Brexit and Trump's presidency. Be under no illusion:

British and American nativism supports European populism implicitly and, in less guarded moments, explicitly.

The French president envisages a more integrated EU economy, more adept at combating the US and Asia. Macron's European regeneration means 'more Europe' – that is, tax harmonisation and particularly corporate tax harmonisation. It will not just be about the rate at which corporate tax is levied, but also the way tax is assessed. For services such as Google Ads, this implies the tax will be levied in the country where the ad is placed, as opposed to where Google is domiciled, which is Ireland.

Commercially, the new Europe could end up being the gospel according to EU Competition Commissioner Margrethe Vestager, made flesh in the guise of Emmanuel Macron.

IRELAND'S CALL

What do all these developments mean for the Renaissance Nation, the 21st-century trading state?

We must make a choice. We can stay outside the new integrationist EU, using our veto to block any changes to our tax code, but this confrontation risks siding with tax avoiders or 'corporate deserters', as former US President Barack Obama described them. In addition, 'Official Ireland' is unlikely to step off the integrationist wagon even if an economically deeper Europe is not in our interest.

Is there any way Ireland can use the tumult in the years ahead to our advantage, remaining a premier destination for mobile capital, investment and talent? Can we remain a trading state, like the Hanseatic cities, ensuring our citizens are prosperous?

It is possible, but we must take the lead and redefine the relationship between the nation state and international companies. Unless you believe globalisation is about to come to a shuddering halt, investment will remain global, corporations' supply chains will remain multinational and money will move like water to the place of least resistance.

Here's the way the system works now. The multinational sets up in a country, creating jobs and paying as little tax as it can. The company gets access to the market. In the case of Ireland, our attraction is enhanced by the fact that multinationals based here have the concession to trade with the EU. It's a free pass.

In return, we get only tax and jobs – and if we don't have the local talent to fill those jobs, educated Europeans come without needing visas. Because Ireland is tolerant, cosmopolitan and liberal, more and more companies want to come here as their key employees are happy to live here. It is a self-reinforcing dynamic, whereby good people beget investment capital, which begets more talented people which begets more capital, driving wages and tax revenue upwards. But tax and wages are income; the real question is what happens to the wealth of the multinationals? We have seen in previous chapters the difference between wealth and income. This distinction between income and wealth in economics is not well understood by politicians, which is not surprising because income is short-term, and so too is politics. Wealth is longer term and inheritable.

The lion's share of the riches made by multinationals goes to shareholders in the form of rising share prices and dividends. Only a tiny fraction goes back to workers in the form of income and to the host state in the form of taxes.

WHAT DO WE WANT?

The tumult in the world gives Ireland a chance to change this system in such a way that many more Irish people might benefit and that multinationals could embrace.

We could reinvent the relationship between the state and the corporation. In so doing, we could remain fully European but with an American sense of corporate innovation that would enrich all Irish citizens. Investment would continue to flow in here, mirroring that of the successful city-states of the past.

According to the US Bureau of Economic Analysis, American multinationals in 2016 made $146 billion (or €126 billion) profit in Ireland.[149] Our corporation tax rate is 12.5%, so they should be paying about €16 billion a year in tax. But they paid only €9 billion.[150] This means that almost €7 billion is missing, because these companies use a myriad of loopholes to avoid even our low rates of tax.

The net is tightening, and companies such as Apple are moving money to offshore structures to avoid tax. But these companies know they are on the wrong side of global opinion, and they want a way out.

Deals are done when both sides have something to gain from reaching an agreement.

Multinationals in Ireland want a new deal which minimises their immediate tax outgoings while remaining tax-compliant.

We want them to stay here, but we want something more. We want a share in their wealth, not just wages and tax income.

What about proposing that multinationals take the difference between what they owe and ought to pay, roughly €7 billion, and pay this to us in shares? We would then set up an Irish sovereign wealth fund composed of the shares of multinationals based here. These are the shares of the best-performing companies in the world across some of the fastest-growing sectors of the global economy. This fund could grow rapidly, creating a real source of wealth for this country, which could be between €110 billion and €140 billion over a decade – €23,000 per Irish person.

In such a way, we could treat the multinational presence as akin to an oil find, much as Norway has banked its oil windfall. Thus we wouldn't just get income, we would share in the wealth of the companies and put aside this wealth for future generations – into a fund that could not be used to finance day-to-day government spending.

Nor would this fund necessarily be used to fund pensions; it could be used as a start-up fund. The Irish economy needs a vibrant start-up scene and not just a multinational sector. Pledging liquid shares of globally traded companies as collateral against investment funds for start-ups would lead to a surge in local innovation.

Multinationals already pay their workers in a combination of wages and share options, so the concept isn't too radical. They would be paying the host country in a similar split between tax and share options. In addition, this initiative would reduce their immediate tax bill, which would drop immediately into their bottom line.

Politically, this would be a form of wealth redistribution in a country with significant levels of wealth inequality. It would give all Irish citizens a stake they don't currently have. It would also give poorer people equity, the main instrument underpinning financial security.

It would get us out of a potential scrap with Brussels, turning the threats of Trump and Brexit into a huge opportunity and putting us one step ahead of Europe, while keeping both feet firmly within the EU.

Geo-strategically, converting unpaid and future taxes into shares would place Ireland at the cutting edge of globalisation. Ireland could become a leader in framing a new relationship between the nation state and the global multinational company. Pledging shares in a wealth fund to the average citizen would give everyone a greater stake in the country, underpinning the Radical Centre and militating against the radical right and left that we see threatening other countries.

Looking ahead, we will need to get these significant economic initiatives in order before we face possibly the biggest challenge of all for our Renaissance Nation. One hundred years after partition, they haven't gone away, you know.

It's time to look at the Nordies.

CHAPTER 33

THE FINAL FRONTIER

CULTURAL FAULT LINES

D id you know that an episode of *Star Trek* was banned in Ireland and Britain? *Star Trek* is many things, but is it really so incendiary as to be worthy of censorship? The twelfth episode (of course it would have to be the twelfth) in the third series of *Star Trek: The Next Generation* was never shown on terrestrial television in Ireland or Britain. In that episode, Lieutenant Commander Data, musing about terrorism in Northern Ireland from the vantage point of the year 2364, noted that Ireland had been reunited in 2024.

This episode was due to be aired in 1990 but was pulled by the censors in both jurisdictions for fear it might encourage political violence.

For many in the Republic, the North is indeed the final frontier, a remote galaxy populated by a different species. But that was then and this is now; today, the frontier may be coming closer and more quickly than you might have imagined. While it mightn't be at the warp-speed of the *Starship Enterprise*, the march towards a United Ireland appears to be accelerating at a pace that few of us appreciate or maybe even want to entertain.

Up until recently, talk of Irish unity was the preserve of romantic nationalists and five-pint Provos who find their inner Pádraig Pearse after a few gargles. However, the reality is that the demographic clock is ticking relentlessly towards the day when self-identifying Catholics outnumber self-identifying Protestants. While sectarian identity doesn't absolutely translate into voting intention, as the Catholic population grows, the chance of a nationalist majority seeking the reunification of the country grows too.

Unification would have been on the cards in time, but Brexit has accelerated everything. It has forced many in the Republic to focus on something that they were not ready for. It has also changed the minds of many in the middle ground in the North, facing the dilemma of either being in a union with London outside the EU or being in a United Ireland within the EU. Polls are now suggesting a significant majority of Northerners will opt for the latter.

As history shows us, once enormous political processes such as a call for unification are set in train and become part of mainstream political conversations, expectations are raised on both sides and a momentum builds which becomes extremely difficult to reverse. The window has been opened.

Perhaps there is evidence of a heightened sense that reunification could be a looming possibility in the increasingly neurotic public displays of fanatical loyalism in Protestant areas of Northern Ireland. I have been travelling around the North recently, taking in the views from rural Markethill in south Armagh to the prosperous King's Road, Belmont and Stormont suburbs of east Belfast, and from coastal fishing villages of the Ards Peninsula to the council estates of Cookstown in Tyrone. I am now seeing Union Jacks and even UVF flags where I never saw them before. The anxiety of unionism about the ticking demographic clock is captured by this 'backs-to-the-wall' psychosis displayed in extravagant loyalist pageantry on the streets. They know it's coming, so the bonfires on the Twelfth are getting more gargantuan.

While *Star Trek*'s Commander Data might have been out by a decade or two, the population data indicates that he wasn't too far off.

THE TIES THAT BIND

Unlike many citizens of the Renaissance Nation, the North is not the final frontier for me. It has been part of my story for many years. I suppose it started when my paternal grandparents emigrated from Scotland to Ireland at the turn of the last century. Like many Scots, their families had been over and back from Ulster for generations. For a young 'mixed' couple, brought up in the intense sectarianism of Edwardian Scotland, Dublin was a liberal oasis. Difficult as it is to believe, pre-independence Dublin was tolerant, or at least it appeared that way compared to the harsh religious strictures of 'Wee-Free'-dominated western Scotland. This is how the McWilliamses ended up in Dalkey in 1914. They chose Dalkey because other Scottish relatives had been stationed in nearby Dún Laoghaire with the Royal Navy and told my painter and decorator grandfather that there would be lots of work around there 'doing up' the big homes of the admiralty in Killiney.

The working assumption was the same admiralty would be around for a while. But, within a decade, the Royal Navy and its officer class was gone. Things can change much quicker than anyone expects.

Sixteen years later, my late father was born in Ballycastle, County Antrim, because, rather inexplicably, my heavily pregnant Scottish grandmother was on her way by boat across the straits to visit her sister twenty miles away from the Mull of Kintyre on the Scottish islands. So, technically, my dad's from Antrim. On the other side, my mother is from west Cork, which is geographically, emotionally and psychologically about as far from north Antrim as it is possible on the island.

I am the product of two of Ireland's polar opposites. For my first 25 years, my Cork DNA dominated any other genes that might have had the temerity to try to make themselves known. (Anyone with Cork blood will know that the Rebel County entertains few competitors.) Growing up, the North was a foreign country, a violent reminder of the sectarianism that my grandparents had tried to escape. Like most southerners, I rarely crossed the border and my Antrim–Scottish heritage, or any association with the North, so obvious in my surname, was something I rarely considered, until I met Sian at a County Down wedding in July 1994.

Being best man is always a tricky business; being best man at a northern–southern union during the Troubles comes with a whole new set of challenges. Obviously, the speech is a minefield. When you are involved in a ceremony officiated by the moderator of the Presbyterian Church in Ireland, you begin to understand that the cultural fault-lines between the North and the South are not so much well-signposted differences as disguised incendiary devices primed to go off at any time, even when you think you are on safe ground.

Unlike the Renaissance Nation, the brethren up the road take their religion seriously.

The morning of the wedding, sweating after a big night out at Ned's bar in Holywood, County Down, the groom and myself sat down with the minister in the austere surroundings of Ballygilbert Presbyterian Church just outside Bangor. My Catholicism is so lapsed as to be totally useless in situations like this but, worse still, as befits a Dún Laoghaire liberal, the groom had not even been baptised. There was a bit of 'a lapsed Catholic and an atheist walk into a bar' feel to it all. Nothing triggers the hungover heebie-jeebies like the sight of a minister with Bible in hand. He solemnly produced the good book and demanded to know which verses we had chosen. The lad might as well have been speaking Swahili.

Later, at three on the dot, the guilty pair of us stood at the altar waiting for the bride. The entire right side of the church was full; punctual Northern Presbyterians, Anglicans, Methodists and the odd be-bonneted Plymouth brethren great-aunt, sitting erect, expectant. Not much smiling going on, but as I've learnt, that's their way in God's house. It is understood everywhere that brides are usually late, but congregations – smiling or not – are supposed to turn up on time. Opposite the grimacing Protestants, almost every pew on the left side, the southern side, was empty. The southerners had, almost to a man and woman, observed the great Irish ritual of the swift one before the big do. The Cultra Inn up the road was jammed with tuxedos rented from Blacktie.

Eventually abandoning the pagan at the altar, I had to barrel down the A2 towards Belfast, in the minister's shiny red Vauxhall, to shoo these

Dublin reprobates out of the boozer and get them into the church. The bride's driver, her staunch Presbyterian father, had been put under strict instructions to keep circumnavigating Bangor. It was going to be a long day and it would take more than champagne, confetti and the trickiest speech of my life to break the cultural ice.

The bridesmaid couldn't stop laughing at these ridiculous Dubliners, their casual attitudes to ritual and their rather pathetic best man, who was trying to keep the whole chaotic show on the road, one off-the-cuff remark away from catastrophe. But in the end, reader, she married me and we haven't stopped laughing since.

So began my 25-year education with the intricacies of Northern Ireland. It's been a long matriculation. Just when you think you are ahead, you are pulled back to earth. For example, for our own wedding we chose the neutral territory of Connemara, neither Belfast nor Dublin. It took a while to find a working Protestant vicar out there. But we did eventually. I thought we were doing everything right and the Northern brethren would be delighted with a Protestant service deep in enemy territory. We all arrived on time, made sure to say 'Awww-men' rather than 'Ay-men', read from something called the *Book of Common Prayer*, inserted 'for thine is the kingdom, the power and the glory' at the end of the 'Our Father' – which they called 'The Lord's Prayer' – and tried to belt out unsingable, obscure Protestant hymns. I thought it was the most Protestant thing I'd ever been at, until the vicar announced that the service was over and my mother-in-law, sitting behind me, leant over and whispered to my father-in-law:

'That was a little bit Roman, Billy.'

You can't win with these people!

But winning and losing has been the problem with the North since partition. For one side to win, the other has to lose. Looking ahead, perhaps the greatest challenge to the Renaissance Nation is how we deal with unification and the lead up to it. Can we do this without jeopardising the liberal, tolerant, commercially dynamic characteristics that underpin the Radical Centre?

DEMOGRAPHIC REALITY

Let's consider demographics. The latest census that we have from the North is the 2011 census which shows that Protestants and Catholics are almost evenly split.[151]

Digging deeper, the data reveals the proportion of Catholics and Protestants in various age groups. Of the elderly, those over 90, 64% are Protestant and 25% are Catholic. A total of 9% had no declared religion.[152] This division reflects the religious status quo when these people were born in the 1920s, and more or less reflects the realities of the Treaty. The numbers underscore the sectarian buffer that was supposed to ensure that Northern Ireland would remain Protestant and unionist. However, that didn't envisage the dramatic flight of middle-class Protestants to universities in Scotland and England. Few came back. Today, that sectarian buffer is wafer-thin and getting thinner.

When you look to the future, you see that the Catholic population will soon form a majority and this could happen as early as the next decade. Protestant Northern Ireland is old, shrinking and nervous; the Catholic six counties are young, expanding and confident.

In the census, when you look at the cohort of children born since 2008, the picture changes completely. Compared to the over-90s, amongst whom Protestants outnumber Catholics easily, the corresponding figure for the young is 34% Protestant and 45% Catholic. In one (admittedly long) lifetime, the Catholic population in the youngest cohort has nearly doubled, while the Protestant cohort has almost halved.[153]

Even accounting for the significant rise in those professing no religion, the census numbers suggest we are on the road to a United Ireland.

THE PRICE OF PARTITION

Historically, emigration has always been a good indicator of economic frailty. Between 1841 and 1951, the population of the Republic's 26 counties fell by 55% compared to just 17% in the six counties of Northern Ireland, underscoring how advanced the northeast's economy used to be.[154] As a result of this, a myth has evolved that the North was always – at least until very recently – economically more advanced than the South. Equally, it has regularly been argued that a significant number of Northern Irish Catholics believe that staying with the UK is the right thing to do for their back pocket, possibly because of the UK's ongoing subvention to the Northern economy.

Up until the emergence of the 'growth freak' that is the modern Irish Republic, such Northern confidence might have seemed reasonable. But when you look closely at the economic numbers, you can see that this is not the case today and has not been for some time.

It is unfashionable to say it, but the union has been an economic calamity for Northern Ireland. All the people have suffered – Catholic and Protestant, unionist and nationalist.

If we go back to 1907, 70% of the industrial output of the entire island of Ireland came from the six counties that would go on to become Northern Ireland, with activity largely centred on Belfast.[155] This was where all Irish industry was; northern entrepreneurs and inventors were at the forefront of industrial innovation. By 1911, Belfast was the biggest city in Ireland with a population of 386,947 – comfortably outstripping that of Dublin at 304,802[156] – and was also growing rapidly. The northeast was by far the richest part of the island.

According to the 1911 census, Protestants in Ireland accounted for 26% of the total population, yet occupational returns suggest that they made up an outsized 40% of the industrial workforce.[157] In 1926 manufacturing accounted for just 7% of employment in the Republic compared with 29% in Northern Ireland.[158] For most other small European countries at the time, manufacturing employment stood at around 25%, reinforcing just how backward and poor the Republic would have seemed to Northerners.

Fast-forward to today and the collapse of the once-dynamic Northern economy versus that of the Republic is shocking. The tolerant Radical Centre is far wealthier than the more religiously observant Northern Ireland. Having been a fraction of the North's at independence, the Republic's industrial output is now far greater than that of Northern Ireland. Exports of goods from the Republic are around €120 billion, while exports from the North come to a paltry €8 billion.[159, 160] This obviously reflects the influence of multinationals, but it also underscores just how far ahead the Republic's industrial base is. Producing 15 times more exports underscores a vast difference in terms of the globalisation of business.

In the same way that emigration was a good proxy for economic frailty, immigration is a good indicator of economic success. People move to places where they feel their kids will have a better life. Today in the Republic, one in six people are foreign-born.[161] In the North, it is less than one in twenty, when you exclude those born in the Republic or Britain.[162]

If immigration tells you about foreign people's choices, direct foreign investment tells you about the choices made by foreign capital. People ascribe much of the economic travails to the Troubles. That is fair enough. There is little doubt that the bombing and the violence of the Troubles destroyed much of the commercial and retail fabric of the North, but if the North's economic decline can be ascribed to the Troubles, the North's economy would have grown more rapidly than the Republic's since 1998. This has not happened.

Over the years, the dependent nature of the Northern Irish economy has become endemic, with handouts from Whitehall replacing the urge to pay for itself. This is evidenced again by the DUP's recent approach to propping up Teresa May's government with a ransom which has nothing to do with making Northern Ireland self-sufficient – in fact, you could argue that it is nothing more than another subsidy in a subsidy-junkie's shopping basket. More subsidies will make the Northern economy more, not less, fragile.

There is much talk about the UK's subvention to Northern Ireland and how the Republic could not afford the North. When you look at the numbers it becomes clear this is just that – talk. The subvention is just over €10 billion annually.[163] When seen from the perspective of the North, with its total GDP of under €50 billion,[164] it looks like a significant figure, but when seen from the perspective of Dublin, it is not. For example, as one demonstration of the dynamism of the Republic's economy, between the signing of the Good Friday Agreement in 1998 and 2014, American corporations alone invested over €310 billion or $400 billion in the

Republic.[165] This figure is equivalent to 38 years of the British government's annual subvention to keep the North afloat!

Furthermore, when expressed as a percentage of national income, which is the normal way financial markets assess whether national expenditure is sustainable or not, Northern Ireland would cost less than 4% of the Irish Republic's GDP annually.[166] Of course, even this manageable figure would end up lower because the combined Irish GDP of the Republic combined with the North would be close to €350 billion, reducing the subvention as a percentage of income yet more. In short, in pure budgetary terms, there is little doubt that the Republic's economy could absorb the North even before the commercial dynamism of unification kicks in.

However, the budgetary reality does tell us another story. Today, the Republic's budget deficit is less than 1% of GDP, easily financed.[167] In contrast, if the North had to pay for itself in the morning, its budget deficit would be about 27% of its GDP![168] Therefore, the budgetary arithmetic tells us Northern Ireland clearly cannot exist as an independent, financially solvent entity. It is a lost child in search of foster parents.

Income earned and living standards in Northern Ireland remain below the UK average. Of the UK's 12 economic regions, Northern Ireland had the third-lowest gross value added per capita in 2016 (£19,997 or €22,442), considerably below the UK's average (£26,621 or €29,876) and well below the corresponding figure for the Republic in the same year (€57,000 or £50,808 at current exchange rates).[169, 170] Northern Ireland still exhibits significant economic dependency on the public sector, which accounts for about 70% of the region's GDP and employs roughly 30% of its workforce, while a high proportion of working-age individuals have no qualifications.[171]

In terms of income per head, Northern Ireland's per capita GDP is similar to that of the border region of Ireland, which is about 38% lower than the national average. As such, in a United Ireland, per capita GDP would be 11% lower than the current national average in Ireland.[172]

At partition, it was so different. The North was industrial and rich, the South agricultural and poor. Now the contrast couldn't be greater. This is due to the concubine nature of the Northern state. If you don't have to pay your bills, you become dependent and you do not confer dignity to the noble pursuit of commercial self-expression. Seen through the lens of the Renaissance Nation, where the state and religion need to back off to allow the questioning 'have a go' citizen to express their individuality, it is hard to envisage a less supportive backdrop to risk-taking and commercial endeavour than the combination of the suffocating state and religious dogma that characterises the North. A way to look at this is that one part of the country was forced to pay its own way, disciplined by the bond markets, and the other was allowed to sit back and take handouts. Ultimately each of these systems led to profoundly different outcomes.

The Republic's economy is roughly six times larger, generated by a workforce that is only two and a half times bigger; average income per head in the Republic, at €39,873, dwarfs the €23,700 across the border.[173]

Dublin is three times bigger than Belfast, far more cosmopolitan, and home to hundreds of international companies.

My Northern relatives joke that, when we first met and they came 'down south', the roads would suddenly become more potholed and the panel-beaten cars all appeared to be ancient. Today, the opposite is the case. To these proper Northern petrol-heads, the state of motors and the roads is a crucial bell-weather. But maybe a better bell-weather in the twenty-first century is the state of restaurants because this reveals to us not just how much money people have in their back pockets, but how they spend it.

THE TRIPADVISOR INDEX OF THE NORTHERN ECONOMY

Before we head out in search of that mythical place called 'Middle Ulster', let me introduce a new indicator of economic development: the TripAdvisor Index of economic vibrancy. This measures the number of restaurants reviewed on TripAdvisor in any town.[174] In economic terms, restaurants capture not just economic dynamism and disposable income, but demography and social vibrancy, all of which, when added to hard numbers, help give us a sense of a place.

Bear this in mind as we head up North.

During the summer I was asked to speak at an event at Seamus Heaney HomePlace in Bellaghy on the western shores of Lough Neagh, down the road from my mother-in-law's home of Portglenone, a village so religious that it supports a Cistercian monastery and six different churches, including the First, Third and Free Presbyterians. The family are members of the First Presbyterian; I haven't the nerve to ask what happened to the Second crowd.

The road from Dublin to Bellaghy in south Derry takes you through four of the six counties of Northern Ireland. You cross the border in south Down, drive through the fascinating county of Armagh, into east Tyrone, before heading on up to County Derry.

Seamus Heaney HomePlace in Bellaghy is a beautiful, peaceful building erected symbolically on the site of the old RUC station in the middle of this deeply nationalist village, home to two of the ten hunger strikers. On this warm June evening, lads were sitting on the kerb outside the Taphouse Bar, talking Gaelic football. You can't get away from the local GAA team, the Wolfe Tones. Across Main Street in the Golden City Chinese takeaway, the Chinese owner, with a brilliant Belfast shipyard accent, is serving up a mean spice bag in his Bellaghy 'Tones GAA jersey. No mistaking what foot he kicks with.

One of the first things you notice in the North is not the flags and painted kerbstones but the proliferation of Chinese takeaways. There must be more Chinese takeaways per head in Northern Ireland than in any other place on earth. And, as political correctness has not reached these shores, the takeaway down the road in Stewartstown is simply called 'Chinaman'. I suspect the Equality Authority down here might have something to say about that.

The other thing you notice, as well as outsized devotion to obscure fundamentalist sects, is an equally outsized devotion to motorbikes, engine oil and heavy metal, which, like the noble spice bag, appear to cross the sectarian divide.

Heading back south from Bellaghy towards Cookstown, flags mark out the territory. A huge UVF banner tells me that the 'Mid Ulster County Council is run by the IRA Army Council'. Somehow, I don't feel like getting out of the car to question the two shaved heads in Rangers trackies outside the bookies about the veracity of that claim. From east Tyrone, we cross into Armagh, where the landscape changes as we approach Armagh City, home of Christianity in Ireland. This is orchard country. As well as the brilliant white motorhome, a bit of sponge cake, Shloer or anything by Stiff Little Fingers, another thing the Northerner loves is a garden centre. This neck of the woods is coming down with them.

Armagh City is framed by two huge competing cathedrals, one Anglican, one Catholic, both called St Patrick's. The city's architecture is Georgian and monumental, all porch fanlights and sash windows. As the North tends to have a more Victorian urban landscape, Georgian Armagh feels closer to Dublin than to Belfast. Majestic cut-stone terraces surround the very British-looking Mall, resplendent with a war monument and cricket crease. This bright morning, passing the Boer War memorial, three lads in the vivid orange jerseys of Armagh GAA confuse those of us who thought that orange was the new black. Indeed, the Orange Order itself was founded up the road in Loughgall and here in Chapel Street the bunting and makeshift triumphal arch is up for the Twelfth. However, unionists are in a minority not just in the city but in the whole county.

What really interests me in Armagh is culture – not historic culture but living culture. I'm interested in how people live today. This is where the TripAdvisor Index comes into play. I am here to find out how Northern Ireland lives and how it differs from the Renaissance Nation. After all, if we are talking about a United Ireland, we'd better know what we are dealing with.

The TripAdvisor Index reveals that the North is another country in a very different sense. Take the two cities of Kilkenny and Armagh, two similar-sized provincial Irish towns, both with city status, both marketed as great places to visit. Armagh, like Kilkenny, has a vibrant cultural life. The John Hewitt Summer School is a significant literary event each year. Armagh also hosts various art galleries and libraries, prides itself on fine dining and, with its history and architecture, is an urban gem. But – and here's the big but – whereas TripAdvisor has reviews of 176 restaurants in Kilkenny, it has just 43 in Armagh.

Kilkenny has more than four times more restaurants than Armagh, reflecting a totally divergent social scene, a much more evolved tourist industry, a much more sophisticated local economy and profoundly different levels of income and willingness to spend and consume. People from the Northern galaxy are different after all. The TripAdvisor Index sheds light on the other side of the economy, how people spend their money, where and how often. It tells us that culture matters and this culture is different not just in the flags-and-banners sense, but in an everyday-life sense.

Leaving Armagh and driving towards Dublin, not too far south we arrive at the village of Markethill, which each summer hosts the world's largest Lambeg drumming contest. This village is home to three chippers on one roundabout and the most enormous Orange arch, trumpeting Protestant victories at Derry, Aughrim, Enniskillen and the mother of them all, the Boyne. Three men are painting the railings of the Orange Hall, beside the Big Panda takeaway. The huge banner at the edge of the village urges me to 'Fear God, Honour the King and Love the Brotherhood'.

Somehow, I don't think that message will catch on with the Radical Centre.

CAUSE FOR OPTIMISM?

It is easy in the North to find radical unionism and radical nationalism, but where is the Northern Radical Centre? What about the people who go out to the restaurants, socialise with each other, and want to live in a place that is reasonable, progressive and not defined by religion? Could what looks like a deeply traditionalist, blinkered, religiously observant society set off on the same predictable journey towards liberalism and individual dignity as the Renaissance Nation? Places change, people change and cultures change.

Thinking back to the summer of 1994, when I met my wife-to-be in Belfast, just after the Shankill Road bombing, the Greysteel and Loughlinisland massacres, the first tentative ceasefires were paving the way for the final ceasefires. In 1994 the IRA were still bombing in our name, deploying Articles 2 and 3 of our constitution as warped legalistic cover for their campaign. Yet by 1998 the Republic had voted overwhelmingly to drop the claim on Northern Ireland. We changed.

In 1994 divorce was illegal in Ireland, contraception was not freely or widely available, being gay – although decriminalised in 1993 – was frowned upon, gay marriage was unheard of, abortion was illegal and the idea of successfully delivering change on either of the latter stances by a national referendum was regarded as liberal dreaming. But both have now happened. Can you imagine Jack Charlton's national football team wearing LGBTQ colours on their shirts?

In 1994, as I pretended to the Presbyterian minister that I had heard of the Book of Deuteronomy, Ireland had hardly any immigrants, the economy was backward, unemployment was in double digits and the idea that the economy of Ireland would emerge as a world-beater would have been dismissed as a Flann O'Brien-esque fantasy. The very notion of a gay Taoiseach would have been laughed off in the mid-1990s. But all these things happened and happened quickly.

Could Northern Ireland do something similar and would this make unification easier? Unfortunately, there is a strain within the unionist tribe that won't accept the Renaissance Nation. Once we were too Catholic for them; now we are too liberal!

Also, there may be a substantial proportion of the Radical Centre population that doesn't want unification – the cost of it and the threat of civil war if extreme loyalism decides to fight. It may be the case that the biggest enemy of unification is not unionism but soft-focus southern patriots, who are happy to mingle with Rory Best in the bar after internationals at the Aviva but are in no mood to risk their comforts to pay for the dole of feral Rangers fans.

CUSTODY OF THE CHILD

The future of Northern Ireland is a bit like a custody battle where neither side – Ireland nor Britain – is particularly sure that they want the child, but both know that the child can't survive, financially or emotionally, without them. As we've noted, with a budget deficit of 27% of GDP, Northern Ireland cannot survive economically on its own.

Four years ago, I appeared on the BBC Northern Ireland programme *Let's Talk*, presented by the extremely able Mark Carruthers, possibly the best current affairs anchor on the island. I found myself sandwiched between Maze escapee and Sinn Féin member Gerry Kelly and a fella called Jim Allister, who believes Arlene Foster isn't unionist enough. It was an unusual position, given what you now know about me and my relationship with Northern Ireland. The conversation went down the usual sectarian rabbit hole, which got so mad that I ended up having to explain to the uber-unionist that the Battle of the Boyne had in fact taken place in that foreign country called the Republic of Ireland. With all the focus on history, obviously geography wasn't a strong suit.

It was quite depressing, the Sinn Féiners, like the unionists, seeing everything through their own tribal lens. After the show I spoke to a few of the younger audience members and those conversations were much more hopeful. They were much less entrenched and more reasonable and these views are borne out by the survey data.

For example, while proposals to legalise abortion in cases of foetal abnormality or rape/incest were defeated 59–40 and 64–30 in the NI Assembly in 2016, attitudes on the ground are more liberal:[175] 83% feel it should 'probably' or 'definitely' be legal in the case of fatal foetal abnormalities; 78% in the case of incest/rape; and 76% if there's a threat to the mother's physical or mental health. That said, support for women's right to choose remains fairly weak, with 60% saying abortion should probably/definitely be illegal if a woman does not want to have a child.[176] This attitude is similar to where the Renaissance Nation was in 2000. People change.

When it comes to attitudes towards LGBTQ people, 77% describe themselves as not prejudiced at all towards gay men. The young are much more tolerant: 83% of 18–24-year-olds are not prejudiced at all versus 61% of the over-65s. While 79% of young people would be comfortable with having a gay MP, just 59% of over-65s would. When it comes to their own child, however, just 54% of over-65s would be comfortable with them being gay, compared to 70% of the youth. Reflecting attitudes that wouldn't have been out of place in the Republic twenty years ago, 38% of the older generation would find two men holding hands on the street offensive, compared to just 7% of the young. And, while they seem to love a good march up North, nearly half of the over-65s feel there should be fewer of the gay pride variety, while under one in five of the 18–24-year-olds feel this way.[177]

When it comes to same-sex marriages, an overwhelming 72% of those aged under 35 feel they should enjoy the same rights as traditional marriages, but 54% of the over-65s feel they should not be valid. Indeed, a majority of those aged over 65 feel change has gone too far in promoting equality for gays and lesbians.[178]

So, on social issues, it's clear there is a massive generation divide in the North. Can you see where this might be going?

My contention is that once Ireland became liberal, we became rich, because tolerance on issues of personal morality changes the value system of the society and this also confers dignity on the great adventure of commercial self-expression which drives innovation, in turn fuelling the economy. In September 2018, an unprecedented public letter signed by 29 of Northern Ireland's largest businesses mapped out precisely that route as the road to prosperity in the North.

The signatories include major multinationals Santander, Coca Cola and IBM; domestic giants Bank of Ireland, Ulster Bank and BT; consulting firms Deloitte and PwC and other leading Northern employers.

The letter advocated support for same-sex marriage, claiming it is both the right thing to do in itself, so people can 'live free from discrimination, prejudice or exclusion', and also made the Renaissance Nation connection with the economy, arguing that liberalism is essential to 'attract the best talent to Northern Ireland and to retain the skilled staff we already have'. The letter concludes 'equality contributes to an environment of creativity and excellence,' adding 'our people should have the same rights, entitlements, responsibilities and freedoms enjoyed elsewhere'.

Northern businesses, looking enviously South, understand the connection between the triumph of the liberal Radical Centre and the wealth of the Renaissance Nation.

Now consider recent Northern attitudes to identity and nationality. The survey bears out the fact that the Protestant population is older, more anxious and is looking to the past, with the Catholics more likely to look to the future positively. In all, just 22% of those aged 18–24 identify as British, compared to 51% of those aged over 65. But evidencing a growing middle ground, perhaps most telling is the fact that those aged 18–24 see the biggest cohort identifying as Northern Irish – as opposed to British or Irish and all the baggage that comes with them.[179] These are Rory McIlroy's people.

Indeed, while overall there are more nationalists (23%) than unionists (16%) amongst the young, the majority (54%) see themselves as neither.[180] Asked in 1998 about the prospects of a United Ireland within the next 20 years – that is, by 2018 – 42% felt it was either quite or very likely.[181] Brexit has changed this because, like any unnecessary ultimatum, it forces people to take sides, amplifying division. The majority of people in the North didn't want Brexit; they wanted to stay in the EU. The impact has been to push more Northerners towards a United Ireland. Given that Brexit was championed exclusively by the DUP, a party implacably opposed to Irish unity, that tactic must be up there with the Irish Home Rule Party supporting the First World War in the annals of great unprompted Irish political blunders.

Latest polls indicate that, despite an increase in people identifying as Northern Irish, a whopping 60% of Northerners say they would be in favour of Northern Ireland entering a political and economic alliance with the Republic if it would help jobs and the economy.[182]

Is the Renaissance Nation prepared for this? Could the Radical Centre hold?

Passing through the invisible border, back to the Renaissance Nation, with our Mamils, Banana Republicans and Sliotar Moms, our tolerant, soft middle and our relentless commercial self-expression, the North seems like that final frontier. But while *Star Trek*'s Commander Data may have been wrong on his timing on Irish unity, as someone else once said, it is not going away, you know; and Brexit certainly has made planning more urgent.

The Renaissance Nation has to prepare for unification. This means that, unlike what happened during the UK's Brexit campaign, Ireland and Britain need to be completely honest with ourselves about the costs and the consequences of such a move. Any politicians or group that try to sugar-coat the outlays, or indeed exaggerate the fears concerning the social and economic implications of this new Ireland will be doing the country a grave disservice.

In the end, demography is destiny and the numbers indicate that Irish unity, or a new form of shared Ireland, is our destiny in our lifetimes. Almost a century after partition, our world has come full circle. It is time to rewrite the already heavily edited Irish script once more.

Forty years ago, when Pope John Paul II visited Ireland, could anyone have dreamt that we could reimagine Ireland so completely and create a radically different society from the one that went before? But we did it. We changed. The Renaissance Nation was the result. Where other economies have wilted, fallen away or veered off to the political extremes, the Irish economy accepted the challenges of globalisation, seized the opportunity afforded to it and has grown much more quickly than any of our neighbours. Relative to the rest of Europe, the country has moved from grinding poverty and narrow dogma to significant wealth and a vibrant openness in one generation. It's not perfect but it's pretty impressive and pretty impressive is – well, pretty impressive.

The heroes of this triumph were ordinary people, the Radical Centre, those quiet revolutionaries, driven by millions of little personal mutinies, who not only dreamt of a better future, but delivered it.

These are the people whose energies will be called upon again to re-engineer Ireland. The next challenge demands vision and determination, but also generosity and understanding. It will involve putting ourselves in other people's shoes, understanding their insecurities and convincing them that they too are part of a great new national project of which they can be proud, where their story gets equal billing and their tunes are also heard.

Game on.

BIBLIOGRAPHY

Ariely, Dan. *Predictably irrational.* New York: HarperCollins, 2008

Birnbach, Lisa, ed. *The official preppy handbook.* Workman Pub., 1980

Bregman, Rutger. *Utopia for realists: And how we can get there.* Bloomsbury Publishing, 2017

Brooks, David. *Bobos in paradise: The new upper class and how they got there.* Simon and Schuster, 2010

Brooks, David. *On paradise drive: How we live now (and always have) in the future tense.* Simon and Schuster, 2004

Brooks, David. *The road to character.* Random House, 2015

Canetti, Elias. *Crowds and power.* Vol. 190. Macmillan, 1984

Chancellor, Edward. *Devil take the hindmost: A history of financial speculation.* Farrar, Straus and Giroux, 1999

Cowen, Tyler. *In praise of commercial culture.* Harvard University Press, 2000

Cowen, Tyler. *The complacent class: The self-defeating quest for the American dream.* St. Martin's Press, 2017

Daly, Tom. *The Rás: The Story of Ireland's Unique Bike Race.* Collins Press, 2012

Diamond, Jared. *The world until yesterday: What can we learn from traditional societies?* Penguin, 2013

Ellmann, Richard, Mark Hussey, and George Whitmore. *James Joyce.* Sussex Publications, 1982

Florida, Richard. *The rise of the creative class and how it's transforming work, leisure, community and everyday life* (Paperback Ed.). Basic Books, 2004

Foster, Robert Fitzroy. *WB Yeats: A life.* Oxford University Press on Demand, 1998

Frank, Robert H. *Luxury fever: Why money fails to satisfy in an era of excess.* Simon and Schuster, 2001

Frank, Robert H., and Philip J. Cook. *The winner-take-all society: Why the few at the top get so much more than the rest of us.* Random House, 2010

Friedman, Thomas L. *Thank you for being late: An optimist's guide to thriving in the age of accelerations* (version 2.0, with a new Afterword). Picador/Farrar Straus and Giroux, 2017

Fussell, Paul. *Class: A guide through the American status system.* Simon and Schuster, 1992

Galbraith, John Kenneth, and Alan Crook. *The affluent society.* Houghton Mifflin, 1958

George, Henry. *Progress and poverty: An enquiry into the cause of industrial depressions, and of increase of want with increase of wealth. The remedy.* K. Paul, Trench & Company, 1879

Gilbert, Dennis L. *The American class structure in an age of growing inequality.* Sage Publications, 2017

Goodhart, David. *The road to somewhere: The populist revolt and the future of politics.* Oxford University Press, 2017

Kiberd, Declan. *Ulysses and us: The art of everyday living.* Faber & Faber, 2010

Krugman, Paul R. *The great unravelling: From boom to bust in three scandalous years.* Penguin, 2003

Krugman, Paul. *The accidental theorist: And other dispatches from the dismal science.* WW Norton & Company, 2010

Leadbeater, Charles. *Up the down escalator: Why the global pessimists are wrong.* Viking, 2002

McCloskey, Deirdre N. *Bourgeois dignity: Why economics can't explain the modern world.* University of Chicago Press, 2010

McCloskey, Deirdre N. *Bourgeois equality: How ideas, not capital or institutions, enriched the world* (Vol. 3). University of Chicago Press, 2016

McCloskey, Deirdre N. *The bourgeois virtues: Ethics for an age of commerce.* University of Chicago Press, 2010

Pinker, Steven. *Enlightenment now: The case for reason, science, humanism, and progress.* Penguin, 2018

Robinson, Ken. *Out of our minds: Learning to be creative.* John Wiley & Sons, 2011

Schwarz, Barry. *The paradox of choice: Why more is less.* Harper Collins e-books, 2004

Simsek, Kara. *So you think you're a hipster?* Dog'n'Bone, 2013

Taleb, Nassim Nicholas. *Antifragile: How to live in a world we don't understand* (Vol. 3). Allen Lane, 2012

Taleb, Nassim Nicholas. *Skin in the game: Hidden asymmetries in daily* life. Random House, 2018

Young, Michael. *The rise of the meritocracy.* Routledge, 2017

NOTES

1. Maddison Project Database, version 2018. Bolt, Jutta, Robert Inklaar, Herman de Jong and Jan Luiten van Zanden (2018), 'Rebasing "Maddison": new income comparisons and the shape of long-run economic development', Maddison Project Working Paper 10, available for download at www.ggdc.net/maddison

2. Broadberry & Klein, 'Aggregate and Per Capita GDP in Europe, 1870–2000: Continental, Regional and National Data with Changing Boundaries', 27 October 2011, https://www.nuffield.ox.ac.uk/users/Broadberry/EuroGDP2.pdf.

3. O'Gráda & O'Rourke, 'Irish economic growth since 1945', *Economic growth in Europe since 1945*, 1996, https://researchrepository.ucd.ie/handle/10197/412.

4. Ibid.

5. Maddison Project Database, version 2018; 1990$ benchmark. Bolt, Jutta, Robert Inklaar, Herman de Jong and Jan Luiten van Zanden (2018), 'Rebasing "Maddison": new income comparisons and the shape of long-run economic development', Maddison Project Working Paper 10, available for download at www.ggdc.net/maddison.

6. Maddison Project Database, version 2018. Bolt, Jutta, Robert Inklaar, Herman de Jong and Jan Luiten van Zanden (2018), 'Rebasing "Maddison": new income comparisons and the shape of long-run economic development', Maddison Project Working Paper 10, available for download at www.ggdc.net/maddison.

7. *The Economist*, Special Report: The luck of the Irish, 14 October 2004, https://www.economist.com/special-report/2004/10/14/the-luck-of-the-irish.

8. *Irish Independent*, 10 September 2018, https://www.independent.ie/business/irish/employment-in-multinationals-reaches-a-record-high-36460410.html.

9. Hybrid Index is composed of three separate measures of Irish economic output: Real GDP Per Capita (1921–1974) sourced from the Maddison Project Database, version 2018; Real GNI Per Capita (1974–1994) & Real Modified GNI Per Capita (1995–2016) both sourced from CSO, Quarterly National Accounts.

10. Maddison Project Database, version 2018. Bolt, Jutta, Robert Inklaar, Herman de Jong and Jan Luiten van Zanden (2018), 'Rebasing "Maddison": new income comparisons and the shape of long-run economic development', Maddison Project Working Paper 10, available for download at www.ggdc.net/maddison.

11. European Commission AMECO Database, Private final consumption expenditure at current prices per head of population (HCPHP), https://ec.europa.eu/info/business-economy-euro/indicators-statistics/economic-databases/macro-economic-database-ameco/ameco-database_en.

12. Ibid.

13. United Nations, 2016 Human Development Report, 'Table 2: Trends in the Human Development Index, 1990–2015', http://hdr.undp.org/en/composite/trends.

14. Ibid.

15. Fahey, Fitzgerald & Maitre (ESRI), The Economic and Social Implications of Demographic Change, *Journal of the Statistical and Social Inquiry Society of Ireland*, 27(5), 1 January 1998, https://www.esri.ie/publications/the-economic-and-social-implications-of-demographic-change/.

16. World Bank Data, Labor force participation rate 2017, female (% of female population ages 15+) (modeled ILO estimate), https://data.worldbank.org/indicator/SL.TLF.CACT.FE.ZS.

17. Ibid.

18. CSO, Women and Men in Ireland 2016, https://www.cso.ie/en/releasesandpublications/ep/p-wamii/womenandmeninireland2016/.

19. *Irish Times*, 17 August 2018, https://www.irishtimes.com/news/education/girls-outperform-boys-in-majority-of-leaving-cert-subjects-1.3598751.

20. *Irish Times*, 14 February 2017, https://www.irishtimes.com/news/education/fifty-years-after-free-secondary-education-what-big-idea-do-we-need-in-2017-1.2967984.

21. Department of Education & Skills, 'Retention Rates of Pupils in Second Level Schools: 2010 Entry Cohort', November 2017, https://www.education.ie/en/Publications/Statistics/Statistical-Reports/retention-rates-of-pupils-in-second-level-schools-2010-entry-cohort.pdf.

22. OECD Data, Adult Education Level, Tertiary (% of 25–64-year-olds, 1989–2015), https://data.oecd.org/eduatt/adult-education-level.htm.

23. CSO, EA005: Population Aged 15 Years and Over 2011 to 2016 by Sex, Highest Level of Ed, Age Group and Census Year, https://www.cso.ie/px/pxeirestat/Statire/SelectVarVal/Define.asp?maintable=EA005&PLanguage=0.

24. World Bank, World Development Indicators, http://databank.worldbank.org/data/reports.aspx?source=world-development-indicators.

25. Ibid.

26. *Quartz*, 24 January 2018, https://qz.com/1187819/country-ranking-worlds-fastest-shrinking-countries-are-in-eastern-europe/.

27. CSO, Historical Earnings 1938–2015, Earnings by Gender, https://www.cso.ie/en/releasesandpublications/ep/p-hes/hes2015/ebg/.

28. EuroFound, The state of trade unionism, 27 February 2001, https://www.eurofound.europa.eu/publications/article/2001/the-state-of-trade-unionism.

29. OECD, Trade Union Density, Administrative Data, https://stats.oecd.org/Index.aspx?DataSetCode=TUD.

30. World Economic Forum, 'The Inclusive Development Index 2018: Summary & Data Highlights', http://www3.weforum.org/docs/WEF_Forum_IncGrwth_2018.pdf.

31. Paul Sweeney, 'The Irish Experience of Economic Lift Off', May 2004, https://www.ictu.ie/download/pdf/celtic_tiger.pdf.

32. Ibid.

33. Data for chart again sourced from Maddison Project Database, version 2018. Bolt, Jutta, Robert Inklaar, Herman de Jong and Jan Luiten van Zanden (2018), 'Rebasing 'Maddison': new income comparisons and the shape of long-run economic development', Maddison Project Working Paper 10, available for download at www.ggdc.net/maddison.

34. Ibid.

35. Pew Research Center, Global Attitudes & Trends, 24 April 2017, http://www.pewglobal.org/interactives/irish-middle-class/.

36. Ibid.

37. Office of the Revenue Commissioners, OECD & IGEES, 'Income Dynamics & Mobility in Ireland: Evidence from Tax Records Microdata', April 2018, https://www.revenue.ie/en/corporate/documents/research/income-dynamics-mobility-ireland.pdf.

38. OECD, Foreign-born population (Total, % of population, 2013 or latest available), https://data.oecd.org/migration/foreign-born-population.htm.

39. Eurostat, Migration and migrant population statistics, https://ec.europa.eu/eurostat/statistics-explained/index.php/Migration_and_migrant_population_statistics.

40. Department of Employment Affairs & Social Protection, Statistics on Personal Public Service Numbers Issued, http://www.welfare.ie/en/Pages/Personal-Public-Service-Number-Statistics-on-Numbers-Issued.aspx.

41. *Poslovni*, 16 March 2016, http://www.poslovni.hr/hrvatska/5500-hrvata-lani-otislo-u-irsku-i-vecina-je-uspjela-prosjecna-placa-245-veca-nego-kod-nas-310312.

42. ESS Round 8: European Social Survey Round 8 Data (2016). Data file edition 2.0. NSD – Norwegian Centre for Research Data, Norway – Data Archive and distributor of ESS data for ESS ERIC.

43. Based on GDP at constant market prices sourced from CSO, Quarterly National Accounts Q4 2017 Statistical Release, https://www.cso.ie/en/releasesandpublications/er/na/quarterlynationalaccountsquarter42017/.

44. *Irish Times*, 28 September 2018, https://www.irishtimes.com/life-and-style/abroad/more-irish-people-still-emigrating-than-moving-back-1.3236979.

45. Central Bank of Ireland, Quarterly Financial Accounts Q4 2017 – Statistical Release, 4 May 2018, https://www.centralbank.ie/docs/default-source/statistics/data-and-analysis/financial-accounts/quarterly-financial-accounts-for-ireland-q4–2017.pdf?sfvrsn=2.

46. Prof. John FitzGerald, 'National Accounts for a Global Economy: the Case of Ireland', TEP Working Paper No. 0418, May 2018, https://www.tcd.ie/Economics/TEP/2018/tep0418.pdf. Also see 'Large multinationals make up only fraction of real economy', Irish Times, 3 August 2018, https://www.irishtimes.com/business/economy/large-multinationals-make-up-only-fraction-of-real-economy-1.3584634 and 'Getting a fix on multinational input to Irish economy', *Irish Times*, 26 May 2017, https://www.irishtimes.com/business/economy/getting-a-fix-on-multinational-input-to-irish-economy-1.3096205.

47. European Commission, SBA Factsheet, https://dbei.gov.ie/en/Publications/Publication-files/2017-SBA-Fact-Sheet.pdf.

48. CSO, Foreign Direct Investment in Ireland 2015, https://www.cso.ie/en/releasesandpublications/ep/p-fdi/fdi2015/.

49. European Commission SBA Factsheet, https://dbei.gov.ie/en/Publications/Publication-files/2017-SBA-Fact-Sheet.pdf.

50. *Irish Times*, 6 April 2018, https://www.irishtimes.com/business/economy/more-than-60-companies-formed-every-day-in-irish-economy-1.3451975.

51. The Journal, 5 February 2018, http://www.thejournal.ie/business-startups-smes-starting-a-business-3833411-Feb2018/.

52. European Commission, SBA Factsheet, https://dbei.gov.ie/en/Publications/Publication-files/2017-SBA-Fact-Sheet.pdf.

53. Ibid.

54. Ibid.

55. Ibid.

56. Ibid.

57. Maddison Project Database, version 2018. Bolt, Jutta, Robert Inklaar, Herman de Jong and Jan Luiten van Zanden (2018), 'Rebasing "Maddison": new income comparisons and the shape of long-run economic development', Maddison Project Working Paper 10, available for download at www.ggdc.net/maddison.

58. RTÉ, 1 November 2017, https://www.rte.ie/news/business/2017/1101/916698-the-economic/. Also see, GoBus timetable, https://www.gobus.ie/timetable.php?map=28 & City Link timetable, https://www.citylink.ie/timetables.

59. United States Energy Information Administration, https://www.eia.gov/beta/.

60. Paul Sweeney, 'The Irish Experience of Economic Lift Off', May 2004, https://www.ictu.ie/download/pdf/celtic_tiger.pdf.

61. CSO, VSA18: Births and Birth Rate per 1,000 Population by Sex, Year and Statistic, https://www.cso.ie/px/pxeirestat/Statire/SelectVarVal/Define.asp?maintable=VSA18&PLanguage=0.

62. EVS (2011): EVS – European Values Study 1981 – Integrated Dataset. GESIS Data Archive, Cologne. ZA4438 Data file Version 3.0.0, doi:10.4232/1.10791.

63. Global Entrepreneurship Monitor, Global Report 2017/18, https://www.gemconsortium.org/report/50012.

64. *Irish Times*, 30 November 2015, https://www.irishtimes.com/news/education/baptisms-remain-popular-as-mass-attendance-declines-1.2448687.

65. CSO, Marriages 2017: Statistical Release, 29 March 2018, https://www.cso.ie/en/releasesandpublications/er/mar/marriages2017/.

66. *Irish Independent*, 29 April 2016, https://www.independent.ie/style/beauty/what-is-irish-womens-obsession-with-faking-it-with-beauty-we-investigate-34663873.html.

67. NewsTalk & RED C, 20 March 2017, https://www.newstalk.com/Newstalk-survey-sheds-light-on-Irish-porn-habits.

68. *Irish Times*, 25 June 2018, https://www.irishtimes.com/life-and-style/homes-and-property/what-salary-will-buy-a-typical-house-around-ireland-1.3540068.

69. *The Journal* & NERI, 17 January 2013, http://www.thejournal.ie/readme/high-earner-ireland-755580-Jan2013/.

70. Tasc, 'The Distribution of Wealth in Ireland', December 2015, https://www.tasc.ie/download/pdf/the_distribution_of_wealth_in_ireland_final.pdf.

71. CSO, Irish Babies' Names 2016, 31 May 2017, https://www.cso.ie/en/releasesandpublications/ep/p-ibn/irishbabiesnames2016/.

72. CSO, Census 2016 Small Area Population Statistics, Theme 2: Migration, ethnicity, religion and foreign languages, https://www.cso.ie/en/census/census2016reports/census2016smallareapopulationstatistics/.

73. CSO, Census of Population 2016 – Profile 7 Migration and Diversity, https://www.cso.ie/en/releasesandpublications/ep/p-cp7md/p7md/p7anii/.

74. Eurostat, Immigration by age group, sex and level of human development of the country of birth, https://ec.europa.eu/eurostat/en/web/products-datasets/-/MIGR_IMM10CTB.

75. Eurostat, Migration and migrant population statistics, Figure 1, https://ec.europa.eu/eurostat/statistics-explained/index.php/Migration_and_migrant_population_statistics#Migrant_population:_almost_22_million_non-EU_citizens_living_in_the_EU.

76. Eurostat, Migration and migrant population statistics, Figure 5, https://ec.europa.eu/eurostat/statistics-explained/index.php/Migration_and_migrant_population_statistics#Migrant_population:_almost_22_million_non-EU_citizens_living_in_the_EU.

77. Eurostat, Immigration by age group, sex and level of human development of the country of birth, https://ec.europa.eu/eurostat/en/web/products-datasets/-/MIGR_IMM10CTB.

78. Ibid.

79. CSO, CNA21: Population (Town and Rural) by Five Year Age Group, Sex, Marital Status, Year and Statistic, https://www.cso.ie/px/pxeirestat/Statire/SelectVarVal/Define.asp?maintable=CNA21.

80. Sport Ireland & IPSOS MRBI, Irish Sports Monitor Annual Report 2017, https://www.sportireland.ie/Research/Irish%20Sports%20Monitor%202017%20-%20Half%20Year%20Report/Irish%20Sports%20Monitor%202017.pdf.

81. Cycling Ireland, Annual General Meeting, 11 November 2017, http://www.cyclingireland.ie/downloads/cycling_ireland_annual_report_agm2017.pdf.

82. Ibid.

83. Ibid.

84. BicyclyingTrade.com, 11 December 2015, http://www.bicyclingtrade.com.au/world/global-cycling-market-is-worth-53-9-billion.

85. Ibid.

86. CSO, E6037: Population aged 15 years and over at work, usually resident and present in the state 2011 to 2016 by county of place of work, county of usual residence and census year, https://www.cso.ie/px/pxeirestat/Statire/SelectVarVal/Define.asp?maintable=E6037&PLanguage=0.

87. *Irish Times*, 21 October 2017, https://www.irishtimes.com/life-and-style/people/m50-blues-ireland-s-busiest-road-dublin-s-biggest-car-park-1.3259694.

88. Ibid.

89. Ibid.

90. *Irish Times*, 9 June 2018, https://www.irishtimes.com/life-and-style/travel/ireland/london-could-become-a-park-city-could-dublin-follow-its-lead-1.3519144.

91. *Irish Times*, 9 January 2017, https://www.irishtimes.com/news/politics/quango-cull-audacious-promises-of-2011-amounted-to-little-1.2929535.

92. Ibid.

93. FÁS: €47,795; Science Foundation Ireland: €83,000; National Council for Curriculum and Assessment: €66,000; National Council for Special Education: €56,500; National Education Welfare Board: €54,800; Higher Education Authority (HEA): €54,795; Grangegorman Development Agency: €57,798; State Examinations Commission: €57,190; The National Qualifications Authority of Ireland (NQAI): €52,392; Comhairle Um Oideachas Gaeltachta agus Gaelscolaíochta: €50,000 approx; Léargas and the National Centre for Guidance in Education (NCGE): €49,610; Gaisce: €60,712; The Further Education and Training Awards Council (FETAC): €64,220. Irish Times, 15 February 2011, https://www.irishtimes.com/news/education/who-earns-what-in-our-education-quangos-1.573001.

94. Davy, Economic Insights: Public Sector Pay – Avoiding the Mistakes of the Past, March 2017, https://www.davy.ie/research/public/printPdf.htm?id=publicsectorpay20170327_24032017.htm.

95. Ibid.

96. CSO, CNA02: Students at School or College Usually Resident in the State by Sex, Means of Travel, Year and Statistic, https://www.cso.ie/px/pxeirestat/Statire/SelectVarVal/Define.asp?maintable=CNA02&PLanguage=0.

97. National Youth Council of Ireland, 24 October 2017, http://www.youth.ie/nyci/Almost-half-millennials-non-standard-contracts-Particular-concern-over-one-third-young-people.

98. Data provided by Dr Kevin Cunningham, Ireland Thinks, https://www.irelandthinks.ie/.

99. Daft.ie, House Price Report Q2 2018, https://www.daft.ie/report/2018-Q2-houseprice-daftreport.pdf & Rental Price Report Q1 2018, https://www.daft.ie/report/2018-Q1-rentalprice-daftreport.pdf. Also see CSO, Residential Property Price Index May 2018, https://www.cso.ie/en/releasesandpublications/ep/p-rppi/residentialpropertypriceindexmay2018/ & Earnings and Labour Costs Annual 2017, https://www.cso.ie/en/releasesandpublications/er/elca/earningsandlabourcostsannualdata2017/.

100. Irish Times, 10 September 2013, https://www.irishtimes.com/business/technology/timeline-the-history-of-the-iphone-1.1522373.

101. TechCrunch, 13 March 2008, https://techcrunch.com/2008/03/13/aol-buys-bebo-for-750-million/.

102. Irish Times, 10 September 2013, https://www.irishtimes.com/business/technology/timeline-the-history-of-the-iphone-1.1522373.

103. Ibid.

104. Apple, 14 July 2008, https://www.apple.com/ie/newsroom/2008/07/14iPhone-App-Store-Downloads-Top-10-Million-in-First-Weekend/.

105. Telegraph, 7 September 2012, https://www.telegraph.co.uk/technology/news/9525267/Airbnb-The-story-behind-the-1.3bn-room-letting-website.html.

106. Business Insider, 10 August 2017, http://uk.businessinsider.com/airbnb-total-worldwide-listings-2017-8?r=US&IR=T.

107. HotelNews.com, 14 February 2017, http://hotelnewsnow.com/Articles/115537/Updated-infographic-Look-at-hotel-industrys-largest.

108. Wired.com, 22 September 2008, https://www.wired.com/2008/09/since-apple-lau/.

109. Intel, Transistors to Transformations, https://www.intel.com/content/dam/www/public/us/en/documents/corporate-information/museum-transistors-to-transformations-brochure.pdf. See also, Science, 20 February 2009, http://science.sciencemag.org/content/323/5917/1000.

110. Irish Times, 2 October 2008, https://www.irishtimes.com/news/facebook-to-set-up-international-hq-in-dublin-1.829528.

111. Satoshi Nakamoto, 'Bitcoin: A Peer-to-Peer Electronic Cash System', https://bitcoin.org/bitcoin.pdf.

112. The Mirror, 3 April 2018, https://www.mirror.co.uk/tech/history-spotify-how-swedish-streaming-12291542.

113. The Verge, 8 July 2018, https://www.theverge.com/2018/7/8/17542612/drake-scorpion-1-billion-streams-first-week-record.

114. Irish Times, 6 January 2009, https://www.irishtimes.com/business/waterford-wedgwood-placed-in-receivership-1.1232378.

115. Wired.com, 4 February 2014, https://www.wired.com/2014/02/decade-facebooks-innovations/.

116. Wired.com, 19 February 2014, https://www.wired.co.uk/article/whatsapp-exclusive.

117. *MTV News*, 26 June 2009, http://www.mtv.com/news/1614812/michael-jacksons-death-overloads-google-twitter/.

118. *Reuters*, 15 September 2009, https://www.reuters.com/article/us-facebook/facebook-says-becomes-free-cash-flow-positive-idUSTRE58E7ZK20090915.

119. *New York Times*, 1 February 2012, https://dealbook.nytimes.com/2012/02/01/tracking-facebooks-valuation/.

120. Twitter Blog, 6 November 2009, https://blog.twitter.com/official/en_us/a/2009/retweet-limited-rollout.html.

121. *The Guardian*, 16 December 2009, https://www.theguardian.com/science/2009/dec/16/cancer-genome-sequences-genetic-mutations.

122. Internet Live Stats, http://www.internetlivestats.com/.

123. Facebook, https://newsroom.fb.com/company-info/.

124. *Quartz*, 27 August 2017, https://qz.com/1057510/facebook-has-more-people-than-any-major-religion-except-christianity/.

125. IAB, 1 November 2017, https://iabireland.ie/mobile-adoption-and-usage-is-prevalent-in-ireland-and-globally-mobile-devices-are-an-integral-part-of-consumers-daily-lives/.

126. RTÉ, 21 December 2017, https://www.rte.ie/news/business/2017/1221/928973-cso-businesses-and-social-media/.

127. Credit Union, 'A Guide to Social Media for Credit Unions', https://www.creditunion.ie/files/Social%20Media%20explained%20FINAL%20Jan%202011.pdf.

128. Connector.ie, http://connector.ie/infographic/.

129. Ibid.

130. Ibid.

131. *New York Times*, 8 November 2016, https://www.nytimes.com/2016/11/09/technology/for-election-day-chatter-twitter-ruled-social-media.html.

132. *New York Times*, 19 November 2016, https://www.nytimes.com/2016/11/20/jobs/quit-social-media-your-career-may-depend-on-it.html.

133. David McWilliams, *Ireland's Great Wealth Divide*, 2015.

134. Ibid.

135. Tasc, 'The Distribution of Wealth in Ireland', December 2015, https://www.tasc.ie/download/pdf/the_distribution_of_wealth_in_ireland_final.pdf.

136. Credit Suisse, Global Wealth Report (2010–2017), https://www.credit-suisse.com/corporate/en/research/research-institute/global-wealth-report.html.

137. Tasc, 'The Distribution of Wealth in Ireland', December 2015, https://www.tasc.ie/download/pdf/the_distribution_of_wealth_in_ireland_final.pdf.

138. Expatistan.com, https://www.expatistan.com/cost-of-living/country/comparison/germany/ireland.

139. Ibid.

140. Ibid.

141. Ibid.

142. Office of the Revenue Commissioners, Annual Report 2017, https://www.revenue.ie/en/corporate/press-office/annual-report/2017/ar-2017.pdf.

143. *Irish Times*, 17 October 2017, https://www.irishtimes.com/business/economy/services-sector-now-accounts-for-75-of-employment-in-ireland-1.3259240.

144. Daft.ie, House Price Report Q2 2018, https://www.daft.ie/report/2018-Q2-houseprice-daftreport.pdf. See also CSO, Earnings and Labour Costs Annual 2017: Statistical Release, 29 June 2018, https://www.cso.ie/en/releasesandpublications/er/elca/earningsandlabourcostsannualdata2017/.

145. CSO, E4074: Population aged 18 years and over still living with their parents 2011 to 2016 by Age Group, Principal Economic Status, Sex, Aggregate Town or Rural Area and Census Year, https://www.cso.ie/px/pxeirestat/Statire/SelectVarVal/Define.asp?maintable=E4074&PLanguage=0.

146. CSO, CNA21: Population (Town and Rural) by Five Year Age Group, Sex, Marital Status, Year and Statistic, https://www.cso.ie/px/pxeirestat/Statire/SelectVarVal/Define.asp?maintable=CNA21.

147. *Irish Times*, 1 August 2018, https://www.irishtimes.com/business/economy/ireland-s-reliance-on-five-huge-multinationals-is-a-threat-to-the-economy-1.3582410.

148. World Integrated Trade Solutions, https://wits.worldbank.org/CountryProfile/en/Country/IRL/Year/LTST/TradeFlow/EXPIMP/Partner/by-country. See also, Department of Foreign Affairs & Trade, Ireland and Britain – A unique Economic Partnership, https://www.dfa.ie/media/dfa/alldfawebsitemedia/ourrolesandpolicies/ourwork/statevisit2014/Economic-Facts.pdf.

149. United States Bureau of Economic Analysis, Ireland – International Trade and Investment Country Facts, https://apps.bea.gov/international/factsheet/factsheet.cfm.

150. Office of the Revenue Commissioners, Annual Report 2017, https://www.revenue.ie/en/corporate/press-office/annual-report/2017/ar-2017.pdf.

151. Northern Ireland Census 2011, Detailed Characteristics Statistics Outputs, Table DC2114NI: Religion By Age By Sex, https://www.nisra.gov.uk/statistics/census/2011-census.

152. Ibid.

153. Ibid.

154. John Bradley, 'The History of Economic Development in Ireland, North and South'. In Proceedings-British Academy, 98, 35–68. https://www.britac.ac.uk/pubs/proc/files/98p035.pdf.

155. Andy Bielenberg, 'Industrial growth in Ireland; c. 1790–1910', Diss. London School of Economics and Political Science, 1994, http://etheses.lse.ac.uk/1326/1/U062811.pdf.

156. John Bradley, 'The History of Economic Development in Ireland, North and South'. In Proceedings-British Academy, 98, 35–68. https://www.britac.ac.uk/pubs/proc/files/98p035.pdf.

157. Andy Bielenberg, 'Industrial growth in Ireland; c. 1790–1910', Diss. London School of Economics and Political Science, 1994, http://etheses.lse.ac.uk/1326/1/U062811.pdf.

158. Michael Hennigan, FinFacts, 10 August 2017, http://www.finfacts.ie/Irish_finance_news/articleDetail.php?Brexit-Northern-Ireland-s-industry-eclipsed-by-Republic-s-after-1961-803.

159. CSO, QuickTables: Annual External Trade: Goods Exports and Imports (€m), https://www.cso.ie/multiquicktables/quickTables.aspx?id=tsa01.

160. Northern Ireland Statistics and Research Agency, Broad Economy Sales and Exports Statistics, https://www.nisra.gov.uk/statistics/business-statistics/broad-economy-sales-and-exports-statistics.

161. OECD, Foreign-born population (Total, % of population, 2013 or latest available), https://data.oecd.org/migration/foreign-born-population.htm.

162. Northern Ireland Census 2011, Detailed Characteristics Statistics Outputs, Table DC2107NI: Country of Birth by Age by Sex, https://www.nisra.gov.uk/statistics/census/2011-census.

163. *Belfast Telegraph*, 24 May 2017, https://www.belfasttelegraph.co.uk/business/news/northern-ireland-public-spending-highest-in-uk-14020-per-head-35747632.html. See also, Fact Check NI, 24 May 2016, https://www.factcheckni.org/facts/how-dependent-is-stormont-on-westminster-subvention/ and Irish Times, 15 March 2017, https://www.irishtimes.com/opinion/a-united-ireland-would-be-worse-off-than-the-republic-1.3010177.

164. Eurostat, Regional gross domestic product by NUTS 2 regions (€ millions), https://ec.europa.eu/eurostat/tgm/table.do?tab=table&init=1&language=en&pcode=tgs00003&plugin=1. See also, House of Commons Library, Briefing Paper No. 05795, 'Regional And Local Economic Growth Statistics', 5 September 2018, https://researchbriefings.parliament.uk/ResearchBriefing/Summary/SN05795#fullreport.

165. *Irish Times*, 3 March 2016, https://www.irishtimes.com/business/economy/us-investment-in-ireland-totals-310bn-report-finds-1.2558447.

166. CSO, National Income and Expenditure 2017, GDP at Current prices, https://www.cso.ie/en/releasesandpublications/ep/p-nie/nie2017/summary/. Assuming Northern Ireland subvention cost of 10–11 billion per annum.

167. CSO, Government Finance Statistics – Annual, April 2018, https://www.cso.ie/en/releasesandpublications/er/gfsa/governmentfinancestatisticsapril2018/.

168. *Irish Times*, 15 March 2017, https://www.irishtimes.com/opinion/a-united-ireland-would-be-worse-off-than-the-republic-1.3010177.

169. Kristin Archick, United States Congressional Research Service, Northern Ireland: Current Issues and Ongoing Challenges in the Peace Process, 12 March 2018, https://fas.org/sgp/crs/row/RS21333.pdf.

170. CSO, N1721: T.21 Gross Value Added at Current Basic Prices by Industrial Sector Nace Rev 2 and Year, 2017 Figure, https://www.cso.ie/px/pxeirestat/Statire/SelectVarVal/Define.asp?maintable=N1721&PLanguage=0. Also see CSO, PEA15: Annual Population Change by Component and Year, 2017 Figure, https://www.cso.ie/px/pxeirestat/Statire/SelectVarVal/Define.asp?maintable=PEA15&PLanguage=0.

171. Kristin Archick, United States Congressional Research Service, Northern Ireland: Current Issues and Ongoing Challenges in the Peace Process, 12 March 2018, https://fas.org/sgp/crs/row/RS21333.pdf.

172. *Irish Times*, 15 March 2017, https://www.irishtimes.com/opinion/a-united-ireland-would-be-worse-off-than-the-republic-1.3010177.

173. Sluggerotoole.com, 26 March 2018, https://sluggerotoole.com/2018/03/26/is-northern-ireland-dramatically-poorer-than-the-republic/.

174. As noted by Steve Moore of Volteface at Kilkenomics, 2017.

175. Ann Marie Gray, ARK Nothern Ireland, Research Update No. 115, 'Attitudes to Abortion in Northern Ireland', http://www.ark.ac.uk/publications/updates/update115.pdf.

176. Northern Irish Life & Times Survey, ARK Northern Ireland, Abortion Module, 2016, http://www.ark.ac.uk/nilt/results/abortion.html.

177. Northern Irish Life & Times Survey, ARK Northern Ireland, Lesbian, Gay, Bisexual and Transgender (LGBT) Issues Module, 2013, http://www.ark.ac.uk/nilt/results/lgbt.html.

178. Ibid.

179. Northern Irish Life & Times Survey, ARK Northern Ireland, Community Relations Module, 2017, http://www.ark.ac.uk/nilt/results/comrel.html.

180. Ibid.

181. Northern Irish Life & Times Survey, ARK Northern Ireland, Political Attitudes Module, Variable UNTDIREL, 1998, http://www.ark.ac.uk/nilt/1998/Political_Attitudes/UNTDIREL.html. See also, same module polled in 2017, http://www.ark.ac.uk/nilt/2017/Political_Attitudes/UNTDIREL.html

182. Northern Irish Life & Times Survey, ARK Northern Ireland, Political Attitudes Module, Variable NIROIALL, 2017, http://www.ark.ac.uk/nilt/2017/Political_Attitudes/NIROIALL.html.